THE
AGE
OF
REASON

THE AGE OF REASON

BY THOMAS PAINE

with a biographical introduction by
PHILIP S. FONER

A Citadel Press Book
Published by Carol Publishing Group

THE
AGE
OF
REASON

INTRODUCTION
THOMAS PAINE—WORLD CITIZEN
AND DEMOCRAT

"HIS name is Paine, a gentleman about two years from England —a man who, General Lee says, has genius in his eyes." So John Adams described the author of the widely-discussed pamphlet, *Common Sense,* published anonymously early in 1776.

Thomas Paine, the man with "genius in his eyes," was born January 29, 1737, at Thetford in Norfolk, England, of a Quaker father and an Anglican mother. His father was a poor corset-maker who could barely afford to send his son to a free school where he was taught just enough to master reading, writing and arithmetic. At thirteen young Paine began to work with his father as a staymaker; three years later he ran away from home, went to sea and served as a sailor on a privateer in the Seven Years' War. He returned to London after two eventful voyages which included a terrific sea-battle and lived by finding such occupations as he could. He worked for a while as a staymaker; then became a government worker, holding a minor job in the collection of the excise, and, after he was dismissed from this post, was employed in 1767 in a school at Kensington. A year later he was working for the government again as an excise officer at Lewes, Sussex. He had married in 1759, but the marriage was cut short by the death of his wife a year later. His second marriage in 1771 was cut short by a legal separation.

During these years Paine took steps to supplement the meagre education he had received at the Thetford Grammar School. From his pitiful earnings as a staymaker and exciseman, he purchased books and scientific apparatus such as a pair of globes. When he lived in London during the period 1757–59, he attended in his spare time the lectures on Newtonian astronomy given by Benjamin Martin, James Ferguson, and Dr. Bevis. He continued his process of self-education throughout his life, convinced that "every person of learning is finally his own teacher." "I seldom passed five minutes of my life however circumstanced," he once observed, "in which I did not acquire some knowledge." No one who traces his lifelong pursuit of education and notes the authors he cites in his writings, will lightly accept the conventional sneer that Paine displayed an "immense ignorance" throughout his career.

Both his Quaker background and his study of Newtonian science influenced his thinking along progressive lines, though neither probably had the effect that some writers have stressed.[1] Unquestionably Paine was influenced to some degree by his acquaintance with the religion of his father, for the Quakers were pioneers in many humanitarian enterprises, including anti-slavery, women's rights and prison reform. Undoubtedly, too, by revealing to Paine a harmonious and universal order guided by divinely-created law, Newtonian science greatly influenced his political and religious thinking. But life itself was an extremely important teacher. During the first thirty-seven years of his life he saw enough misery in England, enough of the contrast between the affluence of the upper classes and the poverty and suffering of the masses to influence his thinking for the remainder of his days.

In the England of his youth and manhood Paine saw the vicious effects of the enclosure system which threw thousands of small, independent farmers into the cities and transformed them from independent yeomanry to landless factory workers and agricultural laborers. All about him he saw thousands struggling in the midst of misery and degradation to eke out an existence, and daily passed "ragged and hungry children, and persons of seventy and eighty years of age, begging in the streets." He knew too from his own intolerably inadequate salary how difficult it was to secure even a subsistence living standard at a time when commodity prices were soaring and wages remained practically stationary. He also noticed the vicious operations of the poor laws which almost reduced workers to serfs, witnessed the brutality of the savage criminal code and observed how it was directed chiefly against the lower classes. Nor could he help noticing the burdens imposed upon the poor by the Anglican Church with its tithes and privileges, the role that family influence played in English politics, the

[1] Moncure Daniel Conway, Paine's indefatigable biographer, contended that the most important source for his religious and many of his political ideas was Quakerism. It is generally conceded today by Paine scholars that Conway greatly exaggerated this influence.

Professor Harry Hayden Clark, the most important student of Paine since Conway, argues that Paine's religious concepts and even many of his economic and social ideas had their source in the Newtonian concept of the universe. Although Professor Clark had made a great contribution to the study of Paine in revealing the Newtonian influence on his thought, it is the opinion of the present writer that he has erred in the same manner that Conway did by overemphasizing this influence. Certainly Professor Clark succeeds only in turning Paine upside down when he argues that his political ideas grew out of his religious ideas. See his important article, "Toward a Reinterpretation of Thomas Paine," *American Literature,* vol. V, May, 1933, pp. 133–145, and his valuable introduction to *Thomas Paine: Representative Selections,* New York, 1944.

inequalities of the rotten-borough system (in Thetford alone thirty-one persons elected two members of the House of Commons), and the corruption that characterized government administration. ·

These experiences left their mark upon Paine. Himself a working man, he was to use his pen, time and again, in an effort to improve the status of the laboring classes. Indeed, his earliest known prose composition and his first important pamphlet, *The Case of the Officers of Excise,* was written to achieve this purpose. In 1772 he was chosen by excisemen to address Parliament in their behalf requesting higher wages. After the pamphlet was written, Paine spent the winter of 1772–73 trying to influence members of Parliament to grant the underpaid excisemen an increase of wages. Regarded as a trouble-maker by the authorities for attempting to organize his fellow excisemen, he was dismissed from the service.

Paine lost his government job on April 8, 1774. A week later he was forced to sell his shop and possessions to escape imprisonment for debt. Having tasted the bitter dregs of British tyranny long enough, Paine decided to begin life all over again in the New World. He left England in October, 1774, and on November 30 landed in America bearing a letter of introduction from Benjamin Franklin whom he had approached in London. Franklin's letter to his son-in-law, Richard Bache, recommended Paine as "an ingenious worthy young man," who might make good in Philadelphia as "a clerk, or assistant tutor in a school, or assistant surveyor."

Arriving in America armed with Franklin's letter, Paine speedily obtained employment with Robert Aitken, a Philadelphia printer. Soon he became the editor of the *Pennsylvania Magazine* which Aitken had started with very little success to publish. On March 4, 1775, the man who had left England branded as a ne'er-do-well wrote a joyful letter to his benefactor. "Your countenancing me," he informed Franklin, "has obtained for me many friends and much reputation . . . I have been applied to by several gentlemen to instruct their sons . . . and a printer and bookseller here, a man of reputation and property, Robert Aitken, . . . has applied to me for assistance. He had not above six hundred subscribers when I first assisted him. We now have upwards of fifteen hundred and daily increasing . . ."

For eighteen months, beginning with the second number in February, 1775, Paine served as editor of the *Pennsylvania Magazine,* and during this time he published enough important articles in this and other journals to be remembered as a significant figure in American history, even if he had never written anything else. A few weeks after his arrival in America, Paine wrote an article entitled, "African Slavery in America," which ranks as the best of the early attacks upon slavery in this country. Paine put the enslavement of the Negro people on a level with "murder, robbery, lewdness, and barbarity," and called upon Americans immediately to "discontinue and renounce it, with grief and abhorrence." When the article was printed on March 8, 1775, Paine gained a wide reputation for his liberal views, and won for himself the friendship of Dr. Benjamin Rush and other important figures in literary and philosophical circles.

The time was ripe for the activity of a lover of liberty when Paine arrived in America. The struggle between England and her colonies had been raging since 1763, and the very atmosphere breathed revolutionary slogans. In his early articles for the *Pennsylvania Magazine,* however, Paine did not deal with any of the pressing political problems confronting the colonists in their quarrel with the mother country. In part this was due to the insistence of his timid publisher, for Aitken was determined not to antagonize any wealthy subscribers who viewed the revolutionary movement with alarm. But it was also due to Paine's belief that it was still possible to reconcile the differences between England and her colonies. Soon a rush of events showed him the futility of this outlook. On April 19, 1775, the battle of Lexington and Concord was fought, an event which convinced Paine that "all plans, proposals, etc.," to settle the conflict by compromise were "like the almanacks of the last year; which though proper then, are superceded and useless now." And on June 15 Washington was appointed commander-in-chief of the Continental army. A day later the battle of Bunker Hill occurred.

Moved by these and other events of a similar nature, Paine started to use his pen to aid the revolutionary movement. On September 16, 1775, he published a poem in the *Pennsylvania Evening Post* entitled, "The Liberty Tree," the last stanza of which attacked the king as well as Parliament and issued a call

> From the East to the West blow the trumpet to arms,
>> Thro' the land let the sound of it flee:
> Let the far and the near all unite with a cheer,
>> In defense of our Liberty Tree.

But Paine was already forming the outlines of a much more important call to arms, for he discovered that poetry was not enough to convince men in high circles that it was time to open a "new system" in America. He was determined to change "the sentiments of the people from dependence to Independence and from the monarchial to the republican form of government . . ." This was no simple task to accomplish. While the mass of the artisans, mechanics and day-laborers in the urban centres and many small farmers in the rural districts were prepared for such a step, many of the members of the colonial aristocracy were by no means ready to follow Paine down the road leading to Independence and Republicanism. Independence, they feared, would bring to an end the rule of the upper classes in America, and Republicanism signified nothing less than anarchy and mob-rule. Better to tolerate the tyranny of the British government, they reasoned, than to chance the dangers of a democratic upheaval in America.

Paine moved quickly to meet and overcome these fears and hesitations. In a short article, "A Serious Thought," published in the *Pennsylvania Journal* on October 18, 1775, he sharply projected the idea of independence. Discussing the barbaric conduct of the British in India and criticizing England for her treatment of the Indians in America and for having "employed herself in the most horrid of all traffics, that of human flesh . . . [and] ravaged the hapless shore of Africa, robbing it of its unoffending inhabitants to cultivate her stolen dominions in the West," he went on to say: "When I reflect on these, I hesitate not for a moment to believe that the Almighty will finally separate America from Britain. Call it Independence or what you will, if it is the cause of God and humanity it will go on."

In December, 1775, Paine showed the manuscript of a pamphlet he had finished to David Rittenhouse and Dr. Benjamin Rush, and the latter, according to his own account, suggested to him the title for the work and found a publisher, Robert Bell, with sufficient courage to print it. The work came off the press on January 10, 1776. It was entitled *Common Sense*.

Paine was not the first person to advocate independence in America; John Adams had done so, for example, even before *Common Sense* was published. Nevertheless, the influence and power of this fifty-page pamphlet can hardly be exaggerated. "With the publication of *Common Sense* in January 1776," writes John C. Miller in his *Origins of the American Revolution* (p. 468), "Tom Paine broke the ice that was slowly congealing the revolutionary movement." And Evarts B. Greene, the distinguished historian of the Revolutionary era, observes in his recently-published study, *The Revolutionary Generation* (p. 209), "Thomas Paine's *Common Sense,* more than any other single piece of writing, set Americans to thinking of the possibility and desirability of an independent place among the nations."

Written in simple, plain, and direct language easily read and understood by all, *Common Sense* became overnight a best-seller; shortly after its publication almost a half a million copies were sold, and many of its most trenchant paragraphs were reprinted in newspapers all over the country. Soon the common people were quoting sections from the booklet which hammered home the need for separation, held up hereditary monarchy to contempt, denounced the British ruling classes for exploiting the lower classes in America and in England, and urged the colonies to declare themselves free and independent states so that they might establish in America a haven of refuge for the oppressed peoples of Europe. More cautious and conservative Americans quoted other sections, particularly the arguments Paine advanced in support of a declaration of independence: the prospect that by independence America could remain aloof from the European conflicts into which she was constantly being drawn by her connection with the British Empire; the possibilities of enormous markets in all of Europe for merchants and farmers once the restrictions imposed by the British on American economic life were broken, and the great certainty of obtaining foreign aid in the war for independence.[2] Shortly after reading the booklet many upper class Americans who had hesitated to support independence for fear of meeting the power of the British singlehanded and did not yet clearly see the advantages of separation, declared with Washington that they were ready "to shake off all connections with a state so unjust and unnatural."

Terrified by the influence of Paine's booklet, the Tories sought frantically to nullify its effects upon the people. Several answers to Paine's

[2] Paine argued that France would aid America if she declared herself independent. *Common Sense* was itself an important factor in helping mobilize French support for the American cause. It was translated promptly into French, with the expurgation of anti-monarchist passages, and published in Paris on May 4, 1776. Silas Deane, American Commissioner to France, wrote home on August 18, 1776, that the booklet "has a greater run, if-possible here than in America." Professor Aulard, historian of the French Revolution, has observed that "the bold phrases of Thomas Paine's republican pamphlet, *Common Sense,* resounded throughout France." See "The Deane Papers . . . ," *New York Historical Society Collections,* vol. I, p. 214, and A. Aulard, *The French Revolution: A Political History.* London, 1910, vol. I, p. 112.

"artful, insidious, and pernicious" work were published, the most important attack consisting of a series of letters signed "Cato," which were first printed in the *Philadelphia Gazette* beginning in April, 1776. Paine immediately wrote four letters in reply, known as *The Forester's Letters,* in which he expanded and amplified many of the arguments he had first advanced in favor of independence in *Common Sense.* Widely reprinted in contemporary newspapers, these articles strengthened the popular demand for immediate independence. This demand in turn influenced the appointment on June 28 by the Continental Congress of a committee of five to draft a declaration of independence.

Although primarily absorbed during these exciting months with the battle against tyranny abroad, Paine did not entirely ignore the struggle for democracy in America. Together with Benjamin Franklin and other progressive leaders in Pennsylvania, he assisted in mobilizing the popular forces for the enactment of a liberal state constitution. Supported by the Philadelphia artisans and the western farmers, these men gradually swept away all vestiges of aristocratic rule in the state. Drawn up by Paine and Franklin, the Pennsylvania constitution, adopted late in 1776, provided for universal suffrage, democratic representation, complete religious freedom, and a unicameral legislature, elected annually. It was by far the most advanced state constitution adopted during the American Revolution, and Paine took pride in his part in shaping the document, although he later questioned the wisdom of a unicameral legislature.[3]

But Paine was doing more than writing Constitutions. In August, 1776, he joined the Pennsylvania Associators as voluntary secretary to General Roberdeau and, on September 19 was appointed aide-de-camp to General Greene who was at Fort Lee in New Jersey. By this time Washington's army, badly defeated in the battle of Long Island, was retreating toward New Jersey and, in November and December streamed across the state in disorderly fashion toward Philadelphia. It was a dark hour for the American cause. Morale in the army and on the home front was at its lowest ebb; a feeling prevailed that the enemy was invincible and that the war might as well end now. Naturally, the Tory speakers and newspapers emphasized that there was no hope for America other than in capitulation, and the flight of Congress from Philadelphia to Baltimore made these arguments seem plausible.

[3] For an excellent analysis of the Pennsylvania Constitution, see J. Paul Selsam, *The Pennsylvania Constitution of 1776*, Philadelphia, 1936.

Seated by a campfire near Newark, New Jersey, Paine started work on an appeal to the people in this hour of crisis. When he was finished, he rushed to Philadelphia and published in the *Pennsylvania Journal* of December 19, 1776, his *Crisis I,* and almost immediately it was issued in three pamphlet editions. His opening words in these days of adversity, "These are the times that try men's souls," rang out like a bugle and heartened the little band of patriots left with Washington. The soldiers who heard the words of Paine's great document—Washington ordered it read to his men—were inspired to face the floes, a blizzard and the swift current of the Delaware River on Christmas Eve and achieve the victory at Trenton which gave the Americans new courage.

Between 1776 and 1783 Paine published thirteen numbered essays and three extra numbers of *The Crisis* papers, each one signed "Common Sense." All were perfectly timed and perfectly adapted to the needs of the time. Did Lord Howe issue a proclamation urging Americans to negotiate a peace? Paine immediately answered him, exposed his proposal and attacked his Tory sympathizers in America. Did the Conway Cabal seek to oust Washington? Paine rushed to press to counteract this conspiracy. Did England send over a Commission for the purpose of winning the Americans away from the French? Paine issued a *Crisis* pamphlet which thoroughly ridiculed the negotiated peace overtures and was influential in compelling the Commission to return to England empty-handed. Was there a danger that the war would be lost because of financial difficulties? Paine published his *Crisis Extraordinary* to prove that it would cost more to submit than to support the war financially. "Can it then be a question," he concluded after estimating the costs of defending the country and governing it after the war as two and three-quarters millions sterling, "whether it is better to raise two millions to defend the country, and govern it ourselves, and only three quarters of a million afterwards, or pay six millions to have it conquered and let the enemy govern it?" Finally, did it appear that the American victory would be rendered valueless by the absence of a strong union? Paine reminded the people that they could not help but "be strongly impressed with the advantage, as well as the necessity of strengthening that happy union which has been our salvation."

Reprinted in most of the northern papers and in some of those in the South, the *Crisis* enormously aided the American cause and contributed to no small extent to ultimate victory. George Washington, Robert Morris, and Robert R. Livingston wrote early in 1782 that Paine had been "of considerable utility to the common cause by several of his Publications," and secured from Congress a salary of $800 a year to enable him to continue to use his "abilities" in "informing the People and rousing them into action."

In addition to "informing the people and rousing them into action," Paine held various posts in the national and state governments during the war. In 1777 Congress appointed him secretary to the Committee on Foreign Affairs, in which capacity he did much to obtain supplies, a large loan and military assistance from France. The fact that his services were appreciated moved him deeply. In a letter recently discovered, he wrote Franklin in Paris, on October 24, 1778: "I have the pleasure of being respected and I feel a little of that satisfactory kind of pride that tells me I have some right to it." [4]

A month after this letter was written Paine became involved in a controversy with Silas Deane that abruptly brought his pleasure to an end, caused a torrent of abuse and defamation to be heaped on his head, and ultimately cost him his job as secretary to the Committee on Foreign Affairs.

The crux of the debate between Paine and Silas Deane centred on the question whether the supplies furnished the United States by France before the Franco-American alliance of 1778, through Caron de Beaumarchais, adventurer and playwright, were a gift from the king of France or comprised a loan to the United States. Deane, attempting to profit personally from French aid to the United States and, as it was established later, had conspired with the British (for a considerable sum) against the American Revolution, maintained that the transactions were of a purely commercial nature and demanded payment of a five percent commission on purchases made for the American government. Paine supporting the position of Arthur Lee, also American Commissioner to France, charged that Deane was simply conspiring to defraud Congress of money. On December 14, 1778, in a letter *To Silas Deane, Esq're,* in the *Pennsylvania Packet,* Paine launched his public attack upon Deane. Answers from Deane's supporters followed, and Paine was compelled to continue the controversy. As he did so, however, he was also forced, to prove his contentions, to quote from secret documents to which he had access as secretary of the Committee on Foreign Affairs. Soon afterwards he had to resign his post owing to the opposi-

[4] Dixon Wecter, "Thomas Paine and the Franklins," *American Literature,* vol. XII, November, 1940, p. 313.

tion of those in Congress, who feared that his revelations jeopardized the alliance with France, as well as of those who considered Paine entirely too radical and believed he should never have been appointed in the first place. Gouverneur Morris, archconservative, told Congress that it was unseemly that the office of Secretary of Foreign Affairs should be held by "a mere adventurer *from England,* without fortune, without family or connexions, ignorant even of grammar."

Paine's resignation did not end the controversy over Silas Deane. For many months articles on the subject appeared daily in the Philadelphia press. Most of them were printed over pseudonyms, but it is known that Paine, Arthur Lee, Richard Henry Lee, and Timothy Matlock penned those denouncing Deane, while Deane, Robert Morris, Matthew Clarkson, William Duer, and Gouverneur Morris spoke for the opposition. As the war of words continued other issues emerged, though in many ways they were related to the general question at issue. Paine had entered the controversy over Deane not merely because he wished to save Congress money, but also because he felt that the type of profiteering disclosed by Deane's conduct was too general in the country and endangered the revolutionary cause. He developed this theme in articles to the press after his resignation, pointing particularly to Robert Morris whose firm held important public contracts while he was conducting congressional business, and who was associated with Silas Deane in personal as well as governmental transactions.[5] Paine publicly attacked Morris for his business associations with Deane, suggested that the State legislatures investigate such activities by all former and present delegates to Congress, and expressed the hope that the Pennsylvania legislature would take the lead.

It is clear, therefore, that what started out as a debate over the role of an American Commissioner to France had become a struggle between radicals and conservatives in Pennsylvania. Here the wealthy merchants and professional aristocrats had been organizing since early in 1777 to overthrow the democratic State Constitution which committed the cardinal sin of allowing the common people according to their number a voice in their government. But the friends of the Constitution—mechanics and small farmers—also were organized to defend their charter

---

[5] On one occasion Morris wrote to Deane, then in France: "It seems to me that the present oppert'y of improving our fortunes ought not to be lost, especially as the very means of doing it will contribute to the service of our country at the same time." See Thomas P. Abernathy, "Commercial Activities of Silas Deane in France," *American Historical Review,* vol. XXXIX, pp. 477–485.

of liberty. Paine, spokesman for the city artisans and mechanics, took his stand with the friends of the constitution he had helped to write. In articles to the press he defended the document and attacked those who sought to deprive the people of their democratic rights.[6]

Paine also spoke for the people, especially the artisans, in his articles denouncing monopolizing practices which caused the cost of living to soar and were responsible for reducing the morale of workers who found it difficult to secure wage-increases. He was present at a mass meeting held on the 27th of May in the State House yard where a series of resolutions were adopted denouncing combinations "for raising the prices of goods and provisions." He also served on a Committee of Inspection before which leading merchants suspected of unscrupulous business methods were forced to appear.

In the State elections which took place on October 12, 1779, the Constitutionalists won a resounding victory and, as a reward for his part in arousing popular support for the Constitution, the new Assembly elected Paine its Clerk. Actually, his position was more important than the name implies, for he was the close friend and advisor of Assembly leaders and influenced important legislation.

In his new position Paine soon had an opportunity to see one of his dreams realized. Late in 1775, in his short article entitled "A Serious Thought," he had looked forward to the day when God "shall have blest us, and made us a people *dependent only upon Him,* then may our gratitude be shown by an act of continental legislation, which shall put a stop to the importation of Negroes for sale, soften the hard fate of those already here, and in time procure their freedom." Five years later, as Clerk of the Pennsylvania Assembly, Paine wrote the "Preamble to the Act Passed by the Pennsylvania Assembly March 1, 1780," which provided for the gradual emancipation of Negro slaves in the state. It was the first legislative measure passed in America for the emancipation of slaves.

While serving as Clerk, Paine was called upon to read to the Assembly Washington's appeal, dated May 28, 1780, for assistance to pay, feed and clothe his troops. "I assure you," Washington wrote in this letter, "every idea you can form of our distresses will fall short of the reality. There is such a combination of circumstances to exhaust the patience

[6] All of Paine's letters and articles on the Deane controversy appear in the second volume of the present edition of his writings. For excellent background material see Robert L. Brunhouse, *The Counter-Revolution in Pennsylvania,* Philadelphia, 1942.

of the soldiery that it begins at length to be worn out, and we see in every line of the army the most serious features of mutiny and sedition." Paine did not forget this appeal after he finished reading. Leaving the assembly hall he drew out one thousand dollars due him on salary, sent five hundred dollars to Blair McClenaghan, a prominent merchant, and included a plea for the men of wealth to rally to aid the cause. "I feel the utmost concern," Paine wrote, "that the fairest cause that men ever engaged in, and with the fairest prospect of success should now be sunk so low, and that not from any new ability in the enemy but from a wilful neglect and decay of every species of public spirit in ourselves." He went on to point out that much financial assistance could not be expected from the artisans and small farmers, since it was "now hard time with many poor people." It remained, therefore, for the wealthy to fill the gap, which they should rush to do for "as it is the rich that will suffer most by the ravages of an Enemy it is not only duty but true policy to do something spirited." He hoped his five hundred dollars— "and if that is not sufficient I will add 500 more"—would inaugurate a movement to rescue the cause in this dark hour. He was willing to bury all past political differences and cooperate with any patriotic society "no matter who may complete it." [7] Acting upon Paine's suggestion, several wealthy merchants and bankers in Philadelphia, with Robert Morris at their head, started the Bank of Pennsylvania to supply the army with provisions.

Undoubtedly Paine's action in this crisis marked a change in his attitude toward men like Morris whom he had publicly denounced only a few months before. It does not, however, mark, as some writers have asserted, the beginning of a conservative trend in Paine's thinking. The simple fact is that the author of *Common Sense* had enough common sense to realize that the American Revolution could not be successful unless all classes willing to support the war were united, and he did not exclude men of wealth from this unity. Paine fully appreciated what Washington had meant when he wrote that everything had to give way to the primary task of winning the war—factional disputes, class antagonisms, even personal quarrels. "The present situation of our public affairs," the commander-in-chief once observed, "affords abundant causes of distress, we should be very careful how we aggravate or multiply them, by private bickerings. . . . All little differences and animosities, calculated to increase the unavoidable evils of the times, should be for-

[7] Thomas Paine *Mss.*, New York Historical Society

gotten, or at least postponed." [8] Paine was not merely willing to forget or postpone but even to cooperate with his former enemies to rescue "the fairest cause that Men ever engaged in."

National unity meant unity among the states as well as among different classes. Paine, therefore, turned his attention late in 1780 to the problem of eliminating state antagonisms and rivalries in the hope that he could convince them to cooperate for the well-being of the entire nation. The immediate issue that aroused his attention was the delay in the ratification of the Articles of Confederation because of a conflict over claims to land in the west. Congress had adopted the Articles on November 17, 1777, and submitted them to the several states for ratification. Maryland, having definite western limits, refused to ratify the new frame of government until Virginia ceded her claims to western land to the national government.

Paine's pamphlet, *Public Good,* published in Philadelphia on December 30, 1780, demolished Virginia's claims to land in the west, contended that the land should belong not to the individual states but to the United States because they had been secured by the united effort of all the states during the war, and concluded by calling for a stronger central government. He urged the convening of "a continental convention, for the purpose of forming a continental constitution, defining and describing the powers and authority of Congress."

Two years later, in 1782–83, Paine spoke out again for a stronger central government and once again emphasized the need to adhere to "the principle of union," which he correctly regarded as "our magna charta—our anchor in the world of empires." In an effort to obtain a revenue to carry on the war Congress proposed a five-per-cent duty on imported articles, the money to be used to pay the interest on loans to be made in Holland. Unanimous consent of the states was necessary to grant Congress the power to levy this duty, and, when Rhode Island refused her assent an *impasse* was created. In this situation Paine once again demonstrated his grasp of the needs of the time by publishing a series of letters addressed to the people of Rhode Island urging them to consent to the five-per-cent impost plan. Signing himself "A Friend to Rhode Island and the Union," he reminded his readers that all the embarrassments faced by the new Republic "are ascribable to the loose and almost disjointed condition of the Union. . . ." We need "to talk

[8] Philip S. Foner, editor, *George Washington: Selections from His Writings,* New York, 1944, pp. 22–23.

less about our independence," he argued, "and more about our union." Independence without a strong union would be meaningless, for "the union of America is the foundation-stone of her independence; the rock on which it is built." It was "the great Palladium of our liberty and safety." [9]

To bring this message to the people of Rhode Island, Paine even went to the trouble to visit the state at his own expense. He made the trip in the dead of winter on a horse he borrowed from a friend in New Jersey. Unfortunately neither his presence nor his letters to the *Providence Gazette* produced any effect and he was forced to leave the state without accomplishing anything.

It is clear that Paine was among the first to point out, even before the American Revolution was over, the need for a stronger central government to replace the weak Articles of Confederation. Little wonder, therefore, that in later years he was enraged to discover the Federalists claiming for themselves the sole distinction of having favored a stronger central government to take the place of the Articles of Confederation. He observed in 1802 that if "by *Federalist* is to be understood one who was for cementing the Union by a general government operating equally over all the States, in all matters that embraced the common interest, . . . *I ought to stand first on the list of Federalist.*" For had he not as early as 1780 and 1782 recognized that "the continental belt was too loosely buckled"?

At the end of the Revolution Paine found himself poverty-stricken. In a moving memorial to Congress, endorsed by Washington, he set forth his services to America and begged for financial assistance. His revolutionary writings had circulated widely, but he had not profited from their sale. Indeed, he had contributed from his own pocket to make them available to as wide a reading public as possible. Referring to the phenomenal distribution of *Common Sense,* Paine wrote in his memorial:

> "As my wish was to serve an oppressed people, and assist in a just and good cause, I conceived that the honor of it would be promoted by my declining to make even the usual profits of an author, by the publication, and therefore I gave up the profits of the first edition into the hands of Col. Joseph Deane and Mr.

[9] Paine's letters to the people of Rhode Island appear in the second volume of the present edition of his writings. See also Harry Hayden Clark, editor, *Six New Letters of Thomas Paine,* Madison, Wisconsin, 1939.

Thomas Pryor both of the city of Philadelphia to be disposed of by them in any public service or private charity. After this I printed six thousand at my own expense and directed Mr. Bradford to sell them at the price of the printing and paper. It may, perhaps, be said, that as I had made a dangerous step, it was my interest to make it as little so as possible by promoting by every means, the success of the principle on which my own safety rested, but this would be an uncandid way of accounting for public spirit and conduct." [10]

Yet for all his public spirit and conduct he faced a desperate future. "I cannot help viewing my situation as singularly inconvenient," he frankly informed Congress. "Trade I do not understand. Land I have none, or what is equal to none. I have exiled myself from one country without making a home of another; and I cannot help sometimes asking myself, what am I better off than a refugee, and that of the most extraordinary kind, a refugee from the country I have obliged and served, to that which can owe me no good will."

Paine's enemies in Congress were still too powerful and the memorial was buried. Fortunately, two states came to his aid. Pennsylvania gave him £500 in cash, and New York presented him with a confiscated Loyalist farm at New Rochelle, the last grant being recommended because "his literary works, and those especially under the signature of Common Sense, and the Crisis, inspired the citizens of this state with unanimity, confirmed their confidence in the rectitude of their cause, and have ultimately contributed to the freedom, sovereignty, and independence of the United States." He remained on his farm and in the village of Bordentown, New Jersey until 1787, devoting most of his time to inventions such as an iron bridge without piers, and a smokeless candle. These were years when he could truly say, "the natural bent of my mind was to science."

Yet he could not remain entirely aloof from the political scene. Independence did not overnight usher in the era of national prosperity Paine had predicted in *Common Sense*. A few men, to be sure, made money through speculation and investments, but the mass of the small farmers and city mechanics found it difficult to make ends meet. The dumping of British goods on the American market caused a serious

---

[10] "A Representation of the Services of Thomas Paine, 1783," *Mss.,* New York Historical Society. The entire memorial appears in the second volume of the present edition of Paine's writings.

amount of unemployment in urban areas. In the rural districts the farmers faced foreclosures and imprisonment for debt.

In every state the small farmers organized a campaign to obtain paper money and stay laws. Pennsylvania was no exception. Here, however, the battle for paper money legislation merged into a movement to revoke the charter of the Bank of North America which had grown out of the Bank of Pennsylvania founded by Paine, Robert Morris and a group of merchants in 1780. The back-country farmers feared that it would be valueless to obtain paper money legislation if the bank was still in existence, for if the institution refused to accept paper money on the same terms as specie, the public would have no faith in the bills. Accordingly, a bill to repeal the bank's charter was introduced in the Pennsylvania legislature and by April 4, 1786, passed its second reading.

The pro-bank forces now rallied to defeat the repeal bill. James Wilson wrote a pamphlet supporting the bank, but the material was so heavy and couched in such complicated legal terminology that it had little popular appeal. This was the situation when Paine's *Dissertations on Government, The Affairs of the Bank, and Paper Money* came off the press in February, 1786.

Paine was reluctant to enter the controversy over the bank. "It was my intention," he wrote to his "Old Friend," Daniel Clymer, in September, 1786, "at the conclusion of the war to have laid down the pen and satisfied myself with silently beholding the prosperity of my country, in whose difficulties I had done my share, and in the raising of which, to an independent Empire, I had added my mite . . ." [11]

Paine did not join in the popular agitation conducted by the back-country farmers in favor of paper money legislation and in opposition to the bank, because he believed that these measures were unwise and harmful to the general well-being of the country. He felt that the bank was essential for commercial development in Pennsylvania and that its services were indispensable for the growth of the state. To destroy a financial institution did not seem to him to be either progressive or necessary. "The whole community," he wrote in his *Dissertations,* "derives benefit from the operation of the bank . . ." As for paper money, it was nothing more than an unjust balm for those debtors who were determined to steal by depreciation "the widow's dowry and children's portion." In any event, neither a legislature nor the people had the right

[11] Paine to Daniel Clymer, September, 1786, Paine *Mss.,* Historical Society of Pennsylvania.

to revoke certain kinds of economic contracts agreed to by a preceding legislature and another party. This, however, did not mean that a contract could last forever. A legislature could not grant a contract forever, for the simple reason that the present generation could no more bind its children to economic contracts than it could set up a government for posterity.

Paine knew that by joining the pro-bank forces he would invite the charge that he had sold out the people. Such charges were made. A representative from the West referred to him as "an unprincipled author, who let his pen out for hire," and a writer who called himself "Atticus" attacked him as a turn-coat, adding: "I cannot conceive in the wide extent of creation, a being more deserving of our abhorrence and contempt, than a writer, who having formerly vindicated the principles of freedom, abandons them to abet the cause of a faction, who exerts the little talent which Heaven has alloted him, . . . to vilify measures which it is his duty to respect, and . . . [devotes] his pen to the ruin of his country."

These attacks did not halt Paine in his determination to fight the battle to the bitter end, and his will was strengthened by the realization that if the farmers had turned against him the city mechanics and artisans as well as merchants and bankers supported him. The urban workers also opposed paper money legislation fearing the effects of inflation on their living standards and favored the continued existence of the bank as essential for business expansion which meant employment opportunities. In a series of letters to the Philadelphia papers Paine attacked the repeal of the bank's charter and called for its restoration.[12]

[12] Paine's letters to the press during the controversy over the bank appear in the second volume of the present edition of his writings. For an interesting discussion of the conflict in Pennsylvania over the bank, see Janet Wilson, "The Bank of North America and Pennsylvania Politics, 1781–1787," *Pennsylvania Magazine of History and Biography,* vol. LXVI, January, 1942, pp. 3–28.

Paine's role in supporting the bank and in calling for a stronger Union has been cited by several recent students as proof of his conservatism before he left America in 1787, and it is argued that during this period he tended to align himself with men like Hamilton, John Adams, Robert Morris and others who were known as conservatives (see Harry Hayden Clark's introduction to *Six New Letters of Thomas Paine* and J. Dorfman, "The Economic Philosophy of Thomas Paine," *Political Science Quarterly,* vol. LIII, September, 1938, pp. 372–386). Neither of these writers take into account the fact that Paine's views were supported by the urban artisans for whom he was a spokesman. Moreover, to argue that Paine's economic objectives were much the same as Hamilton's is entirely to ignore the fact that Paine, even in the bank controversy, wanted property to serve the welfare of all classes in society, while Hamilton always spoke out for protection only for the

In the fall elections of 1786 Paine's position was upheld by a majority of the voters. A few months later the bank's charter was restored.

In April, 1787, Paine left for Europe to promote his plan to build a single-arch bridge across the Schuylkill river in Philadelphia. He expected to remain abroad no more than a year and to spend most of his time in France where engineering was best understood. He met Jefferson in France, was hailed as a friend of Franklin and a distinguished writer and became acquainted with leading scientists and political liberals. The Academy of Science appointed a committee to study the plans for his bridge and, after an investigation this body reported that "Mr. Paine's Plan of an Iron Bridge is ingeniously imagined, that the construction of it is simple, solid, and proper to give it the necessary strength for resisting the effects resulting from its burden, and that it is deserving of a trial . . ." The report was presented on August 29th. The next day Paine left for England.

In the land of his birth Paine visited his aged mother at Thetford, met and was enthusiastically received by Charles Fox, Lord Landsdowne, Lord Shelburne and Edmund Burke, and began to make plans for the construction of his bridge. But soon he was thinking less and less about his bridge and more and more about the exciting events in France.[13] Science, after all, could not flourish without democracy.

The news of the French Revolution filled Paine with joy. But he was not surprised. He had never regarded the American Revolution as a local affair, "but universal, and through which the principles of all

"rich and well-born." See the excellent refutation of J. Dorfman's contention by Howard Penniman in the *American Political Science Review*, vol. XXXVII, April, 1943, pp. 244–262.

Although Paine and Hamilton both supported a stronger central government at this time, it must be remembered that the former, like Jefferson, did so because he believed that it was necessary to preserve Republicanism in America. He certainly would never have favored the type of central government proposed by Hamilton in the Federal Convention. Evidently the Hamiltonians thought so too, for they were not anxious to have Paine attend the Convention. Unlike some present-day writers they did not regard him as a conservative.

13 Paine's bridge was eventually constructed in England, but he himself received no credit for it and made no profits. When Sir Robert Smyth, Paine's friend, attempted to secure some reward for the original inventor, he received a letter from a subscriber to the construction company admitting that "the first idea was taken from Mr. Paine's bridge exhibited at Paddington." Nothing, however, could be done to compensate Mr. Paine. Thomas Paine to Thomas Jefferson, October 1, 1800, Jefferson Papers, Library of Congress.

lovers of mankind are affected." In his celebrated *Letter to the Abbé Raynal,* published in 1782, Paine had predicted that the American Revolution would influence England and France until "every corner of the mind is swept of its cobwebs, poison and dust, and made fit for the reception of generous happiness."

Paine spent four months in France at the invitation of Lafayette and Condorcet. He gave advice on the formation of a constitution, aided in drawing up the Declaration of the Rights of Man and of the Citizen, and witnessed the uprisings to overthrow despotism and feudal privileges. His heart "leaped with joy" when he received from Lafayette the key of the Bastille for presentation to Washington. "That the principles of America opened the Bastille," he wrote in his letter forwarding the key, "is not to be doubted, and therefore the Key comes to the right place."

Even when he returned to England, Paine's mind was still riveted on events across the channel. He continued to send Lafayette suggestions to be incorporated in the new government, and reported on reactions in England to developments in France. "Here is a courtly and an aristocratical hatred against the principles of the French Revolution . . . ," he wrote to William Short, American representative in France, from London early in June, 1790.[14]

In the fall of 1790 Paine returned to Paris where he mingled again with Brissot, Condorcet, Lafayette and other leaders of the Revolution. A business crisis sent him back again to England. In November he began work on his greatest pamphlet, *The Rights of Man,* in answer to Edmund Burke's *Reflections on the French Revolution* which appeared on November 1, 1790.

Burke's speech "On Reconciliation with America" in 1775 had aroused Paine's admiration for the man who was considered America's greatest English friend. His personal contacts with Burke in England after the American Revolution increased this feeling, and he considered him "a friend to mankind." But he was both terribly shocked and speedily disillusioned after he read Burke's vicious denunciation of the French Revolution in his parliamentary speech on February 9, 1790. Soon after this Paine saw an advertisement of the forthcoming publication of

[14] Paine to William Short June 1, 1790, Short Papers, Library of Congress. See also Harold W. Landin, editor, "Some Letters of Thomas Paine and William Short on the Nootka Sound Crisis," *Journal of Modern History,* vol. XIII, September, 1941, pp. 357–374.

Burke's pamphlet, and promised his friends in France that whenever it appeared he would answer it.[15]

Paine finished the pamphlet in February, 1791, and turned it over to a friend, Johnson, to have it published. After a few copies were issued, this publisher became frightened. Paine then gave the pamphlet to a committee consisting of William Godwin, Thomas Holcroft, and Thomas Hollis, and left for France. From Paris he forwarded a preface for the English edition, and the work appeared on March 13, 1791. The pamphlet sold for three shillings, the same price as Burke's *Reflections,* and it was believed in Tory circles that this expensive format would give it a limited circulation.

The pamphlet immediately gained a wide circulation. Within a few weeks the book sold fifty thousand copies, and on April 5th, Sir Samuel Romilly wrote to a friend in France that "in the course of a fortnight it has gone through three editions; and, what I own has a good deal surprised me, has made converts of many persons who were before enemies to the revolution." The Society for Constitutional Information and other popular societies in England, to whose support Paine gave the large income from the sale, distributed the book all over the British Isles. Soon Englishmen were quoting passages from the *Rights of Man* with as much fervor as Americans had once recited sections from *Common Sense.* Workers, small farmers and liberal members of the middle and upper class used Paine's words to deny Burke's contention of the right of the Parliament of 1688 to bind posterity forever to their settlement, to defend the French Revolution, and many even quoted him to urge Englishmen to follow the example set by their brothers across the channel.

While popular societies in England sang Paine's praises, toasted his name and adopted resolutions thanking him for his "most masterly book," the author himself was busy in France fighting for Republicanism. Louis XVI had been intercepted in his flight to join the royalist émigrés and had been brought back to Paris. On July 1, 1791, Paine and Achille Duchâtelet placarded the streets of Paris with a manifesto

---

[15] Burke's impassioned *Reflections on the French Revolution* also called forth replies from writers like Mary Wollstonecraft, James Mackintosh, Joel Barlow and William Godwin. All of them like Paine argued that governmental institutions were not sacred and unalterable. For a discussion of these booklets, see Walter P. Hall, *British Radicalism, 1791–97,* New York, 1912 and C. H. Lockett, *The Relations of French and English Society, 1763–1793,* London, 1920. See also Frederick Sheldon, "Thomas Paine in England and France," *Atlantic Monthly,* vol. IV, December, 1859, pp. 690–709.

which denounced the king and monarchy and boldly proclaimed that
the time had come to establish a republic. A few days later Paine published in *Lé Republicain,* which he and Condorcet had founded, an
attack on the monarchy. He elaborated his attack on the monarchy
in a public letter to the Abbé Sieyès, who had replied to Paine's article
and had advocated the retention of the king.

Paine returned to England on July 13, 1791. A month later he issued
his *Address and Declaration of the Friends of Universal Peace and
Liberty* in which he again defended the French Revolution. "We have
nothing to apprehend from the poor; for we are pleading their cause,"
he wrote. "And we fear not proud oppression, for we have truth on our
side. We say, and we repeat it, that the French Revolution opens to
the world an opportunity in which all good citizens must rejoice—that
of promoting the general happiness of man."

After the appearance of Burke's reply to the first part of *Rights of
Man,* entitled *An Appeal from the New to the Old Whigs,* Paine started
work on Part II of his great book. It was more of an exposition of Paine's
principles of government and society than a reply to Burke and, as
Vernon L. Parrington has pointed out, was "the maturest elaboration
of Paine's political philosophy. . . ." In this work Paine analyzed the
basic reasons for discontent in contemporary society and offered his
remedy for the misery he saw all about him.

"When in countries that we call civilized," he writes, "we see age
going to the workhouse and youth to the gallows, something must be
wrong in the system of government." "Why is it," he asks, "that scarcely
any are executed but the poor"? Poverty and an evil environment—
"lack of education for the young and a decent livelihood for the old"
—were the reasons for this unfortunate state of affairs, and these conditions prevailed because the government failed to provide for the happiness of the people. In England, of course, one could not expect the
government to act otherwise, for it consisted only of representatives of
special privileges and special interests. "No better reason can be given,"
he declares, "why the house of legislature should be composed entirely
of men whose occupations is in letting landed property than why it
should be composed of those who hire, or brewers, or bakers, or of any
other separate class of men."

Paine did not confine himself to advocating a reform in the composition of the government. He outlined a plan for popular education, for
the relief of the poor, for pensions for aged people, for donations, or

premiums, to be given for births and marriages, together with an allow-
ance for funeral expenses of people dying out of work and away from
their friends, and for State employment and lodging-houses to aid
unemployed workingmen.

To raise a revenue for the operation of his plan, Paine proposed the
levying of a progressive income tax. Not only would this secure the
funds necessary for the proper functioning of the government, but it
would bring about the abolition of primogeniture which was both "unnatural and unjust" and a great waste of the national wealth.

In Part II of the *Rights of Man* Paine also outlined his suggestions for
peaceful and harmonious relations among nations to render wars unnecessary. He advocated the signing of a treaty between England, France,
the United States and Holland under which no new ships were to be
built by any of the signers, while their existing naval establishments were
to be reduced one-half of their existing strength. "If men will permit
themselves," he wrote, "to think as rational beings ought to think, nothing can appear more ridiculous and absurd . . . than to be at the expense of building navies, filling them with men, and then hauling them
out into the ocean to see which can sink each other the fastest." Thus
though not the first Paine was one of the earliest advocates of an international association of nations to outlaw war.[16] He was also one of the
first to prophesy, as he does in Part II of *Rights of Man,* "the independence of South America, and the opening of those countries of immense
extent and wealth to the general commerce of the world."

Part Two had a phenomenal circulation. Thirty thousand copies
were distributed by the political clubs at their own expense among the
poor. Although living in poverty Paine turned over to the London Constitutional Society the thousand pounds which he had received from roy-
alties, enabling it to distribute the book even more widely. Not only did
he arrange for the printing of a cheap edition because the original cost
too much, thereby preventing it from reaching the common people,
but he even gave up the copyright to the public. At least one hundred
thousand copies of the cheap edition were sold in England, Ireland and
Scotland.

[16] Paine first presented his views on the value of an international association of nations
to preserve peace in his *Letter to the Abbé Raynal.* This work may be said to mark an
important transition in Paine's thinking in the sense that after it he began to think more
and more in internationalist terms. See Darrel Abel, "The Significance of the 'Letter to
the Abbé Raynal' in the Progress of Thomas Paine's Thought," *Pennsylvania Magazine of
History and Biography,* vol. LXVI, April, 1942, pp. 176–190.

The influence of *Rights of Man* was by no means confined to England. In America, for example, it became the book of the hour, greatly influenced the rise of the Democratic-Republican Societies, and in turn was scattered broadcast throughout the country by these popular clubs.[17] Thomas Jefferson welcomed the book as an antidote to the "political heresies" of the reactionary Federalists and, when attacked for upholding Paine's principles, wrote that he merited the same censure visited upon the author of *Rights of Man,* "for I profess the same principles." Philip Freneau, editor and poet of the Jeffersonian movement, ran excerpts from Paine's work in his *National Gazette,* and proudly announced on May 31, 1792, as his reason that "there is no American newspaper but might, with credit to itself, now and then occupy part of a column with extracts from a work that so forcibly inculcates the genuine principles of natural and equal liberty." Freneau even wrote a poem entitled "Lines Occasioned by Reading Mr. Paine's Rights of Man," in which he assured the author that America would "Remain the guardian of the Rights of Man."

In the meantime in England a storm was breaking over Paine's head. As Paine himself pointed out later, the first part of *Rights of Man* was met by the government with "profound silence," because they "beheld it as an unexpected gale that would soon blow over." When the Second Part appeared, they tried at first to follow the same course, but their silence had no "influence in stifling the progress of the work." As long, however, that it was published in an expensive edition they were not too worried. But when it began to be distributed in cheap editions at cost, the attitude changed. From "that moment," wrote Paine, "and not before, I expected a prosecution, and the event has proved that I was not mistaken."

There is more to the story. At first Premier Pitt tried to prevent the publication of Part II by bribing the publisher. When this failed, the government sponsored and paid for the publication of a slanderous biography of Paine. Then the press began to raise the false bogey of Jacobinism and instituted a cry against seditious doctrines said to be circulated by emissaries from France who were bribed by "Paris Gold" to overthrow British institutions. Mobs were inspired to burn Paine in effigy; individuals were instructed to wear boots whose hobnails were

[17] In his excellent study of these popular societies Eugene P. Link says that it was "the internationalist Thomas Paine who deserves the credit for fathering the democratic societies." See his *Democratic-Republican Societies, 1790–1800,* New York, 1942, p. 104.

marked "T.P.," so that they could trample upon Paine and his principles, and a great outcry was organized against "the notorious Tom Paine." A Royal Proclamation against seditious writings was issued on May 21, 1792, and on June 8 Paine himself was charged with sedition and his trial was set for December 18.

While British royalty was persecuting Paine, the French nation hailed him as their champion and claimed him for herself. During the first week of September he was elected to represent Calais, Oise, Somme, and Puy de Dome in the National Assembly. "Come, friend of the people," they wrote him, "to swell the number of patriots in an assembly which will decide the destiny of the human race. The happy period you have predicted for the nation has arrived. Come! do not deceive their hopes."

On September 12 Paine made a revolutionary speech to the society of the "Friends of Liberty." The next day, warned by the poet William Blake to flee at once to avoid arrest, Paine went to Dover. There he was able to get by the customs officials and depart for France by showing a letter from Washington. Twenty minutes after he got out to sea the authorities arrived to arrest him. He left behind in the hands of a customs officer at Dover "a printed proof copy" of his *Letter to the Addressers* which he wrote in the summer of 1792 in reply to the charges of seditious libel. In this pamphlet he boldly proceeded to inform his persecutors:

"If to expose the fraud and imposition of monarchy and every species of hereditary government—to lessen the oppression of taxes—to propose plans for the education of helpless infancy, and the comfortable support of the aged and distressed—to endeavor to conciliate nations to each other—to extirpate the horrid practice of war—to promote universal peace, civilization, and commerce—and to break the chains of political superstition, and raise degraded man to his proper rank;—if these things be libellous, let me live the life of a libeller, and let the name of *libeller* be engraven on my tomb!"

On December 18 Paine's *Rights of Man* was prosecuted in England. The author was found guilty of seditious libel before a pensioned judge and a packed jury in London. Since the defendant was absent, the English ruling classes had to content themselves with outlawing him.

The defendant at this very time was receiving a rousing reception in France. Soon after his arrival at Calais, Paine took his seat in the Convention. He speedily discovered that much had happened in France since his last visit to the country, and much of what had happened he could not understand.

In England Paine was associated with the extreme Left, but in France his associates were already becoming the Right. The Girondists, with whom Paine was associated, represented the bourgeoisie of France who viewed the Revolution as their property to be used for their profit and interests. They did not believe in a truly democratic government, and were mainly concerned with keeping the Revolution in check so that the common people would not have too much of a voice in affairs of state. Meanwhile, they were not averse to lining their own pockets through speculation, profiteering and sheer corruption. They frequently mouthed revolutionary slogans, but their conduct indicated that these were merely words. They used Paine and his reputation as a spokesman for the common man for their own purposes, and on more than one occasion pushed him forward to defend a program that they did not dare to advocate openly.[18]

Paine does not appear to have understood much of what was taking place behind the scenes in France. For one thing, he knew nothing of the language; for another, he had never experienced a movement as advanced as that represented by the Jacobins, led by men like Marat, Robespierre, and Saint-Just. Nor for that matter did he fully grasp the changing character of the revolution after 1792. He did not, for example, see that a dictatorship of the people was necessary to save France at a time when the reactionary forces in Europe were uniting with counter-revolutionary elements inside France to destroy the revolution. Nor did he fully grasp the fact that the French Revolution was not and could not be merely a duplication of the American Revolution, for the simple reason that the French masses were fighting to overthrow the burden of centuries of oppression and tyranny, and were compelled to meet the power of reaction throughout Europe in their efforts to achieve their goal.

Paine's difficulties in France came quickly. He arrived in Paris on September 19, 1792, just after the September massacres during which many of the Royalist conspirators in Paris had been executed. Three days later the Convention, responding to the demand of the Parisian masses led by the Jacobins, proclaimed the Republic. On September

---

[18] For an excellent analysis of the role of the Girondists together with several penetrating comments on Paine, see Albert Mathiez, *The French Revolution*, New York, 1928.

25, in an "Address to the People of France," Paine congratulated the Convention "on the abolition of Royalty," but revealed the influence of his Girondist associations by deploring the terror which had been directed against the Royalists.

The Convention had been convened primarily to draft a new constitution and to dispose of the case of Louis XVI. Paine was one of the nine members of the committee for drawing up a Constitution for France. He worked with Danton, Brissot, Condorcet, Sieyès and four others in writing the document, but it was not adopted. Soon afterwards he invited the enmity of the Jacobins by his opposition to the execution of Louis XVI.

After it was revealed during his trial that the king had been conspiring with the French émigrés and the courts of Europe to wage war upon the people of France, the Jacobins demanded the death of the king as a traitor to the country. Having failed to avoid the trial, and having been defeated in their maneuvers to adjourn it, the Girondists sought to soften the verdict on the king. The Girondist leaders themselves did not dare to oppose the death penalty directly, but left it to less important speakers to propose banishment or internment.

In taking his stand in opposition to the execution of the king, Paine was unconsciously doing just what the Girondist leaders wanted him to do. But he had his own reasons for taking his stand. Nor did he share the Girondist attitude on every aspect of the problem. In his letter to the President of the Convention, November 20, 1792, Paine had urged that "Louis Capet" be tried for his role in the conspiracy of the "crowned brigands" against liberty. This was hardly in keeping with the Girondist position at this time. On January 14, 1793, when voting took place on the Girondist proposal that the question of the king's fate be referred to the people, Paine voted with the Mountain (Jacobins) against his own party. When he arose in the Convention to make his plea against the execution of the king (it was read for him in French to the delegates), he made it clear that he did not do so out of any deference to Royalty but because he feared that the execution would give England a useful pretext for declaring war against France, and because he still could not forget that the king had once aided America to gain her independence. He pleaded with the delegates that they should not give "the tyrant of England the triumph of seeing the man perish on the scaffold who had aided my much-beloved America to break his chains."

On January 19, 1793, the Convention heard an address in opposition to the execution delivered for Paine by a delegate who had translated it from the original. Marat interrupted the speaker to charge that the translation was incorrect and that the sentiments could not be those of Paine. The incident revealed that troubled times were in store for Paine.

When the Girondists were overthrown by the Mountain, Paine attended fewer and fewer meetings of the Convention, and after June 2 ceased altogether to appear in the legislative body. Not understanding that the party with which he had been allied had brought misery and hardship upon the people of France, he could not be expected to grasp the necessity for the new radical measures introduced by the Jacobins to cope with enemies of the revolution at home and abroad.

Although Robespierre and his associates took action against most of Paine's former friends directly after the Girondists were overthrown, they did not arrest him until December 28, 1793. And then it is more than likely that had not Gouverneur Morris, the American minister to France from 1792 to 1794, conspired to keep Paine imprisoned, he would have been speedily released. After his arrest Paine appealed to his rights as an American citizen,[19] but Morris, who hated both Paine and his writings and the French Revolution, turned a deaf ear. As one of Morris's biographers puts it: "But the American minister was too clever to let such a fish escape. He told Robespierre that he did not acknowledge Mr. Paine's right to pass as an American." [20] He had also intimated to the Jacobins, who were anxious to gain the support of America against England, that Paine was thoroughly disliked in America and that the United States would not be disturbed if Paine were kept in prison. Meanwhile, Morris let his own government believe that he had done everything possible to help Paine. Not realizing the role the American minister was playing with respect to the government of the United States, Paine later placed the blame for his prolonged stay in prison on Washington and in his *Letter* to the President launched a bitter attack charging him with having deserted both his former friend and supporter and the cause of freedom.

Paine remained in the Luxembourg prison until November 4, 1794. He expected every day would be his last on earth, and it is probable that he was once saved from the guillotine by the mistake of a guard in marking his door. He nearly died because of an ulcer in his side and

[19] Paine had been arrested under a law directed against aliens of hostile nations.
[20] Daniel Walther, *Gouverneur Morris*, New York, 1934, pp. 247–248.

was more dead than alive when rescued from prison by James Monroe who replaced Morris as American minister to France. Even ten months after his release Monroe, who nursed Paine at his own home, did not believe he would live long. "The symptoms have become worse," Monroe wrote on September 15, 1795, "and the prospect now is that he will not be able to hold out more than a month or two at the farthest. I shall certainly pay the utmost attention to this gentleman, as he is one of those whose merits in our Revolution were most distinguished."

Paine eventually recovered, was readmitted to the convention in 1795, offered a pension which he refused, and remained in France until September 1, 1802, when he sailed for the United States.

On his way to prison, December 28, 1793, Paine delivered into the hands of his friend Joel Barlow a manuscript which when published in English in 1794 brought upon him a barrage of vituperation that has lasted until the present day. The work was the first part of *The Age of Reason*. Part II was written during his stay in Monroe's home after his release from prison.

Written when Paine was in his fifty-seventh year, *The Age of Reason* represented the results of years of study and reflection by its author on the place of religion in society. When, at the age of twenty, he attended lectures in London on Newtonian astronomy, he must have been influenced by the thought that as Newton found the laws which govern the world of physics so man could find the laws which govern society by observing nature. Again, he probably reached the conclusion some time later that since the clergy in many countries were on the side of oppression and served the vested interests in the interest of reaction, it was essential for the future of progress that their influence be destroyed. As early as *Common Sense* in 1776, he writes that he "saw the exceeding probability that a revolution in the system of government would be followed by a revolution in the system of religion." Although he says nothing in *Rights of Man* about the need for this "revolution in the system of religion," he makes it clear that the idea was still with him. He states that he has avoided the subject "because I am inclined to believe that what is called the present ministry wish to see contention about religion kept up to prevent the nation turning its attention to subjects of government."

During his stay in France, Paine became convinced that it was no longer possible to avoid the subject. As he noticed the reactionary activities of the clergy as plotters against the Revolution, he became even more convinced that to preserve republican principles it was necessary to destroy the priesthood. He was also worried by the fact that in their hatred of the counter-revolutionary role played by the clergy the people of France "were running headlong into Atheism . . ." At one stroke he might save the true religion, Deism, from atheism and republicanism from despotism. With this in mind he wrote his famous theological treatise.

Thomas Paine was no Atheist, Theodore Roosevelt to the contrary. Together with the foremost liberals and intellectuals in America and Europe, he believed in Deism.[21] And like many of these thinkers, Franklin, Jefferson, Wollaston, etc., he was influenced by the intellectual revolution achieved by Newton and Locke in their discovery of a systematic and harmonious universe whose laws could be ascertained by human reason. After seeing the application of the light of rationalism in the political revolutions in America and in France, it seemed to him that the next step was to apply this same rationalism in religion. In his *Letter to Erskine,* Paine wrote: "Of all the tyrannies that effect mankind, tyranny in religion is the worst; every other species of tyranny is limited to the world we live in; but this attempts to stride beyond the grave, and seeks to pursue us into eternity."

Paine's views about the Bible and religion were in no sense original for every one of them had been expressed by Deists before him. But these men had written heavy treatises for scholars. Paine wrote in his usual simple and clear language for the common man. He took Deism out of the sphere of academic discussions and made it a living creed for the average man. By doing so, of course, he threatened the hold of the clergy upon the people. As long as Deism was confined to intellectuals in the upper middle class and liberal sections of the nobility there was no danger to the vested interests of the priesthood. But once it became, as it did after the publication of *The Age of Reason,* a subject for discussion among the common people, the outlook was entirely different. Men, who had said many times before the same things Paine set down in his work, had been ignored. Paine was forced to endure a barrage of calumny and vituperation such as has been visited upon few men in our history.

In one other respect Paine was different from others who had written

[21] The evolution of Paine's religious opinions toward deism has been recently discussed by Robert P. Falk in the article "Thomas Paine: Deist or Quaker," *Pennsylvania Magazine of History and Biography,* vol. LXII, January, 1938, pp. 52–63.

on the subject. He did not bother to use diplomatic language in expressing the things he did not believe and the reasons for his disbelief in them. As he himself said, he went "marching through the Christian forest with an axe." And as he marched through the Christian forest he destroyed with his axe the stories of creation, the garden of Eden, the Resurrection, Mysteries and Miracles, prophecies and Prophets, and everything else through to Revelation, basing all his arguments on science and reason. After completing his journey through the forest, he concludes: "Of all the systems of religion that ever were invented, there is none more *derogatory to the Almighty,* more unedifying to man, more repugnant to reason, and more contradictory to itself than this thing called Christianity." All this does not mean, however, that Paine denies the greatness of Jesus as a man. "Nothing that is said here can apply," he writes, "even with the most distant disrespect, to the real character of Jesus Christ. He was a virtuous and amiable man. The morality that he preached and practised was of the most benevolent kind . . ."

Paine's entire religious creed is put quite simply. By unaided reason man could know that there is a God, that he has certain duties toward Him and his fellow-man, and that the performance of these duties made for his welfare in the present life and hereafter. He ends his work on a note of hope: "Certain . . . I am that when opinions are free, either in matters of government or religion, truth will finally and powerfully prevail." He could not foresee that there were those who were not interested in allowing opinions to be free and, because he transformed Deism from an aristocratic into a popular movement, would make life miserable for him.

In the winter of 1795–96, shortly after he completed the second part of *The Age of Reason,* and while he was still at the home of Monroe in Paris, Paine wrote his last great pamphlet, *Agrarian Justice.* The work resulted from two separate motivating factors. Paine wished, in the first place, to answer a sermon printed by the Bishop of Llandaff, on "The wisdom and goodness of God in having made both rich and poor." He dismissed this remark with the statement that God "made only male and female, and gave them the earth for their inheritance." He was also moved to write his pamphlet by the struggle in France over the confiscation of *émigré* property. After the local communes had initiated a campaign to enforce the laws calling for the confiscation of such property, the Directory, representing the bourgeoisie who had engineered the overthrow of Robespierre, put a stop to this procedure. At the same time a movement was initiated by the Directory to crush the remnants of the radical forces among the masses to pave the way for the unchallenged rule of the upper classes. In an effort to overthrow the counter-revolution and to seize power to wield it against the upper classes, the radical forces, led by Babeuf, made preparations for a *coup d'état*. Included in the program of the Babouvists were the demands for the abolition of inheritance and the confiscation of the properties of counter-revolutionists, of those who had accumulated wealth from public office, of persons who neglected to cultivate their lands, and of individuals who lived without working. The conspiracy was discovered and crushed in May, 1796.

This was the situation when Paine's *Agrarian Justice* was published. He did not go as far as Babeuf, although he approved of the objective of the insurrection in aiming to remove social inequalities in property. Paine held that there were two kinds of property: natural property (the earth in its uncultivated stage), and "improved" property. He had no intention of taking away "improved" property, but argued that the "earth, in its natural uncultivated state was, and ever would have continued to be, *the common property of the human race*." The introduction of private property added, through cultivation, a "tenfold" value to created earth. At the same time, however, it "dispossessed more than half the inhabitants of every nation of their natural inheritance, without providing . . . an indemnification for that loss, and has thereby created a species of poverty and wretchedness that did not exist before." To remedy this situation and assist the persons thus dispossessed, Paine maintained that every proprietor "of cultivated land" owed to the community a ground-rent for the land which he held. With this sum Paine aimed to set up a National Fund, out of which there would be paid to every person, "when arrived at the age of twenty-one years, the sum of fifteen pounds sterling, as a compensation in part, for the loss of his or her natural inheritance, by the system of landed property," and "the sum of ten pounds per annum, during life, to every person now living, of the age of fifty years, and to all others as they shall arrive at that age."

The system he proposed, Paine maintained, would so organize civilization "that the whole weight of misery can be removed." It would aid the blind, the lame and the aged poor, and at the same time guarantee that the new generation would never become poor. And all this would not be achieved through charity. "It is not charity, but a right," he cried, "not bounty but justice, that I am pleading for." [22] In a burst of indignation over the exploitation of workingmen by employers, he wrote: ". . . if we examine the case minutely it will be found that the accumulation of personal property is, in many instances, the effect of paying too little for the labour that produced it; the consequence of which is, that the working hand perishes in old age, and that the employer abounds in affluence."

Paine remained in France despite his dislike for the reaction that set in with the Directory and continued during Napoleon's Consulate. He felt that France deserved enthusiastic support for seeking to end feudalism and autocracy, and was convinced that even though democracy was not developing as completely as he had hoped, the basic advances of the Revolution in destroying feudal privileges would remain. France was still to him, therefore, the revolutionary republic of Europe and as such merited the assistance of all true democrats, especially in its efforts to defeat England which Paine regarded as the bulwark of reaction in the western world. Britain's defeat in war, he was convinced, would end the rule of the English aristocracy, and pave the way for a democratic republic in England which, in alliance with the United States and France, would guarantee the spread of republicanism throughout the world and international peace. "There will be no lasting peace for France, nor for the world," wrote Paine, "until the tyranny and corruption of the English government be abolished, and England, like Italy, become a sister republic."

Paine submitted a plan to the French Directory for a military expedition against England, whose purpose would be to overthrow the monarchy and assist the people to proclaim a democratic republic. Napoleon, who had not yet revealed his plans of becoming a military dictator, received Paine's proposal enthusiastically and even visited the writer to discuss the possibilities. Paine himself contributed funds he could hardly spare toward the expedition, but it never materialized.

Eventually Paine realized that his usefulness in France was over. He was not molested under the Consulate, but his democratic views such as his support of the Haitian revolution led by Touissant L'Ouverture

[22] Dorfman (*op. cit.*, p. 380), argues that in *Agrarian Justice* Paine was primarily concerned with the protection of property from the dangerous masses and sought to convince the property-holders to give up some of their holdings in order that they might be able to save the rest. This rather than the improvement of the condition of the poor was his aim, he concludes. A mere reading of the book reveals how unjustified is this conclusion. See, however, Penniman, *op. cit.*, p. 251, for an able refutation of this contention.

and his agitation against the slave trade, were looked upon unfavorably. He waited to return to the country which had made him an author.

The fifteen years Paine had spent in Europe since his departure from America had been crowded with world-shaking events, and in most of them he had been an active participant. He had seen the French Revolution uproot hallowed traditions, sweep away feudal remnants and revolutionize class and property relations. He had witnessed the upsurge of the revolutionary movement in England and saw how it was pulverized after Pitt's repressive laws of 1796. He had not fully understood the need for stern measures adopted by the people in meeting and defeating counter-revolution, and his prediction of an easy triumph for republican principles had not been realized. But his faith in the people and the cause of democracy was still unshaken. The measures adopted by the people in their striving for freedom had caused many liberals to blanch and revise their ideas. But they had left his convictions undisturbed. He returned to America convinced that in the end freedom would triumph all over the world.

Soon after his inauguration as President in 1801, Jefferson wrote Paine a cordial letter inviting him to return to the United States on the American warship, *Maryland,* the honored guest of the nation he had helped to found. He assured Paine that the attitude of his presidential predecessors towards him had not been a true reflection of the sentiment of a grateful nation. "I am in hopes you will find us returned generally to sentiments worthy of former times," wrote Jefferson. "In these it will be your glory steadily to have laboured, and with as much effect as any man living. That you may long live to continue your useful labours, and to reap their reward in the thankfulness of nations, is my sincere prayer. Accept assurances of my high esteem and affectionate attachment."

Paine sailed from France on September 1 and landed at Baltimore on October 30, 1802. He was hailed by the Jeffersonians and especially by the advocates of Deism, the "Republican Religion." But the Federalists, the reactionary clergy and others in the anti-democratic camp began the vile attack upon him that was to follow him to his grave. Every paper, Paine wrote to a friend in London, was "filled with applause or abuse."

The abuse, however, soon drowned out the applause. The Federalists hated everything Paine stood for, and they did not forget that he had vigorously denounced Washington and condemned the Alien and Sedition laws of the Adams administration. But primarily they considered his return as a useful stick with which to beat and possibly defeat the Jeffersonians. Hence the Federalist press began a campaign of vilification that probably has no equal in our history. As one student has put it, "the reactionary press exhausted the resources of the dictionary to express the unutterable, only to sink back at last with impotent rage." These newspapers called Paine "the scavenger of faction," "lilly-livered sinical rogue," "loathsome reptile," "demi-human archbeast," "an object of disgust, of abhorrence, of absolute loathing to every decent man except the President of the United States." "What! invite to the United States that lying, drunken, brutal infidel," cried the *New England Palladium* of Boston, "who rejoices in the opportunity of basking and wallowing in the confusion, devastation, bloodshed, rapine and murder, in which his soul delights?" The Philadelphia *Portfolio* urged "every honest and insulted man of dignity . . . to shake off the very dust of his feet and to abandon America" the moment "the loathsome Thomas Paine" started to express his views in this country.[23]

Even Paine's former friends in America began to avoid him. Samuel Adams broke off his friendship and Benjamin Rush refused to have anything to do with him, both giving as their reason that the principles set forth in *The Age of Reason* were too "offensive." For a time Paine even thought that Jefferson had turned against him. When the President postponed their meeting after his arrival in Washington, Paine wrote to Jefferson asking him to return his models. He had hoped, he added, to discuss his scientific plans with the President: "But you have not only shown no disposition towards it, but have, in some measure, by a sort of shyness, as if you stood in fear of federal observation, precluded it. I am not the only one, who makes observations of this kind."

Jefferson replied immediately assuring Paine that he was mistaken and only the fact that he had been busy had prevented their meeting. Praising his models, the President went on: "You have certainly misunderstood what you deem shyness. Of that I have not a thought towards you, but on the contrary have openly maintained in conversation the duty of showing our respect to you and of defying federal calumny in this as in other cases by doing what is Right. As to fearing it, if I ever

[23] For interesting accounts of Paine's return to the United States, see G. Adolph Koch, *Republican Religion*, New York, 1933, pp. 130–146; Frederick Sheldon, "Thomas Paine's Second Appearance in the United States," *Atlantic Monthly*, vol. IV, July, 1859, pp. 1–17, and Dixon Wecter, "Hero in Reverse," *Virginia Quarterly Review*, vol. XVIII, Spring, 1942, pp. 243–259.

could have been weak enough for that, they have taken care to cure me of it thoroughly." [24]

Paine visited Jefferson and discussed political and scientific issues. He refused to accept any public office, but continued to advise the President through correspondence on many important political issues of the day as well as to supply him with ideas on the European situation based on his rich experience abroad. Most of his time, however, was devoted to activity in aiding Elihu Palmer promote the religion of Deism in New York. He contributed articles and letters to the *Prospect* expanding some of the themes he had touched upon in *The Age of Reason*. It was unfortunate in one sense that he concentrated so largely upon religious issues, for it rendered his political activities less useful. But he was forced to elaborate his position to clear himself of unjustified charges, and he believed that the struggle against the reactionary clergy was essential for the further progress of the Jeffersonian cause in America.

But the campaign of slander increased the more he ventured to attack the strong-hold of reaction. On one occasion, when he tried to engage passage from New York to Trenton, the stagedriver refused him a seat. "My stage and horses were once struck by lightning, and I don't want him to suffer again," he told Paine to the amusement of his well-to-do passengers. Later a singer in a New York Presbyterian church was suspended for having visited him. His moderate appetite for brandy was distorted into drunkenness by cartoonists and writers. In 1806 came the greatest effrontery of all when he was denied the right to vote by Federalist officials in New Rochelle on the charge that he was not an American citizen.

Although he led an increasingly harried life, Paine enjoyed the company of "the laboring class of emigrants," and spent many enjoyable days with Robert Fulton, who shared his democratic views, observing his steamboat experiments on the Hudson. For several months in the winter of 1807 he lived with John Wesley Jarvis. The painter wrote to a friend on May 2nd, "I have had Tom Paine living with me for these five months. He is one of the most pleasant companions I have met with for an old man." [25]

[24] Thomas Jefferson to Thomas Paine, January 13, 1803, Jefferson Papers, Library of Congress.
[25] H. E. Dickson, "Day vs. Jarvis," *Pennsylvania Magazine of History and Biography,* vol. lxiii, April, 1939, p. 187.

Paine spent his last years in poverty. Broken in health and reduced in finances, he was forced to move to a miserable lodging house on Fulton Street in New York City. Just before he died on June 8, 1809, two clergymen gained access to his room hoping to hear him recant his heresies. To their question concerning his religious opinions, Paine simply said: "Let me alone; good morning."

Paine was buried on his farm in New Rochelle. But even in the grave it was not considered fitting that the great, militant democrat, Thomas Paine, should enjoy peace and dignity. Curiosity-seekers desecrated his tombstone, and twenty years after his death, William Cobbett, the English reformer who had once joined in the campaign of vilification, stole Paine's bones and shipped them to England. Sometime later the remains disappeared. "As to his bones," wrote Moncure Daniel Conway, "no man knows the place of their rest to this day. His principles rest not. His thoughts, untraceable like his dust, are blown about the world which he held in his heart."

"No writer," Jefferson observed in 1821, "has exceeded Paine in ease and familiarity of style, in perspicuity of expression, happiness of elucidation, and in simple and unassuming language." Paine's writings inspired men of his day in America, in England and in France to live and die for freedom, and left behind in these countries a vision of a world of men free in body and mind. At a time when men and women are seeking to realize that type of world it would be well to read again the words of Thomas Paine who wrote so much and so well to build the heritage of freedom.

Philip S. Foner

THE
AGE
OF
REASON
BY THOMAS PAINE

Editor's Note

EDITOR'S NOTE

The first edition of *The Age of Reason* was printed by Barras in Paris in 1794. Written when the author was in his fifty-seventh year, this famous theological treatise represented the results of years of study and reflection on the place of religion in society. Paine always made it his practice to keep abreast of the latest developments in the field of science, so that when he prepared to begin writing *The Age of Reason* he was in the position to apply all the discoveries in the field of scientific knowledge to incidents related in the Old and New Testaments. In essence, therefore, the work is an application of reason to the Bible, in the light of the Newtonian principles of science, and is devoted chiefly to a careful analysis of the revelations, prophecies, miracles and stories related in that book. Actually, Paine was doing for the English world what had already been done in France by men like Voltaire and Diderot. Moreover, he was doing what Jefferson had advised his nephew Peter Carr to do as early as August 10, 1787. "Fix reason firmly in her seat," wrote Jefferson in his letter of advice, "and call to her tribunal every fact, every opinion. Question with boldness even the existence of a God; because if there be one, He must more approve of the homage of reason, than that of blindfold fear. You will naturally examine first, the religion of your own country. Read the Bible, then, as you would read Livy or Tacitus. . . . Your own reason is the only oracle given you by heaven, and you are answerable, not for the rightness, but the uprightness of the decision." (Philip S. Foner, editor, *Thomas Jefferson: Selections from His Writings*, p. 76.)

Paine was not an atheist. Indeed, in the "Profession of Faith" with which he opens his book he states emphatically: "I believe in one God, and no more; and I hope for happiness beyond this life." Together with many other progressive leaders of the age of enlightenment, Paine was a deist, who believed in "a God of moral truth, and not a God of mystery or obscurity." Well grounded in the science of his day, he conceived of God as the "first cause, the cause of all things." The universe itself, he observed, seemed a singular proof of the beneficence of God: "The Almighty Lecturer, by displaying the principles of science in the structure of the universe, has invited man to study and to imitation. It is as if He had said to the inhabitants of this globe·we call ours: I have made an earth for man to dwell upon, and I have rendered the starry heavens visible, to teach him science and the arts. He can now provide for his own comfort, and learn from my munificence to all to be kind to each other."

Organized religion, Paine wrote, was "set up to terrify and enslave mankind, and monopolize power and profit." The only true theology was "natural philosophy, embracing the whole circle of science." The only true religion was that of deism. "The only religion that has not been invented," he wrote, "and that has in it every evidence of divine originality, is pure and simple deism. It must have been the first and will probably be the last that man believes. . . ."

Paine's interest in religious issues was an essential part of his political thinking. Since the clergy in many countries were on the side of oppression and served the vested interests as a valuable bulwark against democratic reforms, it was essential for the future of progress that these defenders of aristocracy and hereditary privilege be exposed and their influence destroyed. During the French Revolution, Paine became even more convinced of the reactionary role played by the clergy in political affairs as he observed the close alliance that existed between the higher clergy of France and the forces of aristocracy and monarchy. In order to break this alliance and to preserve republican and liberal principles, he determined to destroy the priesthood by exposing the false character of the source of its authority—the Scriptural revelation. Still another motive influenced Paine in writing *The Age of Reason*. He was genuinely alarmed by the growth of atheism, and was convinced that the growing disbelief in God and a future life was due primarily to the disgust men felt for the reactionary and rigid conduct of the clergy. Fearing that the growth of atheism threatened the existence of the only true religion, deism, and determined to save republicanism from despotism, Paine published *The Age of Reason*.

Whereas the first part of *The Age of Reason* deals with revelation in general (possibly because the author did not have a Bible at hand while writing this section), the second discusses the Judaic-Christian account in detail. Examining the books of the Old Testament (with which he was now equipped) in the light of reason, he found them all wanting. He argues that Moses, Joshua, Samuel, David and Solomon did not compose the books bearing their names, and asserts that the Pentateuch was written "by some very ignorant and stupid pretenders to authorship. several hundred years after the death of Moses. . . ."

Paine deals just as sharply with the New Testament, a copy of which was also at his side when he wrote the section. He holds that the Gospels were not written by the apostles and that they appeared centuries after the death of

Christ. Of the existence of Jesus, Paine has no doubt, nor of his crucifixion. He admits the greatness of Jesus as a man but denies that he was a God. "The morality that he preached and practised," he writes, "was of the most benevolent kind, and though similar systems of morality had been preached by Confucius and by some of the Greek philosophers many years before, by the Quakers since, and by many good men in all ages, it has not been exceeded by any." But the immaculate conception was a pure piece of fiction, and the resurrection exceedingly doubtful. Thus Paine repudiates the divine origin of Christianity on the ground that it was too "absurd for belief, too impossible to convince and too inconsistent to practice. . . ."

Since the Christian religion was "an engine of power" functioning in behalf of despotism as well as "a species of Atheism," Paine suggests the introduction of deism which he defines as follows: "Were a man impressed as fully and as strongly as he ought to be with the belief of a God, his moral life would be regulated by the forces of this belief, he would stand in awe of God and of himself, and would not do the thing that could not be concealed from either. To give this belief the full opportunity of force it is necessary that it acts alone. This is deism."

So profoundly were the royalists and reactionaries shocked by Paine's vigorous attack upon one of the principal bulwarks of feudal despotism, that the author was treated with such deep and relentless hatred as to earn for him a discredit which the lapse of more than a century has scarcely succeeded in modifying. A century after his death, Theodore Roosevelt could still speak of Paine as "a filthy little atheist." Volumes were written in reply to *The Age of Reason;* the publisher of the book was found guilty of blasphemy; the work was suppressed and the author again hanged in effigy. Not only was the publisher imprisoned, but anyone who distributed, read or discussed *The Age of Reason* was persecuted by the British ministry, and some were even arrested simply for displaying the portrait of the author.

The chief reason for the campaign of slander and vilification launched against Paine was that he had succeeded in carrying the message of deism to the people. Up to this point the deistic movement had been influential solely among people of education and social prominence. Now it was being spread among the masses. Written in a style easily understood by the average man, distributed free of charge in America and Europe by deistic organizations, the work gained an extensive circulation in cities, villages and towns. Overnight deism became a mass movement, and since it allied itself naturally with republicanism in the political arena it became a vital force in the struggle against reaction.

For detailed and scholarly treatments of the deistic movements and the influence of *The Age of Reason,* see Herbert M. Morais, *Deism in Eighteenth Century America,* New York, 1934, and G. A. Koch, *Republican Religion,* New York, 1933.—*Editor.*

THE
AGE
OF
REASON

BEING AN INVESTIGATION OF TRUE AND FABULOUS THEOLOGY

Part First

TO MY FELLOW-CITIZENS OF THE UNITED STATES OF AMERICA

I PUT the following work under your protection. It contains my opinion upon religion. You will do me the justice to remember, that I have always strenuously supported the right of every man to his own opinion, however different that opinion might be to mine. He who denies to another this right, makes a slave of himself to his present opinion, because he precludes himself the right of changing it.

The most formidable weapon against errors of every kind is reason. I have never used any other, and I trust I never shall.

Your affectionate friend and fellow-citizen,

THOMAS PAINE.

Paris, 8th Pluvôise.
Second year of the French Republic, one and indivisible.
January 27th, O. S. 1794.

THE AUTHOR'S PROFESSION OF FAITH

IT HAS been my intention, for several years past, to publish my thoughts upon religion. I am well aware of the difficulties that attend the subject, and from that consideration, had reserved it to a more advanced period of life. I intended it to be the last offering I should make to my fellow-citizens of all nations, and that at a time when the purity of the motive that induced me to it could not admit of a question, even by those who might disapprove the work. The circumstance that has now taken place in France of the total abolition of the whole national order of priesthood, and of everything appertaining to compulsive systems of religion, and compulsive articles of faith, has not only precipitated my intention, but rendered a work of this kind exceedingly necessary, lest in the general wreck of superstition, of false systems of government and false theology, we lose sight of morality, of humanity and of the theology that is true.

As several of my colleagues, and others of my fellow-citizens of France, have given me the example of making their voluntary and individual profession of faith, I also will make mine; and I do this with all that sincerity and frankness with which the mind of man communicates with itself.

I believe in one God, and no more; and I hope for happiness beyond this life.

I believe in the equality of man; and I believe that religious duties consist in doing justice, loving mercy, and endeavoring to make our fellow-creatures happy.

But, lest it should be supposed that I believe many other things in addition to these, I shall, in the progress of this work, declare the things I do not believe, and my reasons for not believing them.

I do not believe in the creed professed by the Jewish Church, by the Roman Church, by the Greek Church, by the Turkish Church, by the Protestant Church, nor by any church that I know of. My own mind is my own church.

All national institutions of churches, whether Jewish, Christian or Turkish, appear to me no other than human inventions, set up to terrify and enslave mankind, and monopolize power and profit.

I do not mean by this declaration to condemn those who believe otherwise; they have the same right to their belief as I have to mine. But it is necessary to the happiness of man that he be mentally faithful to himself. Infidelity does not consist in believing, or in disbelieving; it consists in professing to believe what he does not believe.

It is impossible to calculate the moral mischief, if I may so express it, that mental lying has produced in society. When a man has so far corrupted and prostituted the chastity of his mind as to subscribe his professional belief to things he does not believe he has prepared himself for the commission of every other crime.

He takes up the trade of a priest for the sake of gain, and in order to qualify himself for that trade he begins with a perjury. Can we conceive any thing more destructive to morality than this?

Soon after I had published the pamphlet "Common Sense," in America, I saw the exceeding probability that a revolution in the system of government would be followed by a revolution in the system of religion. The adulterous connection of church and state, wherever it has taken place, whether Jewish, Christian or Turkish, has so effectually prohibited by pains and penalties every discussion upon established creeds, and upon first principles of religion, that until the system of government should be changed, those subjects could not be brought fairly and openly before the world; but that whenever this should be done, a revolution in the system of religion would follow. Human inventions and priestcraft would be detected; and man would return to the pure, unmixed and unadulterated belief of one God, and no more.

Concerning Missions and Revelations

Every national church or religion has established itself by pretending some special mission from God, communicated to certain individuals. The Jews have their Moses; the Christians their Jesus Christ, their apostles and saints; and the Turks their Mahomet, as if the way to God was not open to every man alike.

Each of those churches show certain books, which they call *revelation,* or the Word of God. The Jews say that their Word of God was given by God to Moses, face to face; the Christians say that their Word of God came by divine inspiration; and the Turks say that their Word of God (the Koran) was brought by an angel from heaven. Each of those churches accuses the other of unbelief; and for my own part, I disbelieve them all.

As it is necessary to affix right ideas to words, I will, before I proceed further into the subject, offer some observations on the word *revelation.* Revelation, when applied to religion, means something communicated *immediately* from God to man.

No one will deny or dispute the power of the Almighty to make such a communication, if He pleases. But admitting, for the sake of a case, that something has been revealed to a certain person, and not revealed to any other person, it is revelation to that person only. When he tells it to a second person, a second to a third, a third to a fourth, and so on, it ceases to be a revelation to all those persons. It is revelation to the first person only, and *hearsay* to every other, and consequently they are not obliged to believe it.

It is a contradiction in terms and ideas, to call anything a revelation that comes to us at second-hand, either verbally or in writing. Revelation is necessarily limited to the first communication—after this it is only an account of something which that person says was a revelation made to him; and though he may find himself obliged to believe it, it cannot be incumbent on me to believe it in the same manner; for it was not a revelation made to *me,* and I have only his word for it that it was made to him. When Moses told the children of Israel that he received the two tables of the commandments from the hands of God, they were not obliged to believe him, because they had no other authority for it than his telling them so; and I have no other authority for it than some historian telling me so. The commandments carry no internal evidence of divinity with them; they contain some good moral precepts, such as any man qualified to be a lawgiver, or a legislator, could produce himself, without having recourse to supernatural intervention.[1]

When I am told that the Koran was written in heaven and brought to Mahomet by an angel, the account comes too near the same kind of hearsay evidence and second-hand authority as the former. I did not see the angel myself and, therefore, I have a right not to believe it.

When also I am told that a woman called the Virgin Mary, said, or gave out, that she was with child without any cohabitation with a man, and that her betrothed husband, Joseph, said that an angel told him so, I have a right to believe them or not; such a circumstance required a much stronger evidence than their bare word for it; but we have not even this—for neither Joseph nor Mary wrote any such matter themselves; it is only reported by others that *they said so*—it is hearsay upon hearsay, and I do not choose to rest my belief upon such evidence.

It is, however, not difficult to account for the credit that was given to the story of Jesus Christ being the Son of God. He was born at a time when the heathen mythology had still some fashion and repute in the world, and that mythology had prepared the people for the belief of such

---

[1] It is, however, necessary to except the declaration which says that God *visits the sins of the fathers upon the children;* it is contrary to every principle of moral justice.—*Author.*

a story. Almost all the extraordinary men that lived under the heathen mythology were reputed to be the sons of some of their gods. It was not a new thing, at that time, to believe a man to have been celestially begotten; the intercourse of gods with women was then a matter of familiar opinion.

Their Jupiter, according to their accounts, had cohabited with hundreds: the story, therefore, had nothing in it either new, wonderful or obscene; it was conformable to the opinions that then prevailed among the people called Gentiles, or Mythologists, and it was those people only that believed it.

The Jews, who had kept strictly to the belief of one God, and no more, and who had always rejected the heathen mythology, never credited the story.

It is curious to observe how the theory of what is called the Christian Church sprung out of the tail of the heathen mythology. A direct incorporation took place in the first instance, by making the reputed founder to be celestially begotten. The trinity of gods that then followed was no other than a reduction of the former plurality, which was about twenty or thirty thousand; the statue of Mary succeeded the statue of Diana of Ephesus; the deification of heroes changed into the canonization of saints; the Mythologists had gods for everything; the Christian Mythologists had saints for everything; the Church became as crowded with the one as the Pantheon had been with the other, and Rome was the place of both. The Christian theory is little else than the idolatry of the ancient Mythologists, accommodated to the purposes of power and revenue; and it yet remains to reason and philosophy to abolish the amphibious fraud.

An Appreciation of the Character of Jesus Christ, and His History

Nothing that is here said can apply, even with the most distant disrespect, to the real character of Jesus Christ. He was a virtuous and an amiable man. The morality that he preached and practised was of the most benevolent kind; and though similar systems of morality had been preached by Confucius, and by some of the Greek philosophers, many years before; by the Quakers since; and by many good men in all ages, it has not been exceeded by any.

Jesus Christ wrote no account of himself, of his birth, parentage, or anything else; not a line of what is called the New Testament is of his own writing. The history of him is altogether the work of other people; and as to the account given of his resurrection and ascension, it was the necessary counterpart to the story of his birth. His historians, having brought him into the world in a supernatural manner, were obliged to take him out again in the same manner, or the first part of the story must have fallen to the ground.

The wretched contrivance with which this latter part is told exceeds every thing that went before it. The first part, that of the miraculous conception, was not a thing that admitted of publicity; and therefore the tellers of this part of the story had this advantage, that though they might not be credited, they could not be detected. They could not be expected to prove it, because it was not one of those things that admitted of proof, and it was impossible that the person of whom it was told could prove it himself.

But the resurrection of a dead person from the grave, and his ascension through the air, is a thing very different as to the evidence it admits of, to the invisible conception of a child in the womb. The resurrection and ascension, supposing them to have taken place, admitted of public and ocular demonstration, like that of the ascension of a balloon, or the sun at noon-day, to all Jerusalem at least.

A thing which everybody is required to believe requires that the proof and evidence of it should be equal to all, and universal; and as the public visibility of this last related act was the only evidence that could give sanction to the former part, the whole of it falls to the ground, because that evidence never was given. Instead of this, a small number of persons, not more than eight or nine, are introduced as proxies for the whole world to say they saw it, and all the rest of the world are called upon to believe it. But it appears that Thomas did not believe the resurrection, and, as they say, would not believe without having ocular and manual demonstration himself. *So neither will I,* and the reason is equally as good for me, and for every other person, as for Thomas.

It is in vain to attempt to palliate or disguise this matter. The story, so far as relates to the supernatural part, has every mark of fraud and imposition stamped upon the face of it. Who were the authors of it is as impossible for us now to know, as it is for us to be assured that the books in which the account is related were written by the persons whose names they bear; the best surviving evidence we now have respecting this affair is the Jews. They are regularly descended from the people who lived in the times this resurrection and ascension is said to have happened, and they say, *it is not true*. It has long appeared to me a strange inconsistency to cite the Jews as a proof of the truth of the story. It is just the same as if a man were to say, I will prove the truth of what I have told you by producing the people who say it is false.

That such a person as Jesus Christ existed, and that he was crucified, which was the mode of execution at that day, are historical relations strictly within the limits of probability. He preached most excellent morality and the equality of man; but he preached also against the corruptions and avarice of the Jewish priests, and this brought upon him the hatred and vengeance of the whole order of priesthood.

The accusation which those priests brought against him was that of sedition and conspiracy against the Roman government, to which the Jews were then subject and tributary; and it is not improbable that the Roman government might have some secret apprehensions of the effects of his doctrine, as well as the Jewish priests; neither is it improbable that Jesus Christ had in contemplation the delivery of the Jewish nation from the bondage of the Romans. Between the two, however, this virtuous reformer and revolutionist lost his life.

Fabulous Bases of Christianity

It is upon this plain narrative of facts, together with another case I am going to mention, that the Christian Mythologists, calling themselves the Christian Church, have erected their fable, which, for absurdity and extravagance, is not exceeded by anything that is to be found in the mythology of the ancients.

The ancient Mythologists tell that the race of Giants made war against Jupiter, and that one of them threw a hundred rocks against him at one throw; that Jupiter defeated him with thunder, and confined him afterward under Mount Etna, and that every time the giant turns himself Mount Etna belches fire. It is here easy to see that the circumstance of the mountain, that of its being a volcano, suggested the idea of the fable; and that the fable is made to fit and wind itself up with that circumstance.

The Christian Mythologists tell that their Satan made war against the Almighty, who defeated him, and confined him afterward, not under a mountain, but in a pit. It is here easy to see that the first fable suggested the idea of the second; for the fable of Jupiter and the Giants was told many hundred years before that of Satan.

Thus far the ancient and the Christian Mythologists differ very little from each other. But the latter have contrived to carry the matter much farther.

They have contrived to connect the fabulous part of the story of Jesus Christ with the fable originating from Mount Etna; and in order to make all the parts of the story tie together they have taken to their aid the traditions of the Jews; for the Christian mythology is made up partly from the ancient mythology and partly from the Jewish traditions.

The Christian Mythologists, after having confined Satan in a pit, were obliged to let him out again to bring on the sequel of the fable. He is then introduced into the Garden of Eden, in the shape of a snake or a serpent, and in that shape he enters into familiar conversation with Eve, who is no way surprised to hear a snake talk; and the issue of this *tête-à-tête* is that he persuades her to eat an apple, and the eating of that apple damns all mankind.

After giving Satan this triumph over the whole creation, one would have supposed that the Church Mythologists would have been kind enough to send him back again to the pit; or, if they had not done this, that they would have put a mountain upon him (for they say that their faith can remove a mountain), or have put him *under* a mountain, as the former mythologists had done, to prevent his getting again among the women and doing more mischief. But instead of this they leave him at large, without even obliging him to give his parole—the secret of which is that they could not do without him; and after being at the trouble of making him, they bribed him to stay. They promised him ALL the Jews, ALL the Turks by anticipation, nine-tenths of the world beside, and Mahomet into the bargain. After this, who can doubt the bountifulness of the Christian Mythology?

Having thus made an insurrection and a battle in heaven, in which none of the combatants could be either killed or wounded—put Satan into the pit—let him out again—gave him a triumph over the whole creation—damned all mankind by the eating of an apple, these Christian Mythologists bring the two ends of their fable together. They represent this virtuous and amiable man, Jesus Christ, to be at once both God and Man, and also the Son of God, celestially begotten, on purpose to be sacrificed, because they say that Eve in her longing had eaten an apple.

EXAMINATION OF THE PRECEDING BASES

Putting aside everything that might excite laughter by its absurdity, or detestation by its profaneness, and confining ourselves merely to an examination of the parts, it is impossible to conceive a story more derogatory to the Almighty, more inconsistent with His wisdom, more contradictory to His power, than this story is.

In order to make for it a foundation to rise upon, the inventors were under the necessity of giving to the being whom they call Satan, a power equally as great, if not greater than they attribute to the Almighty. They have not only given him the power of liberating himself from the pit, after what they call his fall, but they have made that power increase afterward to infinity. Before this fall they represent him only as an angel of limited existence, as they represent the rest. After his fall, he becomes, by their account, omnipresent. He exists everywhere, and at the same time. He occupies the whole immensity of space.

Not content with this deification of Satan, they represent him as defeating, by stratagem, in the shape of an animal of the creation, all the power and wisdom of the Almighty. They represent him as having compelled the Almighty to the *direct necessity* either of surrendering the whole of the creation to the government and sovereignty of this Satan, or of capitulating for its redemption by coming down upon earth, and exhibiting Himself upon a cross in the shape of a man.

Had the inventors of this story told it the contrary way, that is, had they represented the Almighty as compelling Satan to exhibit *himself* on a cross, in the shape of a snake, as a punishment for his new transgression, the story would have been less absurd—less contradictory. But instead of this, they make the transgressor triumph, and the Almighty fall.

That many good men have believed this strange fable, and lived very good lives under that belief (for credulity is not a crime), is what I have no doubt of. In the first place, they were educated to believe it, and they would have believed anything else in the same manner.

There are also many who have been so enthusiastically enraptured by what they conceived to be the infinite love of God to man, in making a sacrifice of Himself, that the vehemence of the idea has forbidden and deterred them from examining into the absurdity and profaneness of the story. The more unnatural anything is, the more it is capable of becoming the object of dismal admiration.

OF THE TRUE THEOLOGY

But if objects for gratitude and admiration are our desire, do they not present themselves every hour to our eyes? Do we not see a fair creation prepared to receive us the instant we are born—a world furnished to our hands, that cost us nothing? Is it we that light up the sun, that pour down the rain, and fill the earth with abundance? Whether we sleep or wake, the vast machinery of the universe still goes on.

Are these things, and the blessings they indicate in future, nothing to us? Can our gross feelings be excited by no other subjects than tragedy and suicide? Or is the gloomy pride of man become so intolerable, that nothing can flatter it but a sacrifice of the Creator?

I know that this bold investigation will alarm many, but it would be paying too great a compliment to their credulity to forbear it upon that account; the times and the subject demand it to be done. The suspicion that the theory of what is called the Christian Church is fabulous is becoming very extensive in all countries; and it will be a consolation to men staggering under that suspicion, and doubting what to believe and what to disbelieve, to see the object freely investigated. I therefore pass on to an examination of the books called the Old and New Testaments.

EXAMINATION OF THE OLD TESTAMENT

These books, beginning with Genesis and ending with Revelation (which, by the bye, is a book of riddles that requires a revelation to explain it), are, we are told, the Word of God. It is, therefore, proper for us to know who told us so, that we may know what credit to give to the report. The answer to this question is that nobody can tell, except that we tell one another so. The case, however, historically appears to be as follows:

When the Church Mythologists established their system, they collected all the writings they could find and managed them as they pleased. It is a matter altogether of uncertainty to us whether such of the writings as now appear under the name of the Old and New Testaments are in the same state in which those collectors say they found them, or whether they added, altered, abridged or dressed them up.

Be this as it may, they decided by *vote* which of the books out of the collection they had made should be the WORD OF GOD, and which should not. They rejected several; they voted others to be doubtful, such as the books called the Apocrypha; and those books which had a majority of votes were voted to be the Word of God. Had they voted otherwise, all the people, since calling themselves Christians, had believed otherwise— for the belief of the one comes from the vote of the other. Who the people were that did all this, we know nothing of; they called themselves by the general name of the Church, and this is all we know of the matter.

As we have no other external evidence or authority for believing these books to be the Word of God than what I have mentioned, which is no evidence or authority at all, I come in the next place to examine the internal evidence contained in the books themselves.

In the former part of this essay, I have spoken of revelation; I now proceed further with that subject for the purpose of applying it to the books in question.

Revelation is a communication of something which the person to whom that thing is revealed did not know before. For if I have done a thing, or seen it done, it needs no revelation to tell me I have done it, or seen it, nor to enable me to tell it, or to write it.

Revelation, therefore, cannot be applied to anything done upon earth, of which man himself is the actor or the witness; and consequently all the historical and anecdotal parts of the Bible, which is almost the whole of it, is not within the meaning and compass of the word revelation, and, therefore, is not the Word of God.

When Samson ran off with the gate-posts of Gaza, if he ever did so (and whether he did or not is nothing to us), or when he visited his Delilah, or caught his foxes, or did anything else, what has revelation to do with these things? If they were facts, he could tell them himself, or his secretary, if he kept one, could write them, if they were worth either telling or writing; and if they were fictions, revelation could not make them true; and whether true or not, we are neither the better nor the wiser for knowing them. When we contemplate the immensity of that Being who directs and governs the incomprehensible WHOLE, of which the utmost ken of human sight can discover but a part, we ought to feel shame at calling such paltry stories the Word of God.

As to the account of the Creation, with which the book of Genesis opens, it has all the appearance of being a tradition which the Israelites had among them before they came into Egypt; and after their departure from that country they put it at the head of their history, without telling (as it is most probable) that they did not know how they came by it. The manner in which the account opens shows it to be traditionary. It begins abruptly; it is nobody that speaks; it is nobody that hears; it is addressed to nobody; it has neither first, second, nor third person; it has every criterion of being a tradition; it has no voucher. Moses does not take it upon himself by introducing it with the formality that he used on other occasions, such as that of saying, *"The Lord spake unto Moses, saying."*

Why it has been called the Mosaic account of the Creation, I am at a loss to conceive. Moses, I believe, was too good a judge of such subjects to put his name to that account. He had been educated among the Egyptians, who were a people as well skilled in science, and particularly in astronomy, as any people of their day; and the silence and caution that Moses observes in not authenticating the account is a good negative evidence that he neither told it nor believed it.

The case is that every nation of people has been world-makers, and the Israelites had as much right to set up the trade of world-making as any of the rest; and as Moses was not an Israelite, he might not choose to contradict the tradition. The account, however, is harmless; and this is more than can be said for many other parts of the Bible.[2]

Whenever we read the obscene stories, the voluptuous debaucheries, the cruel and torturous executions, the unrelenting vindictiveness, with which more than half the Bible is filled, it would be more consistent that we called it the word of a demon than the Word of God. It is a history of wickedness that has served to corrupt and brutalize mankind; and, for my part, I sincerely detest it as I detest everything that is cruel.

We scarcely meet with anything, a few phrases excepted, but what deserves either our abhorrence or our contempt, till we come to the miscellaneous parts of the Bible. In the anonymous publications, the Psalms, and the book of Job, more particularly in the latter, we find a great deal of elevated sentiment reverentially expressed of the power and benignity of the Almighty; but they stand on no higher rank than many other compositions on similar subjects, as well before that time as since.

The Proverbs which are said to be Solomon's, though most probably a collection (because they discover a knowledge of life which his situation excluded him from knowing), are an instructive table of ethics. They are inferior in keenness to the proverbs of the Spaniards, and

---

[2] When Paine refers to the "Bible" he means the Old Testament only.—*Editor.*

not more wise and economical than those of the American Franklin.[3]

All the remaining parts of the Bible, generally known by the name of the Prophets, are the works of the Jewish poets and itinerant preachers, who mixed poetry,[4] anecdote, and devotion together—and those works still retain the air and style of poetry, though in translation.

There is not, throughout the whole book called the Bible, any word that describes to us what we call a poet, nor any word which describes what we call poetry. The case is that the word *prophet,* to which latter times have affixed a new idea, was the Bible word for poet, and the word *prophesying* meant the art of making poetry. It also meant the art of playing poetry to a tune upon any instrument of music.

We read of prophesying with pipes, tabrets and horns—of prophesying with harps, with psalteries, with cymbals and with every other instrument of music then in fashion. Were we now to speak of prophesying with a fiddle, or with a pipe and tabor, the expression would have no meaning or would appear ridiculous, and to some people contemptuous, because we have changed the meaning of the word.

We are told of Saul being among the *prophets,* and also that he prophesied; but we are not told what *they prophesied* nor what *he*

---

[3] Paine is referring to the proverbs in Benjamin Franklin's *Poor Richard's Almanack.*—*Editor.*

[4] As there are many readers who do not see that a composition is poetry unless it be in rhyme, it is for their information that I add this note.

Poetry consists principally in two things—imagery and composition. The composition of poetry differs from that of prose in the manner of mixing long and short syllables together. Take a long syllable out of a line of poetry, and put a short one in the room of it, or put a long syllable where a short one should be, and that line will lose its poetical harmony. It will have an effect upon the line like that of misplacing a note in a song. The imagery in those books, called the Prophets, appertains altogether to poetry. It is fictitious, and often extravagant, and not admissible in any other kind of writing than poetry. To show that these writings are composed in poetical numbers, I will take ten syllables, as they stand in the book, and make a line of the same number of syllables, (heroic measure) that shall rhyme with the last word. It will then be seen that the composition of these books is poetical measure. The instance I shall produce is from Isaiah:

> "*Hear, O ye heavens, and give ear, O earth!*"
> 'Tis God himself that calls attention forth.

Another instance I shall quote is from the mournful Jeremiah, to which I shall add two other lines, for the purpose of carrying out the figure, and showing the intention of the poet:

> "*O! that mine head were waters and mine eyes*"
> Were fountains flowing like the liquid skies;
> Then would I give the mighty flood release,
> And weep a deluge for the human race.—*Author.*

prophesied. The case is, there was nothing to tell; for these prophets were a company of musicians and poets, and Saul joined in the concert, and this was called *prophesying.*

The account given of this affair in the book called Samuel is that Saul met a *company* of prophets; a whole company of them! coming down with a psaltery, a tabret, a pipe and a harp, and that they prophesied, and that he prophesied with them. But it appears afterward that Saul prophesied badly; that is, he performed his part badly; for it is said, that an *"evil spirit from God"* [5] came upon Saul, and he prophesied.

Now, were there no other passage in the book called the Bible than this to demonstrate to us that we have lost the original meaning of the word *prophesy,* and substituted another meaning in its place, this alone would be sufficient; for it is impossible to use and apply the word *prophesy,* in the place it is here used and applied, if we give to it the sense which latter times have affixed to it. The manner in which it is here used strips it of all religious meaning, and shows that a man might then be a prophet, or he might *prophesy,* as he may now be a poet or a musician, without any regard to the morality or immorality of his character. The word was originally a term of science, promiscuously applied to poetry and to music, and not restricted to any subject upon which poetry and music might be exercised.

Deborah and Barak are called prophets, not because they predicted anything, but because they composed the poem or song that bears their name in celebration of an act already done. David is ranked among the prophets, for he was a musician, and was also reputed to be (though perhaps very erroneously) the author of the Psalms. But Abraham, Isaac and Jacob are not called prophets; it does not appear from any accounts we have that they could either sing, play music or make poetry.

We are told of the greater and the lesser prophets. They might as well tell us of the greater and the lesser God; for there cannot be degrees in prophesying consistently with its modern sense. But there are degrees in poetry, and therefore the phrase is reconcilable to the case, when we understand by it the greater and the lesser poets.

It is altogether unnecessary, after this, to offer any observations upon what those men, styled prophets, have written. The axe goes at once to

[5] As those men who call themselves divines and commentators are very fond of puzzling one another, I leave them to contest the meaning of the first part of the phrase, that of *an evil spirit from God.* I keep to my text—I keep to the meaning of the word prophesy.— *Author.*

the root, by showing that the original meaning of the word has been mistaken; and consequently all the inferences that have been drawn from those books, the devotional respect that has been paid to them, and the labored commentaries that have been written upon them, under that mistaken meaning, are not worth disputing about. In many things, however, the writings of the Jewish poets deserve a better fate than that of being bound up, as they now are with the trash that accompanies them, under the abused name of the Word of God.

If we permit ourselves to conceive right ideas of things, we must necessarily affix the idea, not only of unchangeableness, but of the utter impossibility of any change taking place, by any means or accident whatever, in that which we would honor with the name of the Word of God; and therefore the Word of God cannot exist in any written or human language.

The continually progressive change to which the meaning of words is subject, the want of a universal language which renders translation necessary, the errors to which translations are again subject, the mistakes of copyists and printers, together with the possibility of willful alteration, are of themselves evidences that the human language, whether in speech or in print, cannot be the vehicle of the Word of God. The Word of God exists in something else.

Did the book called the Bible excel in purity of ideas and expression all the books that are now extant in the world, I would not take it for my rule of faith, as being the Word of God, because the possibility would nevertheless exist of my being imposed upon. But when I see throughout the greater part of this book scarcely anything but a history of the grossest vices and a collection of the most paltry and contemptible tales, I cannot dishonor my Creator by calling it by His name.

Of the New Testament

Thus much for the Bible; I now go on to the book called the New Testament. The *New* Testament! that is, the *new* will, as if there could be two wills of the Creator.

Had it been the object or the intention of Jesus Christ to establish a new religion, he would undoubtedly have written the system himself, or *procured it to be written* in his life-time. But there is no publication extant authenticated with his name. All the books called the New Testament were written after his death. He was a Jew by birth and by profession; and he was the Son of God in like manner that every other person is—for the Creator is the Father of All.

The first four books, called Matthew, Mark, Luke and John, do not give a history of the life of Jesus Christ, but only detached anecdotes of him. It appears from these books that the whole time of his being a preacher was not more than eighteen months; and it was only during this short time that those men became acquainted with him. They make mention of him at the age of twelve years, sitting, they say, among the Jewish doctors, asking and answering them questions. As this was several years before their acquaintance with him began, it is most probable they had this anecdote from his parents.

From this time there is no account of him for about sixteen years. Where he lived, or how he employed himself during this interval, is not known. Most probably he was working at his father's trade, which was that of a carpenter. It does not appear that he had any school education, and the probability is that he could not write, for his parents were extremely poor, as appears from their not being able to pay for a bed when he was born.

It is somewhat curious that the three persons whose names are the most universally recorded, were of very obscure parentage. Moses was a foundling; Jesus Christ was born in a stable; and Mahomet was a mule driver. The first and last of these men were founders of different systems of religion; but Jesus Christ founded no new system. He called men to the practice of moral virtues and the belief of one God. The great trait in his character is philanthropy.

The manner in which he was apprehended shows that he was not much known at that time; and it shows also, that the meetings he then held with his followers were in secret; and that he had given over or suspended preaching publicly. Judas could not otherwise betray him than by giving information where he was, and pointing him out to the officers that went to arrest him; and the reason for employing and paying Judas to do this could arise only from the cause already mentioned, that of his not being much known and living concealed.

The idea of his concealment not only agrees very ill with his reputed divinity, but associates with it something of pusillanimity; and his being betrayed or, in other words, his being apprehended on the information of one of his followers shows that he did not intend to be apprehended, and consequently that he did not intend to be crucified.

The Christian Mythologists tell us that Christ died for the sins of the world, and that he came on *purpose to die*. Would it not then have been the same if he had died of a fever or of the small-pox, of old age, or of anything else?

The declaratory sentence which, they say, was passed upon Adam, in case he ate of the apple, was not, that *thou shalt surely be crucified,* but, *thou·shalt surely die*—the sentence of death, and not the manner of dying. Crucifixion, therefore, or any other particular manner of dying, made no part of the sentence that Adam was to suffer, and consequently, even upon their own tactics, it could make no part of the sentence that Christ was to suffer in the room of Adam. A fever would have done as well as a cross, if there was any occasion for either.

The sentence of death, which they tell us was thus passed upon Adam, must either have meant dying naturally, that is, ceasing to live, or have meant what these Mythologists call damnation; and, consequently, the act of dying on the part of Jesus Christ, must, according to their system, apply as a prevention to one or other of these two *things* happening to Adam and to us.

That it does not prevent our dying is evident, because we all die; and if their accounts of longevity be true, men die faster since the crucifixion than before; and with respect to the second explanation (including with it the *natural death* of Jesus Christ as a substitute for the *eternal death or damnation* of all mankind), it is impertinently representing the Creator as coming off, or revoking the sentence, by a pun or a quibble upon the word *death*.

That manufacturer of quibbles, St. Paul, if he wrote the books that bear his name, has helped this quibble on by making another quibble upon the word *Adam*. He makes there to be two Adams; the one who sins in fact and suffers by proxy; the other who sins by proxy and suffers in fact. A religion thus interlarded with quibble, subterfuge and pun has a tendency to instruct its professors·in the practise of these arts. They acquire the habit without being aware of the cause.

If Jesus Christ was the being which those Mythologists tell us he was, and that he came into this world to *suffer,* which is a word they sometimes use instead of *to die,* the only real suffering he could have endured would have been *to live*. His existence here was a state of exilement or transportation from heaven, and the way back to his original country was to die. In fine, everything in this strange system is the reverse of what it pretends to be. It is the reverse of truth, and I become so tired of examining into its inconsistencies and absurdities that I hasten to the conclusion of it in order to proceed to something better.

How much or what parts of the books called the New Testament were written by the persons whose names they bear is what we can know nothing of; neither are we certain in what language they were originally written. The matters they now contain may be classed under two heads—anecdote and epistolary correspondence.

The four books already mentioned, Matthew, Mark, Luke and John, are altogether anecdotal. They relate events after they have taken place. They tell what Jesus Christ did and said, and what others did and said to him; and in several instances they relate the same event differently. Revelation is necessarily out of the question with respect to those books; not only because of the disagreement of the writers, but because revelation cannot be applied to the relating of facts by the person who saw them done, nor to the relating or recording of any discourse or conversation by those who heard it. The book called the Acts of the Apostles (an anonymous work) belongs also to the anecdotal part.

All the other parts of the New Testament, except the book of enigmas called the Revelations, are a collection of letters under the name of epistles; and the forgery of letters has been such a common practise in the world that the probability is at least equal, whether they are genuine or forged.

One thing, however, is much less equivocal, which is, that out of the matters contained in those books, together with the assistance of some old stories, the Church has set up a system of religion very contradictory to the character of the person whose name it bears. It has set up a religion of pomp and of revenue, in pretended imitation of a person whose life was humility and poverty.

The invention of a purgatory, and of the releasing of souls therefrom by prayers bought of the church with money; the selling of pardons, dispensations and indulgences, are revenue laws, without bearing that name or carrying that appearance.

But the case nevertheless is that those things derive their origin from the paroxysm of the crucifixion and the theory deduced therefrom, which was that one person could stand in the place of another, and could perform meritorious services for him.

The probability, therefore, is that the whole theory or doctrine of what is called the redemption (which is said to have been accomplished by the act of one person in the room of another) was originally fabricated on purpose to bring forward and build all those secondary and pecuniary redemptions upon; and that the passages in the books upon which the idea or theory of redemption is built have been manufactured and fabricated for that purpose.

Why are we to give this Church credit when she tells us that those books are genuine in every part, any more than we give her credit for everything else she has told us, or for the miracles she says she has performed? That she *could* fabricate writings is certain, because she could write; and the composition of the writings in question is of that kind that anybody might do it; and that she *did* fabricate them is not more inconsistent with probability than that she should tell us, as she has done, that she could and did work miracles.

Since, then, no external evidence can, at this long distance of time, be produced to prove whether the Church fabricated the doctrine called redemption or not (for such evidence whether for or against, would be subject to the same suspicion of being fabricated), the case can only be referred to the internal evidence which the thing carries of itself; and this affords a very strong presumption of its being a fabrication. For the internal evidence is that the theory or doctrine of redemption has for its basis an idea of pecuniary justice and not that of moral justice.

If I owe a person money and cannot pay him, and he threatens to put me in prison, another person can take the debt upon himself and pay it for me; but if I have committed a crime, every circumstance of the case is changed; moral justice cannot take the innocent for the guilty, even if the innocent would offer itself. To suppose justice to do this is to destroy the principle of its existence, which is the thing itself; it is then no longer justice, it is indiscriminate revenge. This single reflection will show that the doctrine of redemption is founded on a mere pecuniary idea corresponding to that of a debt which another person might pay; and as this pecuniary idea corresponds again with the system of second redemption, obtained through the means of money given to the church for pardons, the probability is that the same persons fabricated both the one and the other of those theories; and that in truth there is no such thing as redemption—that it is fabulous, and that man stands in the same relative condition with his Maker as he ever did stand since man existed, and that it is his greatest consolation to think so.

Let him believe this, and he will live more consistently and morally than by any other system; it is by his being taught to contemplate himself as an outlaw, as an outcast, as a beggar, as a mumper, as one thrown, as it were, on a dunghill at an immense distance from his Creator, and who must make his approaches by creeping and cringing to intermediate beings, that he conceives either a contemptuous disregard for everything under the name of religion, or becomes indifferent, or turns what he calls devout.

In the latter case, he consumes his life in grief, or the affectation of it; his prayers are reproaches; his humility is ingratitude; he calls himself a worm, and the fertile earth a dunghill; and all the blessings of life by the thankless name of vanities; he despises the choicest gift of God to man, the GIFT OF REASON; and having endeavored to force upon himself the belief of a system against which reason revolts, he ungratefully calls it *human reason,* as if man could give reason to himself.

Yet, with all this strange appearance of humility and this contempt for human reason, he ventures into the boldest presumptions; he finds fault with everything; his selfishness is never satisfied; his ingratitude is never at an end.

He takes on himself to direct the Almighty what to do, even in the government of the universe; he prays dictatorially; when it is sunshine, he prays for rain, and when it is rain, he prays for sunshine; he follows the same idea in everything that he prays for; for what is the amount of all his prayers but an attempt to make the Almighty change His mind, and act otherwise than He does? It is as if he were to say: Thou knowest not so well as I.

DEFINING THE TRUE REVELATION

But some, perhaps, will say: Are we to have no Word of God—no revelation? I answer, Yes; there is a Word of God; there is a revelation.

THE WORD OF GOD IS THE CREATION WE BEHOLD and it is in *this word,* which no human invention can counterfeit or alter, that God speaketh universally to man.

Human language is local and changeable, and is therefore incapable of being used as the means of unchangeable and universal information. The idea that God sent Jesus Christ to publish, as they say, the glad tidings to all nations, from one end of the earth unto the other, is consistent only with the ignorance of those who knew nothing of the extent of the world, and who believed, as those world-saviors believed, and continued to believe for several centuries (and that in contradiction to the discoveries of philosophers and the experience of navigators), that the earth was flat like a trencher, and that man might walk to the end of it.

But how was Jesus Christ to make anything known to all nations? He could speak but one language, which was Hebrew, and there are in the world several hundred languages. Scarcely any two nations speak the same language, or understand each other; and as to translations, every man who knows anything of languages knows that it is impossible to translate from one language into another, not only without losing a great part of the original, but frequently mistaking the sense; and besides all this, the art of printing was wholly unknown at the time Christ lived.

It is always necessary that the means that are to accomplish any end be equal to the accomplishment of that end, or the end cannot be accomplished. It is in this that the difference between finite and infinite power and wisdom discovers itself. Man frequently fails in accomplishing his ends, from a natural inability of the power to the purpose, and frequently from the want of wisdom to apply power properly. But it is impossible for infinite power and wisdom to fail as man faileth. The means it uses are always equal to the end; but human language, more especially as there is not an universal language, is incapable of being used as an universal means of unchangeable and uniform information, and therefore it is not the means that God uses in manifesting himself universally to man.

It is only in the CREATION that all our ideas and conceptions of a *Word of God* can unite. The Creation speaks a universal language, independently of human speech or human language, multiplied and various as they be. It is an ever-existing original, which every man can read. It cannot be forged; it cannot be counterfeited; it cannot be lost; it cannot be altered; it cannot be suppressed. It does not depend upon the will of man whether it shall be published or not; it publishes itself from one end of the earth to the other. It preaches to all nations and to all worlds; and this *Word of God* reveals to man all that is necessary for man to know of God.

Do we want to contemplate His power? We see it in the immensity of the creation. Do we want to contemplate His wisdom? We see it in the unchangeable order by which the incomprehensible whole is governed. Do we want to contemplate His munificence? We see it in the abundance with which He fills the earth. Do we want to contemplate His mercy? We see it in His not withholding that abundance even from the unthankful. In fine, do we want to know what God is? Search not the book called the Scripture, which any human hand might make, but the Scripture called the creation.

CONCERNING GOD, AND THE LIGHTS CAST ON HIS EXISTENCE AND ATTRIBUTES BY THE BIBLE

The only idea man can affix to the name of God is that of a *first cause,* the cause of all things. And incomprehensible and difficult as it is for a man to conceive what a first cause is, he arrives at the belief of it from the tenfold greater difficulty of disbelieving it.

It is difficult beyond description to conceive that space can have no end; but it is more difficult to conceive an end. It is difficult beyond the power of man to conceive an eternal duration of what we call time; but it is more impossible to conceive a time when there shall be no time.

In like manner of reasoning, everything we behold carries in itself the internal evidence that it did not make itself. Every man is an evidence to himself that he did not make himself; neither could his father make himself, nor his grandfather, nor any of his race; neither could any tree, plant or animal make itself; and it is the conviction arising from this evidence that carries us on, as it were, by necessity to the belief of a first cause eternally existing, of a nature totally different to any material existence we know of, and by the power of which all things exist; and this first cause man calls God.

It is only by the exercise of reason that man can discover God. Take away that reason, and he would be incapable of understanding anything; and, in this case, it would be just as consistent to read even the book called the Bible to a horse as to a man. How, then, is it that people pretend to reject reason?

Almost the only parts of the book called the Bible that convey to us any idea of God are some chapters in Job and the 19th Psalm; I recollect no other. Those parts are true *deistical* compositions, for they treat of the *Deity* through His works. They take the book of creation as the Word of God, they refer to no other book, and all the inferences they make are drawn from that volume.

I insert in this place the 19th Psalm, as paraphrased into English verse by Addison. I recollect not the prose, and where I write this I have not the opportunity of seeing it.

"The spacious firmament on high,
With all the blue ethereal sky,
And spangled heavens, a shining frame
Their great original proclaim.
The unwearied sun, from day to day,
Does his Creator's power display;
And publishes to every land
The work of an Almighty hand.

"Soon as the evening shades prevail,
The moon takes up the wondrous tale,
And nightly to the list'ning earth
Repeats the story of her birth;
While all the stars that round her burn,
And all the planets in their turn,
Confirm the tidings as they roll,
And spread the truth from pole to pole.

"What, though in solemn silence all
Move round this dark, terrestrial ball?
What though no real voice, nor sound,
Amidst their radiant orbs be found?
In reason's ear they all rejoice
And utter forth a glorious voice,
Forever singing, as they shine,
THE HAND THAT MADE US IS DIVINE."

What more does man want to know than that the hand or power that made these things is divine, is omnipotent? Let him believe this with the force it is impossible to repel, if he permits his reason to act, and his rule of moral life will follow of course.

The allusions in Job have, all of them, the same tendency with this Psalm; that of deducing or proving a truth that would be otherwise unknown, from truths already known.

I recollect not enough of the passages in Job to insert them correctly; but there is one occurs to me that is applicable to the subject I am speaking upon. "Canst thou by searching find out God? Canst thou find out the Almighty to perfection?"

I know not how the printers have pointed this passage, for I keep no Bible; but it contains two distinct questions that admit of distinct answers.

First,—Canst thou by searching find out God? Yes; because, in the first place, I know I did not make myself, and yet I have existence; and by *searching* into the nature of other things, I find that no other thing could make itself; and yet millions of other things exist; therefore it is, that I know, by positive conclusion resulting from this search, that there is a power superior to all those things, and that power is God.

Secondly,—Canst thou find out the Almighty to *perfection?* No; not only because the power and wisdom He has manifested in the structure of the creation that I behold is to me incomprehensible, but because even this manifestation, great as it is, is probably but a small display of that immensity of power and wisdom by which millions of other worlds, to me invisible by their distance, were created and continue to exist.

It is evident that both these questions were put to the reason of the person to whom they are supposed to have been addressed; and it is only by admitting the first question to be answered affirmatively that the second could follow. It would have been unnecessary, and even absurd, to have put a second question, more difficult than the first, if the first question had been answered negatively.

The two questions have different objects; the first refers to the existence of God; the second to His attributes; reason can discover the one, but it falls infinitely short in discovering the whole of the other.

I recollect not a single passage in all the writings ascribed to the men called apostles that conveys any idea of what God is. Those writings are chiefly controversial; and the subjects they dwell upon, that of a man dying in agony on a cross, is better suited to the gloomy genius of a monk in a cell, by whom it is not impossible they were written, than to any man breathing the open air of the creation.

The only passage that occurs to me that has any reference to the works of God, by which only His power and wisdom can be known, is related to have been spoken by Jesus Christ as a remedy against distrustful care. "Behold the lilies of the field, they toil not, neither do they spin." This, however, is far inferior to the allusions in Job and in the 19th Psalm; but it is similar in idea, and the modesty of the imagery is correspondent to the modesty of the man.

True Theology and That of Superstition

As to the Christian system of faith, it appears to me a species of Atheism—a sort of religious denial of God. It professes to believe in a man rather than in God. It is a compound made up chiefly of Manism with but little Deism, and is as near to Atheism as twilight is to darkness. It introduces between man and his Maker an opaque body, which it calls a Redeemer, as the moon introduces her opaque self between the earth and the sun, and it produces by this means a religious, or an irreligious, eclipse of light. It has put the whole orbit of reason into shade.

The effect of this obscurity has been that of turning everything upside down, and representing it in reverse, and among the revolutions it has thus magically produced it has made a revolution in theology.

That which is now called natural philosophy, embracing the whole circle of science, of which astronomy occupies the chief place, is the study of the works of God, and of the power and wisdom of God in His works, and is the true theology.

As to the theology that is now studied in its place, it is the study of human opinions and of human fancies *concerning* God. It is not the study of God Himself in the works that He has made, but in the works or writings that man has made; and it is not among the least of the mischiefs that the Christian system has done to the world, that it has abandoned the original and beautiful system of theology, like a beautiful innocent, to distress and reproach, to make room for the hag of superstition.

The Book of Job and the 19th Psalm, which even the Church admits to be more ancient than the chronological order in which they stand in the book called the Bible, are theological orations conformable to the original system of theology.

The internal evidence of those orations proves to a demonstration that the study and contemplation of the works of creation, and of the power and wisdom of God, revealed and manifested in those works, made a great part in the religious devotion of the times in which they were written; and it was this devotional study and contemplation that led to the discovery of the principles upon which what are now called sciences are established; and it is to the discovery of these principles that almost all the arts that contribute to the convenience of human life owe their existence.

Every principal art has some science for its parent, though the person who mechanically performs the work does not always, and but very seldom, perceive the connection.

It is a fraud of the Christian system to call the sciences *human invention;* it is only the application of them that is human. Every science has for its basis a system of principles as fixed and unalterable as those by which the universe is regulated and governed. Man cannot make principles, he can only discover them.

For example: Every person who looks at an almanac sees an account when an eclipse will take place, and he sees also that it never fails to take place according to the account there given. This shows that man is acquainted with the laws by which the heavenly bodies move. But it would be something worse than ignorance, were any church on earth to say that those laws are a human invention.

It would also be ignorance, or something worse, to say that the scientific principles by the aid of which man is enabled to calculate and foreknow when an eclipse will take place are a human invention. Man cannot invent anything that is eternal and immutable; and the scientific principles he employs for this purpose must be, and are of necessity, as eternal and immutable as the laws by which the heavenly bodies move, or they could not be used as they are to ascertain the time when, and the manner how, an eclipse will take place.

The scientific principles that man employs to obtain the foreknowledge of an eclipse, or of anything else relating to the motion of the heavenly bodies, are contained chiefly in that part of science which is called trigonometry, or the properties of a triangle, which, when applied to the study of the heavenly bodies, is called astronomy; when applied to direct the course of a ship on the ocean it is called navigation; when applied to the construction of figures drawn by rule and compass it is called geometry; when applied to the construction of plans or edifices it is called architecture; when applied to the measurement of any portion of the surface of the earth it is called land surveying. In fine, it is the soul of science; it is an eternal truth; it contains the *mathematical demonstration* of which man speaks, and the extent of its uses is unknown.

It may be said that man can make or draw a triangle, and therefore a triangle is a human invention.

But the triangle, when drawn, is no other than the image of the principle; it is a delineation to the eye, and from thence to the mind, of a principle that would otherwise be imperceptible. The triangle does not make the principle, any more than a candle taken into a room that was dark makes the chairs and tables that before were invisible. All the properties of a triangle exist independently of the figure, and existed before any triangle was drawn or thought of by man. Man had no more to do in the formation of these properties or principles than he had to do in making the laws by which the heavenly bodies move; and therefore the one must have the same divine origin as the other.

In the same manner, as it may be said, that man can make a triangle, so also, may it be said, he can make the mechanical instrument called a lever; but the principle by which the lever acts is a thing distinct from the instrument, and would exist if the instrument did not; it attaches itself to the instrument after it is made; the instrument, therefore, cannot act otherwise than it does act; neither can all the efforts of human invention make it act otherwise—that which, in all such cases, man calls the *effect* is no other than the principle itself rendered perceptible to the senses.

Since, then, man cannot make principles, from whence did he gain a knowledge of them, so as to be able to apply them, not only to things on earth, but to ascertain the motion of bodies so immensely distant from him as all the heavenly bodies are? From whence, I ask, *could* he gain that knowledge, but from the study of the true theology?

It is the structure of the universe that has taught this knowledge to man. That structure is an ever-existing exhibition of every principle upon which every part of mathematical science is founded. The offspring of this science is mechanics; for mechanics is no other than the principles of science applied practically.

The man who proportions the several parts of a mill uses the same scientific principles as if he had the power of constructing a universe; but as he cannot give to matter that invisible agency by which all the component parts of the immense machine of the universe have influence upon each other and act in motional unison together, without any apparent contact, and to which man has given the name of attraction, gravitation and repulsion, he supplies the place of that agency by the humble imitation of teeth and cogs.

All the parts of a man's microcosm must visibly touch; but could he gain a knowledge of that agency so as to be able to apply it in practise we might then say that another *canonical book* of the Word of God had been discovered.

If man could alter the properties of the lever, so also could he alter the properties of the triangle, for a lever (taking that sort of lever which is called a steelyard, for the sake of explanation) forms, when in motion, a triangle. The line it descends from (one point of that line being in the fulcrum), the line it descends to, and the chord of the arc which the end of the lever describes in the air, are the three sides of a triangle.

The other arm of the lever describes also a triangle; and the corresponding sides of those two triangles, calculated scientifically, or measured geometrically, and also the sines, tangents and secants generated from the angles, and geometrically measured, have the same proportions to each other as the different weights have that will balance each other on the lever, leaving the weight of the lever out of the case.

It may also be said that man can make a wheel and axis; that he can put wheels of different magnitudes together, and produce a mill. Still the case comes back to the same point, which is that he did not make the principle that gives the wheels those powers. That principle is as unalterable as in the former cases, or rather it is the same principle under a different appearance to the eye.

The power that two wheels of different magnitudes have upon each other is in the same proportion as if the semi-diameter of the two wheels were joined together and made into that kind of lever I have described, suspended at the part where the semi-diameters join; for the two wheels, scientifically considered, are no other than the two circles generated by the motion of the compound lever.

It is from the study of the true theology that all our knowledge of science is derived, and it is from that knowledge that all the arts have originated.

The Almighty Lecturer, by displaying the principles of science in the structure of the universe, has invited man to study and to imitation. It is as if He had said to the inhabitants of this globe that we call ours, "I have made an earth for man to dwell upon, and I have rendered the starry heavens visible, to teach him science and the arts. He can now provide for his own comfort, AND LEARN FROM MY MUNIFICENCE TO ALL, TO BE KIND TO EACH OTHER."

Of what use is it, unless it be to teach man something, that his eye is endowed with the power of beholding to an incomprehensible distance an immensity of worlds revolving in the ocean of space? Of what use is it that this immensity of worlds is visible to man? What has man to do with the Pleiades, with Orion, with Sirius, with the star he calls the North Star, with the moving orbs he has named Saturn, Jupiter, Mars, Venus, and Mercury, if no uses are to follow from their being visible? A less power of vision would have been sufficient for man, if the immensity he now possesses were given only to waste itself, as it were, on an immense desert of space glittering with shows.

It is only by contemplating what he calls the starry heavens, as the book and school of science, that he discovers any use in their being visible to him, or any advantage resulting from his immensity of vision. But when he contemplates the subject of this light, he sees an additional motive for saying, that *nothing was made in vain;* for in vain would be this power of vision if it taught man nothing.

CHRISTIANITY AND EDUCATION, IN THE LIGHT OF HISTORY

As the Christian system of faith has made a revolution in theology, so also has it made a revolution in the state of learning. That which is now called learning was not learning originally. Learning does not consist, as the schools now make it consist, in the knowledge of languages, but in the knowledge of things to which language gives names.

The Greeks were a learned people, but learning with them did not consist in speaking Greek any more than in a Roman's speaking Latin, or a Frenchman's speaking French, or an Englishman's speaking English. From what we know of the Greeks, it does not appear that they knew or studied any language but their own, and this was one cause of their becoming so learned; it afforded them more time to apply themselves to better studies. The schools of the Greeks were schools of science and philosophy, and not of languages; and it is in the knowledge of the things that science and philosophy teach, that learning consists.

Almost all the scientific learning that now exists came to us from the Greeks, or the people who spoke the Greek language. It, therefore, became necessary to the people of other nations who spoke a different language that some among them should learn the Greek language in order that the learning of the Greeks might be made known in those nations, by translating the Greek books of science and philosophy into the mother tongue of each nation.

The study, therefore, of the Greek language (and in the same manner for the Latin) was no other than the drudgery business of a linguist; and the language thus obtained was no other than the means, as it were the tools, employed to obtain the learning the Greeks had. It made no part of the learning itself, and was so distinct from it as to make it exceedingly probable that the persons who had studied Greek sufficiently to translate those works, such, for instance, as Euclid's "Elements," did not understand any of the learning the works contained.

As there is now nothing new to be learned from the dead languages, all the useful books being already translated, the language are become useless, and the time expended in teaching and learning them is wasted. So far as the study of languages may contribute to the progress and communication of knowledge (for it has nothing to do with the *creation* of knowledge), it is only in the living languages that new knowledge is to be found; and certain it is that, in general, a youth will learn more of a living language in one year than of a dead language in seven, and it is but seldom that the teacher knows much of it himself.

The difficulty of learning the dead languages does not arise from any superior abstruseness in the languages themselves, but in their *being dead,* and the pronunciation entirely lost. It would be the same with any other language when it becomes dead. The best Greek linguist that now exists does not understand Greek so well as a Grecian plowman did or a Grecian milkmaid; and the same for the Latin, compared with a plowman or milkmaid of the Romans; and with respect to pronunciation and idiom, not so well as the cows that she milked. It would therefore be advantageous to the state of learning to abolish the study of dead languages and to make learning consist, as it originally did, in scientific knowledge.

The apology that is sometimes made for continuing to teach the dead languages is that they are taught at a time when a child is not capable of exerting any other mental faculty than that of memory; but that is altogether erroneous. The human mind has a natural disposition to scientific knowledge and to the things connected with it.

The first and favorite amusement of a child, even before it begins to play, is that of imitating the works of man. It builds houses with cards or sticks: it navigates the little ocean of a bowl of water with a paper boat, or dams the stream of a gutter and contrives something which it calls a mill; and it interests itself in the fate of its works with a care that resembles affection. It afterwards goes to school, where its genius is killed by the barren study of a dead language, and the philosopher is lost in the linguist.

But the apology that is now made for continuing to teach the dead languages could not be the cause, at first, of cutting down learning to the narrow and humble sphere of linguistry; the cause, therefore, must be sought for elsewhere. In all researches of this kind the best evidence that can be produced is the internal evidence the thing carries with itself, and the evidence of circumstances that unite with it; both of which, in this case, are not difficult to be discovered.

Putting then aside, as a matter of distinct consideration, the outrage

offered to the moral justice of God by supposing Him to make the innocent suffer for the guilty, and also the loose morality and low contrivance of supposing Him to change Himself into the shape of a man, in
order to make an excuse to Himself for not executing His supposed
sentence upon Adam—putting, I say, those things aside as matter of
distinct consideration, it is certain that what is called the Christian system of faith, including in it the whimsical account of the Creation—the
strange story of Eve—the snake and the apple—the ambiguous idea of
a man-god—the corporeal idea of the death of a god—the mythological
idea of a family of gods, and the Christian system of arithmetic, that
three are one, and one is three, are all irreconcilable, not only to the
divine gift of reason that God has given to man, but to the knowledge
that man gains of the power and wisdom of God, by the aid of the sciences and by studying the structure of the universe that God has made.

The setters-up, therefore, and the advocates of the Christian system
of faith could not but foresee that the continually progressive knowledge
that man would gain, by the aid of science, of the power and wisdom
of God, manifested in the structure of the universe and in all the works
of creation, would militate against, and call into question, the truth of
their system of faith; and therefore it became necessary to their purpose
to cut learning down to a size less dangerous to their project, and this
they effected by restricting the idea of learning to the dead study of dead
languages.

They not only rejected the study of science out of the Christian
schools, but they persecuted it, and it is only within about the last two
centuries that the study has been revived. So late as 1610, Galileo, a
Florentine, discovered and introduced the use of telescopes, and by
applying them to observe the motions and appearances of the heavenly
bodies afforded additional means for ascertaining the true structure of
the universe.

Instead of being esteemed for those discoveries, he was sentenced to
renounce them, or the opinions resulting from them, as a damnable
heresy. And, prior to that time, Virgilius was condemned to be burned
for asserting the antipodes, or in other words that the earth was a globe,
and habitable in every part where there was land; yet the truth of this
is now too well known even to be told.

If the belief of errors not morally bad did no mischief, it would make
no part of the moral duty of man to oppose and remove them. There
was no moral ill in believing the earth was flat like a trencher, any more

than there was moral virtue in believing it was round like a globe; neither was there any moral ill in believing that the Creator made no other world than this, any more than there was moral virtue in believing that He made millions and that the infinity of space is filled with worlds.

But when a system of religion is made to grow out of a supposed system of creation that is not true, and to unite itself therewith in a manner almost inseparable therefrom, the case assumes an entirely different ground. It is then that errors not morally bad become fraught with the same mischiefs as if they were. It is then that the truth, though otherwise indifferent itself, becomes an essential by becoming the criterion that either confirms by corresponding evidence, or denies by contradictory evidence the reality of the religion itself.

In this view of the case, it is the moral duty of man to obtain every possible evidence that the structure of the heavens or any other part of creation affords, with respect to systems of religion. But this, the supporters or partisans of the Christian system, as if dreading the result, incessantly opposed, and not only rejected the sciences, but persecuted the professors.

Had Newton or Descartes lived three or four hundred years ago and pursued their studies as they did, it is most probable they would not have lived to finish them; and had Franklin drawn lightning from the clouds at the same time, it would have been at the hazard of expiring for it in the flames.

Later times have laid all the blame upon the Goths and the Vandals; but, however unwilling the partisans of the Christian system may be to believe or to acknowledge it, it is nevertheless true that the age of ignorance commenced with the Christian system. There was more knowledge in the world before that period than for many centuries afterwards; and as to religious knowledge, the Christian system, as already said, was only another species of mythology, and the mythology to which it succeeded was a corruption of an ancient system of theism.[6]

---

[6] It is impossible for us now to know at what time the heathen mythology began; but it is certain, from the internal evidence that it carries, that it did not begin in the same state or condition in which it ended. All the gods of that mythology, except Saturn, were of modern invention. The supposed reign of Saturn was prior to that which is called the heathen mythology, and was so far a species of theism, that it admitted the belief of only one God. Saturn is supposed to have abdicated the government in favor of his three sons and one daughter, Jupiter, Pluto, Neptune and Juno; after this, thousands of other gods and demi-gods were imaginarily created, and the calendar of gods increased as fast as the calendar of saints and the calendars of courts have increased since.

All the corruptions that have taken place in theology and in religion have been produced

It is owing to this long interregnum of science, *and to no other cause,* that we have now to look back through a vast chasm of many hundred years to the respectable characters we call the ancients. Had the progression of knowledge gone on proportionably with that stock that before existed, that chasm would have been filled up with characters rising superior in knowledge to each other; and those ancients we now so much admire would have appeared respectably in the background of the scene. But the Christian system laid all waste; and if we take our stand about the beginning of the sixteenth century, we look back through that long chasm to the times of the ancients, as over a vast sandy desert, in which not a shrub appears to intercept the vision to the fertile hills beyond.

It is an inconsistency scarcely possible to be credited that anything should exist, under the name of a religion, that held it to be *irreligious* to study and contemplate the structure of the universe that God has made. But the fact is too well established to be denied. The event that served more than any other to break the first link in this long chain of despotic ignorance is that known by the name of the Reformation by Luther.

From that time, though it does not appear to have made any part of the intention of Luther, or of those who are called reformers, the sciences began to revive, and liberality, their natural associate, began to appear. This was the only public good the Reformation did; for with respect to religious good it might as well not have taken place. The mythology still continued the same, and a multiplicity of National Popes grew out of the downfall of the Pope of Christendom.

COMPARING CHRISTIANISM WITH PANTHEISM

Having thus shown from the internal evidence of things the cause that produced a change in the state of learning, and the motive for sub-

---

by admitting of what man calls *revealed religion.* The Mythologists pretended to more revealed religion than the Christians do. They had their oracles and their priests, who were supposed to receive and deliver the word of God verbally, on almost all occasions.

Since then, all corruptions, down from Moloch to modern predestinarianism, and the human sacrifices of the heathens to the Christian sacrifice of the Creator, have been produced by admitting of what is called *revealed religion.* The most effectual means to prevent all such evils and impositions is not to admit of any other revelation than that which is manifested in the book of creation, and to contemplate the creation as the only true and real Word of God that ever did or ever will exist; and that everything else, called the Word of God, is fable and imposition.—*Author.*

stituting the study of the dead languages in the place of the sciences, I proceed, in addition to the several observations already made in the former part of this work, to compare, or rather to confront, the evidence that the structure of the universe affords with the Christian system of religion; but, as I cannot begin this part better than by referring to the ideas that occurred to me at an early part of life, and which I doubt not have occurred in some degree to almost every person at one time or other, I shall state what those ideas were and add thereto such other matter as shall arise out of the subject, giving to the whole, by way of preface, a short introduction.

My father being of the Quaker profession, it was my good fortune to have an exceedingly good moral education, and a tolerable stock of useful learning. Though I went to the grammar school,[7] I did not learn Latin, not only because I had no inclination to learn languages, but because of the objection the Quakers have against the books in which the language is taught. But this did not prevent me from being acquainted with the subjects of all the Latin books used in the school.

The natural bent of my mind was to science. I had some turn, and I believe some talent, for poetry; but this I rather repressed than encouraged, as leading too much into the field of imagination. As soon as I was able I purchased a pair of globes, and attended the philosophical lectures of Martin and Ferguson, and became afterward acquainted with Dr. Bevis, of the society called the Royal Society, then living in the Temple, and an excellent astronomer.

I had no disposition for what is called politics. It presented to my mind no other idea than as contained in the word Jockeyship. When, therefore, I turned my thoughts toward matter of government I had to form a system for myself that accorded with the moral and philosophic principles in which I have been educated. I saw, or at least I thought I saw, a vast scene opening itself to the world in the affairs of America, and it appeared to me that unless the Americans changed the plan they were pursuing with respect to the government of England, and declared themselves independent, they would not only involve themselves in a multiplicity of new difficulties, but shut out the prospect that was then offering itself to mankind through their means. It was from these motives that I published the work known by the name of "Common Sense," which was the first work I ever did publish; and so far as I can judge of

[7] The same school, Thetford in Norfolk that the present Counsellor Mingay went to and under the same master.—*Author.*

myself, I believe I should never have been known in the world as an author on any subject whatever had it not been for the affairs of America. I wrote "Common Sense" the latter end of the year 1775, and published it the first of January, 1776. Independence was declared the fourth of July following.

Any person who has made observations on the state and progress of the human mind by observing his own cannot but have observed that there are two distinct classes of what are called thoughts—those that we produce in ourselves by reflection and the act of thinking, and those that bolt into the mind of their own accord. I have always made it a rule to treat these voluntary visitors with civility, taking care to examine, as well as I was able, if they were worth entertaining, and it is from them I have acquired almost all the knowledge that I have. As to the learning that any person gains from school education, it serves only, like a small capital, to put him in a way of beginning learning for himself afterward.

Every person of learning is finally his own teacher, the reason of which is that principles, being a distinct quality to circumstances, cannot be impressed upon the memory; their place of mental residence is the understanding and they are never so lasting as when they begin by conception. Thus much for the introductory part.

From the time I was capable of conceiving an idea and acting upon it by reflection, I either doubted the truth of the Christian system or thought it to be a strange affair; I scarcely knew which it was, but I well remember, when about seven or eight years of age, hearing a sermon read by a relation of mine, who was a great devotee of the Church, upon the subject of what is called *redemption by the death of the Son of God.*

After the sermon was ended, I went into the garden, and as I was going down the garden steps (for I perfectly recollect the spot) I revolted at the recollection of what I had heard, and thought to myself that it was making God Almighty act like a passionate man who killed His son when He could not revenge Himself in any other way, and, as I was sure a man would be hanged who did such a thing, I could not see for what purpose they preached such sermons.

This was not one of that kind of thoughts that had anything in it of childish levity; it was to me a serious reflection, arising from the idea I had that God was too good to do such an action, and also too almighty to be under any necessity of doing it. I believe in the same manner at this moment; and I moreover believe that any system of religion that has anything in it that shocks the mind of a child cannot be a true system.

It seems as if parents of the Christian profession were ashamed to tell their children anything about the principles of their religion. They sometimes instruct them in morals and talk to them of the goodness of what they call Providence, for the Christian mythology has five deities—there is God the Father, God the Son, God the Holy Ghost, the God Providence and the Goddess Nature. But the Christian story of God the Father putting His son to death, or employing people to do it (for that is the plain language of the story) cannot be told by a parent to a child; and to tell him that it was done to make mankind happier and better is making the story still worse—as if mankind could be improved by the example of murder; and to tell him that all this is a mystery is only making an excuse for the incredibility of it.

How different is this to the pure and simple profession of Deism! The true Deist has but one Deity, and his religion consists in contemplating the power, wisdom and benignity of the Deity in His works, and in endeavoring to imitate Him in everything moral, scientifical and mechanical.

The religion that approaches the nearest of all others to true Deism, in the moral and benign part thereof, is that professed by the Quakers; but they have contracted themselves too much by leaving the works of God out of their system. Though I reverence their philanthropy, I cannot help smiling at the conceit that if the taste of a Quaker could have been consulted at the Creation what a silent and drab-colored Creation it would have been! Not a flower would have blossomed its gayeties, nor a bird been permitted to sing.

Quitting these reflections, I proceed to other matters. After I had made myself master of the use of the globes and of the orrery,[8] and conceived an idea of the infinity of space, and the eternal divisibility of matter, and obtained at least a general knowledge of what is called natural philosophy, I began to compare, or, as I have before said, to confront the eternal evidence those things afford with the Christian system of faith.

Though it is not a direct article of the Christian system, that this world

---

[8] As this book may fall into the hands of persons who do not know what an orrery is, it is for their information I add this note, as the name gives no idea of the uses of the thing. The orrery has its name from the person who invented it. It is a machinery of clock-work, representing the universe in miniature, and in which the revolution of the earth round itself and round the sun, the revolution of the moon round the earth, the revolution of the planets round the sun, their relative distances from the sun, as the center of the whole system, their relative distances from each other and their different magnitudes, are represented as they really exist in what we call the heavens.—*Author.*

that we inhabit is the whole of the habitable creation, yet it is so worked up therewith, from what is called the Mosaic account of the Creation, the story of Eve and the apple, and the counterpart of that story, the death of the Son of God, that to believe otherwise, that is, to believe that God created a plurality of worlds, at least as numerous as what we call stars, renders the Christian system of faith at once little and ridiculous, and scatters it in the mind like feathers in the air. The two beliefs cannot be held together in the same mind, and he who thinks that he believes both has thought but little of either.

Though the belief of a plurality of worlds was familiar to the ancients, it is only within the last three centuries that the extent and dimensions of this globe that we inhabit have been ascertained. Several vessels following the tract of the ocean have sailed entirely around the world, as a man may march in a circle and come round by the contrary side of the circle to the spot he set out from.

The circular dimensions of our world, in the widest part, as a man would measure the widest round of an apple or ball, is only twenty-five thousand and twenty English miles, reckoning sixty-nine miles and a half to an equatorial degree, and may be sailed round in the space of about three years.[9]

A world of this extent may, at first thought, appear to us to be great; but if we compare it with the immensity of space in which it is suspended, like a bubble or balloon in the air, it is infinitely less in proportion than the smallest grain of sand is to the size of the world, or the finest particle of dew to the whole ocean, and is therefore but small; and, as will be hereafter shown, is only one of a system of worlds of which the universal creation is composed.

It is not difficult to gain some faint idea of the immensity of space in which this and all other worlds are suspended if we follow a progression of ideas. When we think of the size or dimensions of a room our ideas limit themselves to the walls, and there they stop; but when our eye or our imagination darts into space, that is, when it looks upward into what we call the open air, we cannot conceive any walls or boundaries it can have, and if for the sake of resting our ideas we suppose a boundary, the question immediately renews itself, and asks what is beyond that boundary? —and in the same manner, what is beyond the next boundary? And so

[9] Allowing a ship to sail, on an average, three miles in an hour, she would sail entirely round the world in less than one year, if she could sail in a direct circle; but she is obliged to follow the course of the ocean.—*Author.*

on till the fatigued imagination returns and says, *There is no end*. Certainly, then, the Creator was not pent for room when He made this world no larger than it is, and we have to seek the reason in something else.

If we take a survey of our own world, or rather of this of which the Creator has given us the use as our portion of the immense system of creation, we find every part of it—the earth, the waters, and the air that surrounds it—filled, and, as it were, crowded with life, down from the largest animals that we know of to the smallest insects the naked eye can behold, and from thence to others still smaller, and totally invisible without the assistance of the microscope. Every tree, every plant, every leaf serves not only as a habitation but as a world to some numerous race, till animal existence becomes so exceedingly refined that the effluvia of a blade of grass would be food for thousands.

Since, then, no part of our earth is left unoccupied, why is it to be supposed that the immensity of space is a naked void, lying in eternal waste? There is room for millions of worlds as large or larger than ours, and each of them millions of miles apart from each other. Having now arrived at this point, if we carry our ideas only one thought further, we shall see, perhaps, the true reason, at least a very good reason for our happiness, why the Creator, instead of making one immense world extending over an immense quantity of space, has preferred dividing that quantity of matter into several distinct and separate worlds, which we call planets, of which our earth is one. But before I explain my ideas upon this subject, it is necessary (not for the sake of those who already know, but for those who do not) to show what the system of the universe is.

THE PLAN AND ORDER OF THE UNIVERSE

That part of the universe that is called the solar system (meaning the system of worlds to which our earth belongs, and of which Sol, or in English language, the Sun, is the center) consists, besides the Sun, of six distinct orbs, or planets, or worlds, besides the secondary bodies, called the satellites or moons, of which our earth has one that attends her in her annual revolution around the Sun, in like manner as the other satellites or moons attend the planets or worlds to which they severally belong, as may be seen by the assistance of the telescope.

The Sun is the center, round which those six worlds or planets revolve at different distances therefrom, and in circles concentric to each other. Each world keeps constantly in nearly the same track round the Sun, and continues, at the same time, turning round itself in nearly an upright position, as a top turns round itself when it is spinning on the ground, and leans a little sideways.

It is this leaning of the earth (23½ degrees) that occasions summer and winter, and the different length of days and nights. If the earth turned round itself in a position perpendicular to the plane or level of the circle it moves in around the Sun, as a top turns round when it stands erect on the ground, the days and nights would be always of the same length, twelve hours day and twelve hours night, and the seasons would be uniformly the same throughout the year.

Every time that a planet (our earth for example) turns round itself, it makes what we call day and night; and every time it goes entirely round the Sun it makes what we call a year; consequently our world turns three hundred and sixty-five times round itself in going once round the Sun.[10]

The names that the ancients gave to those six worlds, and which are still called by the same names, are Mercury, Venus, this world that we call ours, Mars, Jupiter and Saturn. They appear larger to the eye than the stars, being many million miles nearer to our earth than any of the stars are. The planet Venus is that which is called the evening star, and sometimes the morning star, as she happens to set after or rise before the Sun, which in either case is never more than three hours.

The Sun, as before said, being the center, the planet or world nearest the Sun is Mercury; his distance from the Sun is thirty-four million miles, and he moves round in a circle always at that distance from the Sun, as a top may be supposed to spin round in the track in which a horse goes in a mill.

The second world is Venus; she is fifty-seven million miles distant from the Sun, and consequently moves round in a circle much greater than that of Mercury. The third world is this that we inhabit, and which is eighty-eight million miles distant from the Sun, and consequently moves round in a circle greater than that of Venus.

The fourth world is Mars; he is distant from the Sun one hundred and thirty-four million miles, and consequently moves round in a circle greater than that of our earth. The fifth is Jupiter; he is distant from the

[10] Those who supposed that the sun went round the earth every 24 hours made the same mistake in idea that a cook would do in fact, that should make the fire go round the meat, instead of the meat turning round itself toward the fire.—*Author.*

Sun five hundred and fifty-seven million miles, and consequently moves round in a circle greater than that of Mars.

The sixth world is Saturn; he is distant from the Sun seven hundred and sixty-three million miles, and consequently moves round in a circle that surrounds the circles, or orbits, of all the other worlds or planets.

The space, therefore, in the air, or in the immensity of space, that our solar system takes up for the several worlds to perform their revolutions in round the Sun, is of the extent in a straight line of the whole diameter. of the orbit, or circle, in which Saturn moves round the Sun, which being double his distance from the Sun, is fifteen hundred and twenty-six million miles and its circular extent is nearly five thousand million, and its globular contents are almost three thousand five hundred million times three thousand five hundred million square miles.[11]

But this, immense as it is, is only one system of worlds. Beyond this, at a vast distance into space, far beyond all power of calculation, are the stars called the fixed stars. They are called fixed because they have no revolutionary motion, as the six worlds or planets have that I have been describing. Those fixed stars continue always at the same distance from each other, and always in the same place, as the Sun does in the center of our system. The probability, therefore, is that each of those fixed stars is also a Sun, round which another system of worlds or planets, though too remote for us to discover, performs its revolutions, as our system of worlds does round our central Sun.

By this easy progression of ideas, the immensity of space will appear to us to be filled with systems of worlds, and that no part of space lies at waste, any more than any part of the globe of earth and water is left unoccupied.

Having thus endeavored to convey, in a familiar and easy manner, some idea of the structure of the universe, I return to explain what I

[11] If it should be asked, how can man know these things? I have one plain answer to give, which is, that man knows how to calculate an eclipse, and also how to calculate to a minute of time when the planet Venus in making her revolutions around the sun will come in a straight line between our earth and the sun, and will appear to us about the size of a large pea passing across the face of the sun. This happens but twice in about a hundred years, at the distance of about eight years from each other, and has happened twice in our time, both of which were foreknown by calculation. It can also be known when they will happen again for a thousand years to come, or to any other portion of time. As, therefore, man could not be able to do these things if he did not understand the solar system, and the manner in which the revolutions of the several planets or worlds are performed, the fact of calculating an eclipse, or a transit of Venus, is a proof in point that the knowledge exists; and as to a few thousand, or even a few million miles, more or less, it makes scarcely any sensible difference in such immense distances.—*Author.*

before alluded to, namely, the great benefits arising to man in consequence of the Creator having made a *plurality* of worlds, such as our system is, consisting of a central Sun and six worlds, besides satellites, in preference to that of creating one world only of a vast extent.

Advantages of Life in a Plurality of Worlds

It is an idea I have never lost sight of that all our knowledge of science is derived from the revolutions (exhibited to our eye and from thence to our understanding) which those several planets or worlds of which our system is composed make in their circuit round the Sun.

Had, then, the quantity of matter which these six worlds contain been blended into one solitary globe, the consequence to us would have been that either no revolutionary motion would have existed, or not a sufficiency of it to give to us the idea and the knowledge of science we now have; and it is from the sciences that all the mechanical arts that contribute so much to our earthly felicity and comfort are derived.

As, therefore, the Creator made nothing in vain, so also must it be believed that He organized the structure of the universe in the most advantageous manner for the benefit of man; and as we see, and from experience feel, the benefits we derive from the structure of the universe formed as it is, which benefits we should not have had the opportunity of enjoying, if the structure, so far as relates to our system, had been a solitary globe—we can discover at least one reason why a *plurality* of worlds has been made, and that reason calls forth the devotional gratitude of man as well as his admiration.

But it is not to us, the inhabitants of this globe, only, that the benefits arising from a plurality of worlds are limited. The inhabitants of each of the worlds of which our system is composed enjoy the same opportunities of knowledge as we do. They behold the revolutionary motions of our earth, as we behold theirs. All the planets revolve in sight of each other and, therefore, the same universal school of science presents itself to all. Neither does the knowledge stop here. The system of worlds next to us exhibits, in its revolutions, the same principles and school of science to the inhabitants of their system as our system does to us, and in like manner throughout the immensity of space.

Our ideas, not only of the almightiness of the Creator, but of His wisdom and His beneficence, become enlarged in proportion as we contemplate the extent and the structure of the universe. The solitary idea of a solitary world rolling or at rest in the immense ocean of space gives place to the cheerful idea of a society of worlds so happily contrived as to administer, even by their motion, instruction to man. We see our own earth filled with abundance, but we forget to consider how much of that abundance is owing to the scientific knowledge the vast machinery of the universe has unfolded.

But, in the midst of those reflections, what are we to think of the Christian system of faith that forms itself upon the idea of only one world, and that of no greater extent, as is before shown, than twenty-five thousand miles? An extent which a man walking at the rate of three miles an hour, for twelve hours in the day, could he keep on in a circular direction, would walk entirely round in less than two years. Alas! what is this to the mighty ocean of space, and the almighty power of the Creator?

From whence, then, could arise the solitary and strange conceit that the Almighty, who had millions of worlds equally dependent on His protection, should quit the care of all the rest, and come to die in our world, because, they say, one man and one woman had eaten an apple? ·

And, on the other hand, are we to suppose that every world in the boundless creation had an Eve, an apple, a serpent and a redeemer? In this case, the person who is irreverently called the Son of God, and sometimes God Himself, would have nothing else to do than to travel from world to world, in an endless succession of deaths, with scarcely a momentary interval of life.

Concerning the Multiplicity of Religions

It has been by rejecting the evidence that the world or works of God in the creation afford to our senses, and the action of our reason upon that evidence, that so many wild and whimsical systems of faith and of religion have been fabricated and set up.

There may be many systems of religion that, so far from being morally bad, are in many respects morally good; but there can be but ONE that is true; and that one necessarily must, as it ever will, be in all things consistent with the ever-existing word of God that we behold in His works. But such is the strange construction of the Christian system of faith that every evidence the heavens afford to man either directly contradicts it or renders it absurd.

It is possible to believe, and I always feel pleasure in encouraging myself to believe it, that there have been men in the world who persuade themselves that what is called a *pious fraud* might, at least under particular circumstances, be productive of some good. But the fraud being once established, could not afterward be explained, for it is with a pious fraud as with a bad action, it begets a calamitous necessity of going on.

The persons who first preached the Christian system of faith, and in some measure combined with it the morality preached by Jesus Christ, might persuade themselves that it was better than the heathen mythology that then prevailed. From the first preachers the fraud went on to the second and to the third, till the idea of its being a pious fraud became lost in the belief of its being true; and that belief became again encouraged by the interests of those who made a livelihood by preaching it.

But though such a belief might by such means be rendered almost general among the laity, it is next to impossible to account for the continued persecution carried on by the Church for several hundred years against the sciences and against the professors of science, if the Church had not some record or some tradition that it was originally no other than a pious fraud, or did not foresee that it could not be maintained against the evidence that the structure of the universe afforded.

Having thus shown the irreconcilable inconsistencies between the real word of God existing in the universe and that which is called *the Word of God,* as shown to us in a printed book that any man might make, I proceed to speak of the three principal means that have been employed in all ages, and perhaps in all countries, to impose upon mankind.

Those three means are mystery, miracle and prophecy. The two first are incompatible with true religion, and the third ought always to be suspected.

With respect to mystery, everything we behold is, in one sense, a mystery to us. Our own existence is a mystery; the whole vegetable world is a mystery. We cannot account how it is that an acorn, when put into the ground, is made to develop itself and become an oak. We know not how it is that the seed we sow unfolds and multiplies itself, and returns to us such an abundant interest for so small a capital.

The fact, however, as distinct from the operating cause, is not a mystery, because we see it, and we know also the means we are to use, which is no other than putting the seed into the ground. We know, therefore, as much as is necessary for us to know; and that part of the operation that we do not know, and which, if we did, we could not perform, the Creator takes upon Himself and performs it for us. We are, therefore, better off than if we had been let into the secret, and left to do it for ourselves.

But though every created thing is, in this sense a mystery, the word mystery cannot be applied to *moral truth,* any more than obscurity can be applied to light. The God in whom we believe is a God of moral truth, and not a God of mystery or obscurity. Mystery is the antagonist of truth. It is a fog of human invention, that obscures truth, and represents it in distortion. Truth never envelops *itself* in mystery, and the mystery in which it is at any time enveloped is the work of its antagonist, and never of itself.

THE BEST WAY TO SERVE GOD

Religion, therefore, being the belief of a God and the practise of moral truth, cannot have connection with mystery. The belief of a God, so far from having anything of mystery in it, is of all beliefs the most easy, because it arises to us, as is before observed, out of necessity. And the practise of moral truth, or, in other words, a practical imitation of the moral goodness of God, is no other than our acting toward each other as He acts benignly toward all.

We cannot *serve* God in the manner we serve those who cannot do without such service; and, therefore, the only idea we can have of serving God is that of contributing to the happiness of the living creation that God has made. This cannot be done by retiring ourselves from the society of the world and spending a recluse life in selfish devotion.

The very nature and design of religion, if I may so express it, prove even to demonstration that it must be free from everything of mystery, and unencumbered with everything that is mysterious. Religion, considered as a duty, is incumbent upon every living soul alike, and, therefore, must be on a level with the understanding and comprehension of all.

Man does not learn religion as he learns the secrets and mysteries of a trade. He learns the theory of religion by reflection. It arises out of the action of his own mind upon the things which he sees, or upon what he may happen to hear or to read, and the practise joins itself thereto.

When men, whether from policy or pious fraud, set up systems of religion incompatible with the word or works of God in the creation, and not only above, but repugnant to human comprehension, they were under the necessity of inventing or adopting a word that should serve as a bar to all questions, inquiries and speculations. The word *mystery* answered this purpose, and thus it has happened that religion, which is in itself without mystery, has been corrupted into a fog of mysteries.

As *mystery* answered all general purposes, *miracle* followed as an occasional auxiliary. The former served to bewilder the mind, the latter to puzzle the senses. The one was the lingo, the other the legerdemain.

But before going further into this subject, it will be proper to inquire what is to be understood by a miracle.

In the same sense that everything may be said to be a mystery, so also may it be said that everything is a miracle, and that no one thing is a greater miracle than another. The elephant, though larger, is not a greater miracle than a mite, nor a mountain a greater miracle than an atom. To an almighty power, it is no more difficult to make the one than the other, and no more difficult to make millions of worlds than to make one.

Everything, therefore, is a miracle in one sense, while in the other sense there is no such thing as a miracle. It is a miracle when compared to our power and to our comprehension, it is not a miracle compared to the power that performs it; but as nothing in this description conveys the idea that is affixed to the word miracle, it is necessary to carry the inquiry further.

Mankind have conceived to themselves certain laws by which what they call nature is supposed to act; and that a miracle is something contrary to the operation and effect of those laws; but unless we know the whole extent of those laws, and of what are commonly called the powers of nature, we are not able to judge whether anything that may appear to us wonderful or miraculous be within, or be beyond, or be contrary to, her natural power of acting.

The ascension of man several miles high in the air would have everything in it that constitutes the idea of a miracle if it were not known that a species of air can be generated several times lighter than the common atmospheric air and yet possess elasticity enough to prevent the balloon in which that light air is inclosed from being compressed into as many times less bulk by the common air that surrounds it.

In like manner, extracting flashes or sparks of fire from the human body, as visibly as from a steel struck with a flint, and causing iron or steel to move without any visible agent, would also give the idea of a miracle if we were not acquainted with electricity and magnetism. So also would many other experiments in natural philosophy, to those who are not acquainted with the subject.

The restoring of persons to life who are to appearance dead, as is practised upon drowned persons, would also be a miracle if it were not known that animation is capable of being suspended without being extinct.

Besides these, there are performances by sleight-of-hand, and by persons acting in concert that have a miraculous appearance, which when known are thought nothing of. And besides these, there are mechanical and optical deceptions. There is now an exhibition in Paris of ghosts or spectres, which, though it is not imposed upon the spectators as a fact, has an astonishing appearance. As, therefore, we know not the extent to which either nature or art can go, there is no positive criterion to determine what a miracle is, and mankind, in giving credit to appearances, under the idea of there being miracles, are subject to be continually imposed upon.

Since, then, appearances are so capable of deceiving, and things not real have a strong resemblance to things that are, nothing can be more inconsistent than to suppose that the Almighty would make use of means such as are called miracles that would subject the person who performed them to the suspicion of being an impostor, and the person who related them to be suspected of lying, and the doctrine intended to be supported thereby to be suspected as a fabulous invention.

Of all the modes of evidence that ever were invented to obtain belief to any system or opinion to which the name of religion has been given, that of miracle, however successful the imposition may have been, is the most inconsistent. For, in the first place, whenever recourse is had to show, for the purpose of procuring that belief (for a miracle, under any idea of the word, is a show), it implies a lameness or weakness in the doctrine that is preached.

And, in the second place, it is degrading the Almighty into the character of a showman, playing tricks to amuse and make the people stare and wonder. It is also the most equivocal sort of evidence that can be set up; for the belief is not to depend upon the thing called a miracle, but upon the credit of the reporter who says that he saw it; and, therefore, the thing, were it true, would have no better chance of being believed than if it were a lie.

Suppose I were to say that when I sat down to write this book a hand presented itself in the air, took up the pen and wrote every word that is herein written; would anybody believe me? Certainly they would not. Would they believe me a whit more if the thing had been a fact? Certainly they would not.

Since, then, a real miracle, were it to happen, would be subject to the same fate as the falsehood, the inconsistency becomes the greater of supposing the Almighty would make use of means that would not answer the purpose for which they were intended, even if they were real.

If we are to suppose a miracle to be something so entirely out of the course of what is called nature that she must go out of that course to accomplish it, and we see an account given of such miracle by the person who said he saw it, it raises a question in the mind very easily decided, which is, is it more probable that nature should go out of her course or that a man should tell a lie? We have never seen, in our time, nature go out of her course; but we have good reason to believe that millions of lies have been told in the same time; it is, therefore, at least millions to one that the reporter of a miracle tells a lie.

The story of the whale swallowing Jonah, though a whale is large enough to do it, borders greatly on the marvelous; but it would have approached nearer to the idea of a miracle if Jonah had swallowed the whale. In this, which may serve for all cases of miracles, the matter would decide itself, as before stated, namely, is it more probable that a man should have swallowed a whale or told a lie?

But suppose that Jonah had really swallowed the whale, and gone with it in his belly to Nineveh and, to convince the people that it was true, had cast it up in their sight, of the full length and size of a whale, would they not have believed him to have been the devil instead of a prophet? Or, if the whale had carried Jonah to Nineveh, and cast him up in the same public manner, would they not have believed the whale to have been the devil, and Jonah one of his imps?

The most extraordinary of all the things called miracles, related in the New Testament, is that of the devil flying away with Jesus Christ, and carrying him to the top of a high mountain, and to the top of the highest pinnacle of the temple, and showing him and promising to him *all the kingdoms of the World.* How happened it that he did not discover America, or is it only with *kingdoms* that his sooty highness has any interest?

I have too much respect for the moral character of Christ to believe that he told this whale of a miracle himself; neither is it easy to account for what purpose it could have been fabricated, unless it were to impose upon the connoisseurs of miracles as is sometimes practised upon the connoisseurs of Queen Anne's farthings and collectors of relics and antiquities; or to render the belief of miracles ridiculous by outdoing miracles, as Don Quixote outdid chivalry; or to embarrass the belief of miracles by making it doubtful by what power, whether of God or of the devil, anything called a miracle was performed. It requires, however, a great deal of faith in the devil to believe this miracle.

In every point of view in which those things called miracles can be placed and considered, the reality of them is improbable and their existence unnecessary. They would not, as before observed, answer any useful purpose even if they were true; for it is more difficult to obtain belief to a miracle than to a principle evidently moral without any miracle.

Moral principle speaks universally for itself. Miracle could be but a thing of the moment, and seen but by a few; after this it requires a transfer of faith from God to man to believe a miracle upon man's report. Instead, therefore, of admitting the recitals of miracles as evidence of any system of religion being true, they ought to be considered as symptoms of its being fabulous. It is necessary to the full and upright character of truth that it rejects the crutch, and it is consistent with the character of fable to seek the aid that truth rejects. Thus much for mystery and miracle.

As mystery and miracle took charge of the past and the present, prophecy took charge of the future and rounded the tenses of faith. It was not sufficient to know what had been done, but what would be done. The supposed prophet was the supposed historian of times to come; and if he happened, in shooting with a long bow of a thousand years, to strike within a thousand miles of a mark, the ingenuity of posterity could make it point-blank; and if he happened to be directly wrong, it was only to suppose, as in the case of Jonah and Nineveh, that God had repented Himself and changed His mind. What a fool do fabulous systems make of man!

PROPHETS AND THEIR PROPHECIES

It has been shown, in a former part of this work, that the original meaning of the words *prophet* and *prophesying* has been changed, and that a prophet, in the sense of the word as now used, is a creature of modern invention; and it is owing to this change in the meaning of the words, that the flights and metaphors of the Jewish poets, and phrases and expressions now rendered obscure by our not being acquainted with the local circumstances to which they applied at the time they were used, have been erected into prophecies and made to bend to explanations at the will and whimsical conceits of sectaries, expounders and commentators.

Everything unintelligible was prophetical, and everything insignificant was typical. A blunder would have served for a prophecy, and a dishclout for a type.

If by a prophet we are to suppose a man to whom the Almighty communicated some event that would take place in future, either there were such men or there were not. If there were, it is consistent to believe that the event so communicated would be told in terms that could be understood, and not related in such a loose and obscure manner as to be out of the comprehension of those that heard it, and so equivocal as to fit almost any circumstance that might happen afterward. It is conceiving very irreverently of the Almighty to suppose that He would deal in this jesting manner with mankind, yet all the things called prophecies in the book called the Bible come under this description.

But it is with prophecy as it is with miracle; it could not answer the purpose even if it were real. Those to whom a prophecy should be told, could not tell whether the man prophesied or lied, or whether it had been revealed to him, or whether he conceited it; and if the thing that he prophesied, or intended to prophesy, should happen, or something like it, among the multitude of things that are daily happening, nobody could again know whether he foreknew it, or guessed at it, or whether it was accidental.

A prophet, therefore, is a character useless and unnecessary; and the safe side of the case is to guard against being imposed upon by not giving credit to such relations.

Upon the whole, mystery, miracle and prophecy are appendages that belong to fabulous and not to true religion. They are the means by which so many *Lo, heres!* and *Lo, theres!* have been spread about the world, and religion been made into a trade. The success of one impostor gave encouragement to another, and the quieting salvo of doing *some good* by keeping up a *pious fraud* protected them from remorse.

Recapitulation

Having now extended the subject to a greater length than I first intended, I shall bring it to a close by abstracting a summary from the whole.

First—That the idea or belief of a Word of God existing in print, or in writing, or in speech, is inconsistent in itself for reasons already assigned. These reasons, among many others, are the want of a universal language; the mutability of language; the errors to which translations are subject; the possibility of totally suppressing such a word; the probability of altering it, or of fabricating the whole, and imposing it upon the world.

Secondly—That the creation we behold is the real and ever-existing Word of God, in which we cannot be deceived. It proclaims His power, it demonstrates His wisdom, it manifests His goodness and beneficence.

Thirdly—That the moral duty of man consists in imitating the moral goodness and beneficence of God, manifested in the creation toward all His creatures. That seeing, as we daily do, the goodness of God to all men, it is an example calling upon all men to practise the same toward each other; and, consequently, that everything of persecution and revenge between man and man, and everything of cruelty to animals, is a violation of moral duty.

I trouble not myself about the manner of future existence. I content myself with believing, even to positive conviction, that the Power that gave me existence is able to continue it, in any form and manner He pleases, either with or without this body; and it appears more probable to me that I shall continue to exist hereafter, than that I should have had existence, as I now have, before that existence began.

It is certain that, in one point, all the nations of the earth and all religions agree—all believe in a God; the things in which they disagree are the redundancies annexed to that belief; and, therefore, if ever a universal religion should prevail, it will not be by believing anything new, but in getting rid of redundancies and believing as man believed at first. Adam, if ever there were such a man, was created a Deist; but in the meantime, let every man follow, as he has a right to do, the religion and the worship he prefers.

END OF THE FIRST PART

AUTOBIOGRAPHICAL INTERLUDE

Thus far I had written on the 28th of December, 1793. In the evening I went to the Hotel Philadelphia (formerly White's Hotel), Passage des Petits Pères, where I lodged when I came to Paris in consequence of being elected a member of the Convention, but had left the lodging about nine months, and taken lodgings in the Rue Fauxbourg St. Denis, for the sake of being more retired than I could be in the middle of the town.

Meeting with a company of Americans at the Hotel Philadelphia, I agreed to spend the evening with them; and as my lodging was distant about a mile and a half, I bespoke a bed at the hotel. The company broke up about twelve o'clock and I went directly to bed. About four in the morning I was awakened by a rapping at my chamber door; when I opened it, I saw a guard and the master of the hotel with them. The guard told me they came to put me under arrestation and to demand the key of my papers. I desired them to walk in, and I would dress myself and go with them immediately.

It happened that Archilles Audibert, of Calais, was then in the hotel; and I desired to be conducted into his room. When we came there I told the guard that I had only lodged at the hotel for that night; that I was printing a work, and that part of that work was at the Maison Bretagne, Rue Jacob; and desired they would take me there first, which they did.

The printing office at which the work was printing was near the Maison Bretagne, where Colonel Blackden and Joel Barlow, of the United States of America, lodged; and I had desired Joel Barlow to compare the proof sheets with the copy as they came from the press. The remainder of the manuscript from page 32 to 76 was at my lodging. But besides the necessity of my collecting all the parts of the work together that the publication might not be interrupted by my imprisonment or by any event that might happen to me, it was highly proper that I should have a fellow-citizen of America with me during the examination of my papers, as I had letters of correspondence in my possession of the President of Congress, General Washington; the Minister of Foreign Affairs to Congress, Mr. Jefferson; and the late Benjamin Franklin; and it might be necessary for me to make a pròces-verbal to send to Congress.

It happened that Joel Barlow had received only one proof sheet of the work, which he had compared with the copy and sent it back to the printing office.

We then went in company with Joel Barlow to my lodging; and the guard, or commissaires, took with them the interpreter to Committee of Surety-General. It was satisfactory to me that they went through the examination of my papers with the strictness they did; and it is but justice that I say they did it not only with civility, but with tokens of respect to my character.

I showed them the remainder of the manuscript of the foregoing work. The interpreter examined it and returned it to me saying, *"It is an interesting work; it will do much good."* I also showed him another manuscript, which I had intended for the Committee of Public Safety. It is entitled, "Observations on the Commerce between the United States of America and France."

After the examination of my papers was finished, the guard conducted me to the prison of the Luxembourg where they left me as they would a man whose undeserved fate they regretted. I offered to write under the procès-verbal they had made that they had executed their orders with civility, but they had declined it.

THE AGE OF REASON

Part Second

PREFACE

I HAVE mentioned in the former part of "The Age of Reason" that it had long been my intention to publish my thoughts upon religion; but that I had originally reserved it to a later period in life, intending it to be the last work I should undertake. The circumstances, however, which existed in France in the latter end of the year 1793 determined me to delay it no longer. The just and humane principles of the Revolution, which philosophy had first diffused, had been departed from. The idea, always dangerous to society, as it is derogatory to the Almighty, that priests could forgive sins, though it seemed to exist no longer, had blunted the feelings of humanity and prepared men for the commission of all crimes.

The intolerant spirit of Church persecutions had transferred itself into politics; the tribunal styled revolutionary supplied the place of an inquisition; and the guillotine of the stake. I saw many of my most intimate friends destroyed, others daily carried to prison, and I had reason to believe, and had also intimations given me that the same danger was approaching myself.

Under these disadvantages, I began the former part of "The Age of Reason"; I had, besides, neither Bible nor Testament [1] to refer to, though I was writing against both; nor could I procure any; notwithstanding which, I have produced a work that no Bible believer, though

[1] Paine continually refers to the Old Testament as the "Bible," and to the New Testament as the Testament.—*Editor.*

writing at his ease, and with a library of Church books about him, can refute.

Toward the latter end of December of that year a motion was made and carried to exclude foreigners from the Convention. There were but two in it, Anacharsis Cloots [2] and myself; and I saw I was particularly pointed at by Bourbon de l'Oise, in his speech on that motion.

Conceiving, after this, that I had but a few days of liberty, I sat down and brought the work to a close as speedily as possible; and I had not finished it more than six hours, in the state it has since appeared, before a guard came there, about three in the morning, with an order signed by the two Committees of Public Safety and Surety-General for putting me in arrestation as a foreigner, and conveyed me to the prison of the Luxembourg.

I contrived, on my way there, to call on Joel Barlow,[3] and I put the manuscript of the work into his hands, as more safe than in my possession in prison; and, not knowing what might be the fate in France either of the writer or the work, I addressed it to the protection of the citizens of the United States.

It is with justice that I say that the guard who executed this order, and the interpreter of the Committee of General Surety who accompanied them to examine my papers, treated me not only with civility, but with respect. The keeper of the Luxembourg, Bennoit, a man of a good heart, showed to me every friendship in his power, as did also all his family, while he continued in that station. He was removed from it, put into arrestation, and carried before the tribunal upon a malignant accusation, but acquitted.

After I had been in the Luxembourg about three weeks, the Americans then in Paris went in a body to the Convention to reclaim me as their countryman and friend; but were answered by the President, Vadier, who was also President of the Committee of Surety-General, and had signed the order for my arrestation, that I was born in England. I heard no more, after this, from any person out of the walls of the prison till the fall of Robespierre, on the ninth of Thermidor—July 27, 1794.

About two months before this event I was seized with a fever that in

[2] Anacharsis Clootz was a leader of the Girondins in France and the author of a pamphlet entitled *Ni Marat ni Roland.—Editor.*

[3] Joel Barlow was the author of the great poem, *The Columbiad* and a close friend of Paine.—*Editor.*

its progress had every symptom of becoming mortal, and from the effects of which I am not recovered. It was then that I remembered with renewed satisfaction, and congratulated myself most sincerely, on having written the former part of "The Age of Reason." I had then but little expectation of surviving, and those about me had less. I know, therefore, by experience, the conscientious trial of my own principles.

I was then with three chamber comrades, Joseph Vanhuele, of Bruges; Charles Bastini and Michael Rubyns, of Louvain. The unceasing and anxious attention of these three friends to me, by night and by day, I remember with gratitude and mention with pleasure. It happened that a physician (Dr. Graham) and a surgeon (Mr. Bond), part of the suite of General O'Hara,[4] were then in the Luxembourg. I ask not myself whether it be convenient to them, as men under the English Government, that I express to them my thanks, but I should reproach myself if I did not; and also to the physician of the Luxembourg, Dr. Markoski.

I have some reason to believe, because I cannot discover any other, that this illness preserved me in existence. Among the papers of Robespierre that were examined and reported upon to the Convention by a Committee of Deputies is a note in the handwriting of Robespierre, in the following words:

"Demander que Thomas Paine soit décrété d'accusation, pour l'intérêts de l'Amerique autant que de la France."

To demand that a decree of accusation be passed against Thomas Paine, for the interest of America, as well as of France.

From what cause it was that the intention was not put in execution I know not, and cannot inform myself, and therefore I ascribe it to impossibility, on account of that illness.

The Convention, to repair as much as lay in their power the injustice I had sustained, invited me publicly and unanimously to return into the Convention, and which I accepted, to show I could bear an injury without permitting it to injure my principles or my disposition. It is not because right principles have been violated that they are to be abandoned.

I have seen, since I have been at liberty, several publications written,

[4] O'Hara was a British officer who officiated for Cornwallis at the Yorktown surrender. He was in prison with Paine and the latter loaned him about $1,500 when he (O'Hara) was released from the jail ahead of Paine.—*Editor.*

some in America and some in England, as answers to the former part of "The Age of Reason." If the authors of these can amuse themselves by so doing, I shall not interrupt them. They may write against the work, and against me, as much as they please; they do me more service than they intend, and I can have no objection that they write on. They will find, however, by this second part, without its being written as an answer to them, that they must return to their work, and spin their cobweb over again. The first is brushed away by accident.

They will now find that I have furnished myself with a Bible and a Testament; and I can say also that I have found them to be much worse books than I had conceived. If I have erred in anything in the former part of "The Age of Reason," it has been by speaking better of some parts of those books than they have deserved.

I observe that all my opponents resort, more or less, to what they call Scripture evidence and Bible authority to help them out. They are so little masters of the subject as to confound a dispute about authenticity with a dispute about doctrines; I will, however, put them right, that if they should be disposed to write any more, they may know how to begin.

THOMAS PAINE.

October, 1795.

CHAPTER I

As to the Old Testament

IT HAS often been said, that anything may be proved from the Bible, but before anything can be admitted as proved by the Bible, the Bible itself must be proved to be true; for if the Bible be not true, or the truth of it be doubtful, it ceases to have authority, and cannot be admitted as proof of anything.

It has been the practise of all Christian commentators on the Bible, and of all Christian priests and preachers, to impose the Bible on the world as a mass of truth and as the Word of God; they have disputed and wrangled, and anathematized each other about the supposeable meaning of particular parts and passages therein; one has said and insisted that such a passage meant such a thing; another that it meant directly the contrary; and a third, that it meant neither one nor the other, but something different from both; and this they have called *understanding* the Bible.

It has happened that all the answers which I have seen to the former part of "The Age of Reason" have been written by priests; and these pious men, like their predecessors, contend and wrangle, and *understand* the Bible; each understands it differently, but each understands it best; and they have agreed in nothing but in telling their readers that Thomas Paine understands it not.

Now, instead of wasting their time and heating themselves in fractious disputations about doctrinal points drawn from the Bible, these men ought to know, and if they do not, it is civility to inform them, that the first thing to be understood is whether there is sufficient authority for believing the Bible to be the Word of God or whether there is not.

There are matters in that book, said to be done by the *express command* of God, that are as shocking to humanity and to every idea we have of moral justice as anything done by Robespierre, by Carrier, by Joseph le Bon, in France, by the English Government in the East Indies, or by any other assassin in modern times. When we read in the books ascribed to Moses, Joshua, etc., that they (the Israelites) came by stealth upon whole nations of people, who, as history itself shows, had given them no offense; *that they put all those nations to the sword; that they spared neither age nor infancy; that they utterly destroyed men, women and children; that they left not a soul to breathe*—expressions that are repeated over and over again in those books, and that, too, with ex-ulting ferocity—are we sure these things are facts? Are we sure that the Creator of man commissioned these things to be done? And are we sure that the books that tell us so were written by His authority?

It is not the antiquity of a tale that is any evidence of its truth; on the contrary, it is a symptom of its being fabulous; for the more ancient any history pretends to be the more it has the resemblance of a fable. The origin of every nation is buried in fabulous tradition, and that of the Jews is as much to be suspected as any other.

To charge the commission of acts upon the Almighty, which, in their own nature and by every rule of moral justice, are crimes, as all assassination is, and more especially the assassination of infants, is matter of serious concern. The Bible tells us, that those assassinations were done by the *express command of God*.

To believe, therefore, the Bible to be true, we must *unbelieve* all our belief in the moral justice of God; for wherein could crying or smiling infants offend? And to read the Bible without horror, we must undo everything that is tender, sympathizing and benevolent in the heart of man. Speaking for myself, if I had no other evidence that the Bible is fabulous than the sacrifice I must make to believe it to be true, that alone would be sufficient to determine my choice.

But in addition to all the moral evidence against the Bible, I will in the progress of this work produce such other evidence as even a priest cannot deny, and show, from that evidence, that the Bible is not entitled to credit as being the Word of God.

But, before I proceed to this examination, I will show wherein the Bible differs from all other ancient writings with respect to the nature of the evidence necessary to establish its authenticity; and this is the more proper to be done, because the advocates of the Bible, in their answers to the former part of "The Age of Reason," undertake to say, and they put some stress thereon, that the authenticity of the Bible is as well established as that of any other ancient book; as if our belief of the one could become any rule for our belief of the other.

I know, however, but of one ancient book that authoritatively challenges universal consent and belief, and that is Euclid's "Elements of Geometry" [5] and the reason is, because it is a book of self-evident demonstration, entirely independent of its author, and of everything relating to time, place and circumstance. The matters contained in that book would have the same authority they now have, had they been written by any other person, or had the work been anonymous, or had the author never been known; for the identical certainty of who was the author makes no part of our belief of the matters contained in the book.

But it is quite otherwise with respect to the books ascribed to Moses, to Joshua, to Samuel, etc.; those are books of *testimony,* and they testify of things naturally incredible; and, therefore, the whole of our belief as to the authenticity of those books rests, in the first place, upon the *certainty* that they were written by Moses, Joshua and Samuel; secondly, upon the credit we give to their testimony.

We may believe the first, that is, we may believe the certainty of the authorship, and yet not the testimony; in the same manner that we may believe that a certain person gave evidence upon a case and yet not believe the evidence that he gave.

But if it should be found that the books ascribed to Moses. Joshua

[5] Euclid, according to Chronological history, lived three years before Christ, and about one hundred years before Archimedes; he was of the city of Alexandria in Egypt.—*Author*

and Samuel were not written by Moses, Joshua and Samuel, every part of the authority and authenticity of those books is gone at once; for there can be no such thing as forged or invented testimony; neither can there be anonymous testimony, more especially as to things naturally incredible, such as that of talking to God face to face, or that of the sun and moon standing still at the command of a man.

The greatest part of the other ancient books are works of genius, of which kind are those ascribed to Homer, to Plato, to Aristotle, to Demosthenes, to Cicero, etc. Here, again, the author is not an essential in the credit we give to any of those works, for, as works of genius, they would have the same merit they have now, were they anonymous.

Nobody believes the Trojan story, as related by Homer, to be true—for it is the poet only that is admired, and the merit of the poet will remain, though the story be fabulous. But if we disbelieve the matters related by the Bible authors (Moses, for instance), as we disbelieve the things related by Homer, there remains nothing of Moses in our estimation, but an impostor.

As to the ancient historians, from Herodotus to Tacitus, we credit them as far as they relate things probable and credible, and no further; for if we do, we must believe the two miracles which Tacitus relates were performed by Vespasian, that of curing a lame man and a blind man in just the same manner as the same things are told of Jesus Christ by his historians. We must also believe the miracle cited by Josephus, that of the sea of Pamphilia opening to let Alexander and his army pass, as is related of the Red Sea in Exodus.

These miracles are quite as well authenticated as the Bible miracles, and yet we do not believe them; consequently the degree of evidence necessary to establish our belief of things naturally incredible, whether in the Bible or elsewhere, is far greater than that which obtains our belief to natural and probable things; and therefore the advocates for the Bible have no claim to our belief of the Bible, because that we believe the things stated in other ancient writings; since that we believe the things stated in these writings no further than they are probable and credible, or because they are self-evident, like Euclid; or admire them because they are elegant, like Homer; or approve of them because they are sedate, like Plato; or judicious, like Aristotle.

Having premised those things, I proceed to examine the authenticity of the Bible, and I begin with what are called the five books of Moses, Genesis, Exodus, Leviticus, Numbers and Deuteronomy. My intention is to show that those books are spurious, and that Moses is not the author of them; and still further, that they were not written in the time of Moses, nor till several hundred years afterward; that they are no other than an attempted history of the life of Moses, and of the times in which he is said to have lived, and also of the times prior thereto, written by some very ignorant and stupid pretenders to authorship several hundred years after the death of Moses, as men now write histories of things that happened, or are supposed to have happened, several hundred or several thousand years ago.

The evidence that I shall produce in this case is from the books themselves, and I shall confine myself to this evidence only. Were I to refer for proof to any of the ancient authors whom the advocates of the Bible call profane authors, they would controvert that authority, as I controvert theirs; I will therefore come on their own ground, and oppose them with their own weapon, the Bible.

In the first place, there is no affirmative evidence that Moses is the author of those books; and that he is the author, is altogether an unfounded opinion, got abroad nobody knows how. The style and manner in which those books are written give no room to believe, or even to suppose, they were written by Moses, for it is altogether the style and manner of another person speaking of Moses.

In Exodus, Leviticus and Numbers (for everything in Genesis is prior to the time of Moses, and not the least allusion is made to him therein), the whole, I say, of these books is in the third person; it is always, *the Lord said unto Moses,* or *Moses said unto the Lord,* or *Moses said unto the people* or *the people said unto Moses;* and this is the style and manner that historians use in speaking of the persons whose lives and actions they are writing. It may be said that a man may speak of himself in the third person, and therefore it may be supposed that Moses did; but supposition proves nothing; and if the advocates for the belief that Moses wrote those books himself have nothing better to advance than supposition, they may as well be silent.

But granting the grammatical right that Moses might speak of himself in the third person, because any man might speak of himself in that manner, it cannot be admitted as a fact in those books that it is Moses who speaks, without rendering Moses truly ridiculous and absurd. For example, Numbers, chap. xii. ver. 3. *Now the man Moses was very meek, above all the men which were upon the face of the earth.*

If Moses said this of himself, instead of being the meekest of men, he was one of the most vain and arrogant of coxcombs; and the advocates for those books may now take which side they please, for both sides are against them; if Moses was not the author, the books are without authority; and if he was the author, the author is without credit, because to boast of *meekness* is the reverse of meekness, and is *a lie in sentiment*.

In Deuteronomy, the style and manner of writing marks more evidently than in the former books that Moses is not the writer. The manner here used is dramatical; the writer opens the subject by a short introductory discourse, and then introduces Moses as in the act of speaking, and when he has made Moses finish his harangue, he (the writer) resumes his own part, and speaks till he brings Moses forward again, and at last closes the scene with an account of the death, funeral and character of Moses.

This interchange of speakers occurs four times in this book; from the first verse of the first chapter to the end of the fifth verse it is the writer who speaks; he then introduces Moses as in the act of making his harangue, and this continues to the end of the 40th verse of the fourth chapter; here the writer drops Moses and speaks historically of what was done in consequence of what Moses, when living, is supposed to have said, and which the writer had dramatically rehearsed.

The writer opens the subject again in the first verse of the fifth chapter, though it is only by saying that Moses called the people of Israel together; he then introduces Moses as before, and continues him, as in the act of speaking, to the end of the 26th chapter. He does the same thing at the beginning of the 27th chapter; and continues Moses, as in the act of speaking, to the end of the 28th chapter. At the 29th chapter the writer speaks again through the whole of the first verse and the first line of the second verse, where he introduces Moses for the last time and continues him, as in the act of speaking, to the end of the 33d chapter.

The writer, having now finished the rehearsal on the part of Moses, comes forward and speaks through the whole of the last chapter; he begins by telling the reader that Moses went to the top of Pisgah; that he saw from thence the land which (the writer says) had been promised to Abraham, Isaac and Jacob; that he, Moses, died there in the land of Moab, but that no man knows of his sepulchre unto this day; that is, unto the time in which the writer lived who wrote the book of Deuteronomy. The writer then tells us, that Moses was 110 years of age when he died—that his eye was not dim, nor his natural force abated;

and he concludes by saying that there arose not a prophet *since* in Israel like unto Moses, whom, says this anonymous writer, the Lord knew face to face.

Having thus shown, as far as grammatical evidence applies, that Moses was not the writer of those books, I will, after making a few observations on the inconsistencies of the writer of the book of Deuteronomy, proceed to show from the historical and chronological evidence contained in those books, that Moses was not, because *he could not be* the writer of them, and consequently that there is no authority for believing that the inhuman and horrid butcheries of men, women and children, told of in those books, were done, as those books say they were, at the command of God. It is a duty incumbent on every true Deist, that he vindicate the moral justice of God against the calumnies of the Bible.

The writer of the book of Deuteronomy, whoever he was (for it is an anonymous work), is obscure, and also in contradiction with himself, in the account he has given of Moses.

After telling that Moses went to the top of Pisgah (and it does not appear from any account that he ever came down again), he tells us that Moses died *there* in the land of Moab, and that *he* buried him in a valley in the land of Moab; but as there is no antecedent to the pronoun *he,* there is no knowing who *he* was that did bury him. If the writer meant that *He* (God) buried him, how should *he* (the writer) know it? or why should we (the readers) believe him? since we know not who the writer was that tells us so, for certainly Moses could not himself tell where he was buried.

The writer also tells us, that no man knows where the sepulchre of Moses is *unto this day,* meaning the time in which this writer lived; how then should he know that Moses was buried in a valley in the land of Moab? for as the writer lived long after the time of Moses, as is evident from his using the expression of *unto this day,* meaning a great length of time after the death of Moses, he certainly was not at his funeral; and on the other hand, it is impossible that Moses himself could say that *no man knows where the sepulchre is unto this day.* To make Moses the speaker would be an improvement on the play of a child that hides himself and cries *nobody can find me;* nobody can find Moses!

This writer has nowhere told us how he came by the speeches which he has put into the mouth of Moses to speak, and therefore we have a right to conclude that he either composed them himself or wrote them from oral tradition. One or the other of these is the more probable, since he has given in the fifth chapter a table of commandments in which that called the fourth commandment is different from the fourth commandment in the twentieth chapter of Exodus.

In that of Exodus the reason given for keeping the seventh day is, "because (says the commandment) God made the heavens and the earth in six days, and rested on the seventh"; but in that of Deuteronomy, the reason given is that it was the day on which the children of Israel came out of Egypt and *therefore,* says this commandment, *the Lord thy God commanded thee to keep the sabbath day.* This makes no mention of the Creation, nor *that* of the coming out of Egypt.

There are also many things given as laws of Moses in this book that are not to be found in any of the other books; among which is that inhuman and brutal law, chapter xxi., verses 18, 19, 20 and 21, which authorizes parents, the father and the mother, to bring their own children to have them stoned to death for what it is pleased to call stubbornness.

But priests have always been fond of preaching up Deuteronomy, for Deuteronomy preaches up tithes; and it is from this book, chap. xxv., ver. 4, that they have taken the phrase, and applied it to tithing, that *"thou shalt not muzzle the ox when he treadeth out the corn";* and that this might not escape observation, they have noted it in the table of contents at the head of the chapter, though it is only a single verse of less than two lines. Oh, priests! priests! ye are willing to be compared to an ox, for the sake of tithes.

Though it is impossible for us to know *identically* who the writer of Deuteronomy was, it is not difficult to discover him *professionally,* that he was some Jewish priest, who lived, as I shall show in the course of this work, at least three hundred and fifty years after the time of Moses.

I come now to speak of the historical and chronological evidence. The chronology that I shall use is the Bible chronology, for I mean not to go out of the Bible for evidence of anything, but to make the Bible itself prove, historically and chronologically, that Moses is not the author of the books ascribed to him. It is, therefore, proper that I inform the reader (such at least as may not have the opportunity of knowing it), that in the larger Bibles, and also in some smaller ones, there is a series of chronology printed in the margin of every page, for the purpose of showing how long the historical matters stated in each page happened, or are supposed to have happened, before Christ, and, consequently, the distance of time between one historical circumstance and another.

I begin with the book of Genesis. In the 14th chapter of Genesis, the writer gives an account of Lot being taken prisoner in a battle between the four kings against five, and carried off; and that when the account of Lot being taken came to Abraham, he armed all his household and marched to rescue Lot from the captors, and that he pursued them unto Dan (ver. 14).

To show in what manner this expression of *pursuing them unto Dan* applies to the case in question, I will refer to two circumstances, the one in America, the other in France.

The city now called New York, in America, was originally New Amsterdam; and the town in France, lately called Havre Marat, was before called Havre de Grace. New Amsterdam was changed to New York in the year 1664; Havre de Grace to Havre Marat in the year 1793. Should, therefore, any writing be found, though without date, in which the name of New York should be mentioned, it would be certain evidence that such a writing could not have been written before, but must have been written after New Amsterdam was changed to New York, and consequently, not till after the year 1664, or at least during the course of that year. And, in like manner, any dateless writing with the name Havre Marat would be certain evidence that such a writing must have been written after Havre de Grace became Havre Marat, and consequently not till after the year 1793, or at least during the course of that year.

I now come to the application of those cases, and to show that there was no such place as *Dan,* till many years after the death of Moses, and consequently that Moses could not be the writer of the book of Genesis, where this account of pursuing them unto *Dan* is given. The place that is called Dan in the Bible was originally a town of the Gentiles called Laish; and when the tribe of Dan seized upon this town they changed its name to Dan, in commemoration of Dan, who was the father of that tribe and the great-grandson of Abraham.

To establish this in proof, it is necessary to refer from Genesis, to the 18th chapter of the book called the book of Judges. It is there said (ver. 27) *that they* (the Danites) *came unto Laish to a people that were quiet and secure, and they smote them with the edge of the sword* (the Bible is filled with murder) *and burned the city with fire; and they built a city* (ver. 28), and dwelt therein, *and they called the name of the city*

Dan, after the name of Dan, their father, howbeit the name of the city was Laish at the first.

This account of the Danites taking possession of Laish and changing it to Dan is placed in the book of Judges immediately after the death of Samson. The death of Samson is said to have happened 1120 years before Christ, and that of Moses 1451 before Christ; and, therefore, according to the historical arrangement, the place was not called Dan till 331 years after the death of Moses.

There is a striking confusion between the historical and the chronological arrangement in the book of Judges. The five last chapters, as they stand in the book, 17, 18, 19, 20, 21, are put chronologically before all the preceding chapters; they are made to be 28 years before the 16th chapter, 266 before the 15th, 245 before the 13th, 195 before the 9th, 90 before the 4th, and 15 years before the 1st chapter. This shows the uncertain and fabulous state of the Bible.

According to the chronological arrangement, the taking of Laish and giving it the name of Dan is made to be 20 years after the death of Joshua, who was the successor of Moses; and by the historical order as it stands in the book, it is made to be 306 years after the death of Joshua, and 331 after that of Moses; but they both exclude Moses from being the writer of Genesis, because, according to either of the statements, no such a place as Dan existed in the time of Moses; and therefore the writer of Genesis must have been some person who lived after the town of Laish had the name of Dan; and who that person was nobody knows, and consequently the book of Genesis is anonymous and without authority.

I proceed now to state another point of historial and chronological evidence, and to show therefrom, as in the preceding case, that Moses is not the author of the book of Genesis.

In the 36th chapter of Genesis there is given a genealogy of the sons and descendants of Esau, who are called Edomites, and also a list, by name, of the kings of Edom, in enumerating of which, it is said (ver. 31), *And these are the kings that reigned in Edom, before there reigned any king over the children of Israel.*

Now, were any dateless writings to be found in which, speaking of any past events, the writer should say, These things happened before there was any Congress in America, or before there was any Convention in France, it would be evidence that such writing could not have been written before, and could only be written after there was a Congress in

America, or a Convention in France, as the case might be; and, consequently, that it could not be written by any person who died before
there was a Congress in the one country or a Convention in the other.

Nothing is more frequent, as well in history as in conversation, than
to refer to a fact in the room of a date; it is most natural so to do, first,
because a fact fixes itself in the memory better than a date; secondly,
because the fact includes the date and serves to excite two ideas at
once; and this manner of speaking by circumstances implies as positively
that the fact alluded to is *past* as if it were so expressed.

When a person speaking upon any matter, says, it was before I was
married, or before my son was born, or before I went to America, or
before I went to France, it is absolutely understood, and intended to be
understood, that he had been married, that he has had a son, that he
has been in America or been in France. Language does not admit of
using this mode of expression in any other sense; and whenever such
an expression is found anywhere it can only be understood in the sense
in which it only could have been used.

The passage, therefore, that I have quoted—"that these are the kings
that reigned in Edom, before there reigned *any* king over the children
of Israel"—could only have been written after the first king began to
reign over them; and, consequently, that the book of Genesis, so far
from having been written by Moses, could not have been written till
the time of Saul at least.

This is the positive sense of the passage; but the expression, *any* king,
implies more kings than one, at least it implies two, and this will carry
it to the time of David; and if taken in a general sense, it carries itself
through all times of the Jewish monarchy.

Had we met with this verse in any part of the Bible that *professed* to
have been written after kings began to reign in Israel, it would have been
impossible not to have seen the application of it. It happens then that
this is the case; the two books of Chronicles which give a history of all
the kings of Israel are *professedly,* as well as in fact, written after the
Jewish monarchy began; and this verse that I have quoted, and all the
remaining verses of the 36th chapter of Genesis, are word for word in
the first chapter of Chronicles, beginning at the 43d verse.

It was with consistency that the writer of the Chronicles could say,
as he has said, 1st Chron., chap. i., ver. 43, *These are the kings that
reigned in the land of Edom, before any king reigned over the children
of Israel,* because he was going to give, and has given, a list of the kings

that had reigned in Israel; but as it is impossible that the same expression could have been used before that period, it is as certain as anything that can be proved from historical language that this part of Genesis is taken from Chronicles, and that Genesis is not so old as Chronicles, and probably not so old as the book of Homer, or as Æsop's "Fables," admitting Homer to have been, as the tables of chronology state, contemporary with David or Solomon, and Æsop to have lived about the end of the Jewish monarchy.

Take away from Genesis the belief that Moses was the author, on which only the strange belief that it is the Word of God has stood, and there remains nothing of Genesis but an anonymous book of stories, fables and traditionary or invented absurdities, or of downright lies. The story of Eve and the serpent, and of Noah and his ark, drops to a level with the Arabian tales, without the merit of being entertaining; and the account of men living to eight and nine hundred years becomes as fabulous as the immortality of the giants of the Mythology.

Besides, the character of Moses, as stated in the Bible, is the most horrid that can be imagined. If those accounts be true, he was the wretch that first began and carried on wars on the score or on the pretense of religion; and under that mask, or that infatuation, committed the most unexampled atrocities that are to be found in the history of any nation, of which I will state only one instance.

When the Jewish army returned from one of their plundering and murdering excursions, the account goes on as follows: Numbers, chap. xxxi., ver. 13:

"And Moses, and Eleazar the priest, and all the princes of the congregation, went forth to meet them without the camp; and Moses was wroth with the officers of the host, with the captains over thousands, and captains over hundreds, which came from the battle; and Moses said unto them, *Have ye saved all the women alive?* behold, these caused the children of Israel, through the council of Balaam, to commit trespass against the Lord in the matter of Peor, and there was a plague among the congregation of the Lord. Now, therefore, *kill every male among the little ones, and kill every woman that hath known a man by lying with him; but all the women-children, that have not known a man by lying with him, keep alive for yourselves."*

Among the detestable villains that in any period of the world have disgraced the name of man, it is impossible to find a greater than Moses, if this account be true. Here is an order to butcher the boys, to massacre the mothers and debauch the daughters.

Let any mother put herself in the situation of those mothers; one child murdered, another destined to violation, and herself in the hands of an executioner; let any daughter put herself in the situation of those daughters, destined as a prey to the murderers of a mother and a brother, and what will be their feelings? It is in vain that we attempt to impose upon nature, for nature will have her course, and the religion that tortures all her social ties is a false religion.

After this detestable order, follows an account of the plunder taken, and the manner of dividing it; and here it is that the profaneness of priestly hypocrisy increases the catalogue of crimes. Ver. 37, *"And the Lord's tribute* of the sheep was six hundred and three score and fifteen; and the beeves were thirty and six thousand, of which the *Lord's tribute* was three score and twelve; and the asses were thirty thousand, of which the *Lord's tribute* was three score and one; and the persons were sixteen thousand, of which the *Lord's tribute* was thirty and two."

In short, the matters contained in this chapter, as well as in many other parts of the Bible, are too horrid for humanity to read or for decency to hear, for it appears, from the 35th verse of this chapter, that the number of women-children consigned to debauchery by the order of Moses was thirty-two thousand.

People in general do not know what wickedness there is in this pretended Word of God. Brought up in habits of superstition, they take it for granted that the Bible is true, and that it is good; they permit themselves not to doubt of it, and they carry the ideas they form of the benevolence of the Almighty to the book which they have been taught to believe was written by His authority. Good heavens! it is quite another thing; it is a book of lies, wickedness and blasphemy; for what can be greater blasphemy than to ascribe the wickedness of man to the orders of the Almighty?

But to return to my subject, that of showing that Moses is not the author of the books ascribed to him, and that the Bible is spurious. The two instances I have already given would be sufficient without any additional evidence to invalidate the authenticity of any book that pretended to be four or five hundred years more ancient than the matters it speaks of, or refers to, as facts; for in the case of *pursuing them unto Dan,* and of *the kings that reigned over the children of Israel,* not even the flimsy pretense of prophecy can be pleaded. The expressions are in the preterite tense, and it would be downright idiotism to say that a man could prophesy in the preterite tense.

But there are many other passages scattered throughout those books that unite in the same point of evidence. It is said in Exodus (another of the books ascribed to Moses), chap. xvi. ver. 34, "And the children of Israel did eat manna forty years *until they came to a land inhabited;* they did eat manna *until they came unto the borders of the land of Canaan."*

Whether the children of Israel ate manna or not, or what manna was, or whether it was anything more than a kind of fungus or small mushroom, or other vegetable substance common to that part of the country, makes no part my argument; all that I mean to show is that it is not Moses that could write this account, because the account extends itself beyond the life and time of Moses. Moses, according to the Bible (but it is such a book of lies and contradictions there is no knowing which part to believe, or whether any), died in the wilderness and never came upon the borders of the land of Canaan; and consequently it could not be he that said what the children of Israel did, or what they ate when they came there.

This account of eating manna, which they tell us was written by Moses, extends itself to the time of Joshua, the successor of Moses; as appears by the account given in the book of Joshua, after the children of Israel had passed the river Jordan, and came unto the borders of the land of Canaan. Joshua, chap. v., ver. 12. *"And the manna ceased on the morrow, after they had eaten of the old corn of the land; neither had the children of Israel manna any more, but they did eat of the fruit of the land of Canaan that year."*

But a more remarkable instance than this occurs in Deuteronomy, which, while it shows that Moses could not be the writer of that book, shows also the fabulous notions that prevailed at that time about giants. In the third chapter of Deuteronomy, among the conquests said to be made by Moses, is an account of the taking of Og, king of Bashan, v. 12. "For only Og, king of Bashan, remained of the race of giants; behold, his bedstead was a bedstead of iron; is it not in Rabbath of the children of Ammon? Nine cubits was the length thereof, and four cubits the breadth of it, after the cubit of a man."

A cubit is 1 foot 9 888-1000ths inches; the length, therefore, of the bed was 16 feet 4 inches, and the breadth 7 feet 4 inches; thus much for this giant's bed. Now for the historical part, which, though the evidence is not so direct and positive as in the former cases, it is nevertheless very presumable and corroborating evidence, and is better than the *best* evidence on the contrary side.

The writer, by way of proving the existence of this giant, refers to his bed as an *ancient relic,* and says, Is it not in Rabbath (or Rabbah) of the children of Ammon? meaning that it is; for such is frequently the Bible method of affirming a thing. But it could not be Moses that said this, because Moses could know nothing about Rabbah nor of what was in it.

Rabbah was not a city belonging to this giant king, nor was it one of the cities that Moses took. The knowledge, therefore, that this bed was at Rabbah, and of the particulars of its dimensions, must be referred to the time when Rabbah was taken, and this was not till four hundred years after the death of Moses; for which see 2 Sam. chap. xii., ver. 26. "And Joab (David's general) fought against *Rabbah of the children of Ammon,* and took the royal city."

As I am not undertaking to point out all the contradictions in time, place, and circumstance that abound in the books ascribed to Moses, and which prove to demonstration that those books could not have been written by Moses, nor in the time of Moses, I proceed to the book of Joshua, and to show that Joshua is not the author of that book, and that it is anonymous and without authority. The evidence I shall produce is contained in the book itself; I will not go out of the Bible for proof against the supposed authenticity of the Bible. False testimony is always good against itself.

Joshua, according to the first chapter of Joshua, was the immediate successor of Moses; he was, moreover, a military man, which Moses was not, and he continued as chief of the people of Israel 25 years, that is, from the time that Moses died, which, according to the Bible chronology, was 1451 years before Christ, until 1426 years before Christ, when, according to the same chronology, Joshua died.

If, therefore, we find in this book, said to have been written by Joshua, reference to *facts done* after the death of Joshua, it is evidence that Joshua could not be the author; and also that the book could not have been written till after the time of the latest fact which it records. As to the character of the book, it is horrid; it is a military history of rapine and murder, as savage and brutal as those recorded of his predecessor in villainy and hypocrisy, Moses; and the blasphemy consists, as in the former books, in ascribing those deeds to the orders of the Almighty.

In the first place, the book of Joshua, as is the case in the preceding books, is written in the third person; it is the historian of Joshua that speaks, for it would have been absurd and vainglorious that Joshua should say of himself, as is said of him in the last verse of the sixth chapter, that *"his fame was noised throughout all the country."* I now come more immediately to the proof.

In the 24th chapter, ver. 31, it is said, "And Israel served the Lord all the days of Joshua, and *all the days of the elders that overlived Joshua."* Now, in the name of common sense, can it be Joshua that relates what people had done after he was dead? This account must not only have been written by some historian that lived after Joshua, but that lived also after the elders that had outlived Joshua.

There are several passages of a general meaning with respect to time scattered throughout the book of Joshua, that carries the time in which the book was written to a distance from the time of Joshua, but without marking by exclusion any particular time, as in the passage above quoted. In that passage, the time that intervened between the death of Joshua and the death of the elders is excluded descriptively and absolutely, and the evidence substantiates that the book could not have been written till after the death of the last.

But though the passages to which I allude, and which I am going to quote, do not designate any particular time by exclusion, they imply a time far more distant from the days of Joshua than is contained between the death of Joshua and the death of the elders. Such is the passage, chap. x., ver. 14, where, after giving an account that the sun stood still upon Gibeon, and the moon in the valley of Ajalon, at the command of Joshua (a tale only fit to amuse children), the passage says, "And there was no day like that, before it, or after it, that the Lord hearkened unto the voice of a man."

This tale of the sun standing still upon mount Gibeon, and the moon in the valley of Ajalon, is one of those fables that detects itself. Such a circumstance could not have happened without being known all over the world. One half would have wondered why the sun did not rise, and the other why it did not set; and the tradition of it would be universal, whereas there is not a nation in the world that knows anything about it.

But why must the moon stand still? What occasion could there be for moonlight in the daytime, and that, too, while the sun shone? As a poetical figure, the whole is well enough; it is akin to that in the song of Deborah and Barak, *The stars in their courses fought against Sisera;* but it is inferior to the figurative declaration of Mahomet to the persons who came to expostulate with him on his goings on: *"Wert thou,"* said he, *"to come to me with the sun in thy right hand and the moon in thy left, it should not alter my career."*

For Joshua to have exceeded Mahomet, he should have put the sun and moon one in each pocket, and carried them as Guy Fawkes carried his dark lantern, and taken them out to shine as he might happen to want them.

The sublime and the ridiculous are often so nearly related that it is difficult to class them separately. One step above the sublime makes the ridiculous, and one step above the ridiculous makes the sublime again; the account, however, abstracted from the poetical fancy, shows the ignorance of Joshua, for he should have commanded the earth to have stood still.

The time implied by the expression *after* it, that is, after that day, being put in comparison with all the time that passed *before* it, must, in order to give any expressive signification to the passage, mean a *great length of time;* for example, it would have been ridiculous to have said so the next day, or the next week, or the next month, or the next year; to give, therefore, meaning to the passage, comparative with the wonder it relates and the prior time it alludes too, it must mean centuries of years; less, however, than one would be trifling, and less than two would be barely admissible.

A distant but general time is also expressed in the 8th chapter, where, after giving an account of the taking of the city of Ai, it is said, ver. 28, "And Joshua burned Ai, and made it a heap forever, a desolation *unto this day";* and again, ver. 29, where, speaking of the king of Ai, whom Joshua had hanged, and buried at the entering of the gate, it is said, "And he raised thereon a great heap of stones, which remaineth unto this day," that is, unto the day or time in which the writer of the book of Joshua lived. And again, in the 10th chapter, where, after speaking of the five kings whom Joshua had hanged on five trees, and then thrown in a cave, it is said, "And he laid great stones on the cave's mouth, which remain unto this very day."

In enumerating the several exploits of Joshua, and of the tribes, and of the places which they conquered or attempted, it is said, chap. xv., ver. 63: "As for the Jebusites, the inhabitants of Jerusalem, the children of Judah could not drive them out; but the Jebusites dwell with the children of Judah *at Jerusalem unto this day."* The question upon this passage is, at what time did the Jebusites and the children of Judah dwell together at Jerusalem? As this matter occurs again in the first chapter of Judges, I shall reserve my observations until I come to that part.

Having thus shown from the book of Joshua itself, without any auxiliary evidence whatever, that Joshua is not the author of that book. and that it is anonymous, and consequently without authority, I proceed as before mentioned, to the book of Judges.

The book of Judges is anonymous on the face of it; and therefore, even the pretense is wanting to call it the Word of God; it has not so much as a nominal voucher; it is altogether fatherless.

This book begins with the same expression as the book of Joshua. That of Joshua begins, chap. i., ver. 1, *"Now after the death of Moses,"* etc., and this of the Judges begins, *"Now after the death of Joshua,"* etc. This and the similarity of style between the two books indicate that they are the work of the same author, but who he was is altogether unknown; the only point that the book proves is that the author lived long after the time of Joshua; for though it begins as if it followed immediately after his death, the second chapter is an epitome or abstract of the whole book, which, according to the Bible chronology, extends its history through a space of 306 years; that is, from the death of Joshua, 1426 years before Christ, to the death of Samson, 1120 years before Christ, and only 25 years before Saul went *to seek his father's asses, and was made king.* But there is good reason to believe, that it was not written till the time of David, at least, and that the book of Joshua was not written before the same time.

In the first chapter of Judges, the writer, after announcing the death of Joshua, proceeds to tell what happened between the children of Judah and the native inhabitants of the land of Canaan. In this statement, the writer, having abruptly mentioned Jerusalem in the 7th verse, says immediately after, in the 8th verse, by way of explanation, "Now the children of Judah *had* fought against Jerusalem and *taken* it"; consequently this book could not have been written before Jerusalem had been taken. The reader will recollect the quotation I have just before made from the 15th chapter of Joshua, ver. 63, where it is said that *the Jebusites dwell with the children of Judah at Jerusalem at this day,* meaning the time when the book of Joshua was written.

The evidence I have already produced to prove that the books I have hitherto treated of were not written by the person to whom they are ascribed, nor till many years after their death, if such persons ever lived, is already so abundant that I can afford to admit this passage with less weight than I am entitled to draw from it. For the case is, that so far as the Bible can be credited as a history, the city of Jerusalem was not taken till the time of David; and consequently that the books of Joshua and of Judges were not written till after the commencement of the reign of David, which was 370 years after the death of Joshua.

The name of the city that was afterward called Jerusalem was originally Jebus, or Jebusi, and was the capital of the Jebusites. The account of David's taking this city is given in II. Samuel, chap. v., ver. 4, etc.; also in I. Chron., chap. xiv., ver. 4, etc. There is no mention in any part of the Bible that it was ever taken before, nor any account that favors such an opinion.

It is not said, either in Samuel or in Chronicles, that they *utterly destroyed men, women and children; that they left not a soul to breathe,* as is said of their other conquests; and the silence here observed implies that it was taken by capitulation, and that the Jebusites, the native inhabitants, continued to live in the place after it was taken. The account, therefore, given in Joshua, that *the Jebusites dwell with the children of Judah* at Jerusalem *at this day* corresponds to no other time than after the taking of the city by David.

Having now shown that every book in the Bible, from Genesis to Judges, is without authenticity, I come to the book of Ruth, an idle, bungling story, foolishly told, nobody knows by whom, about a strolling country-girl, creeping slyly to bed with her cousin Boaz. Pretty stuff indeed, to be called the Word of God! It is, however, one of the best books in the Bible, for it is free from murder and rapine

I come next to the two books of Samuel, and to show that those books were not written by Samuel, nor till a great length of time after the death of Samuel; and that they are, like all former books, anonymous and without authority.

To be convinced that these books have been written much later than the time of Samuel, and consequently not by him, it is only necessary to read the account which the writer gives of Saul going to seek his father's asses, and of his interview with Samuel, of whom Saul went to inquire about those lost asses, as foolish people nowadays go to a conjuror to inquire after lost things.

The writer, in relating this story of Saul, Samuel and the asses, does not tell it as a thing that has just then happened, but as an ancient *story in the time this writer lived;* for he tells it in the language or terms used at the time that *Samuel* lived, which obliges the writer to explain the story in the terms or language used in the time the *writer* lived.

Samuel, in the account given of him, in the first of those books, chap. ix., is called *the seer;* and it is by this term that Saul inquires after him, ver. 11, "And as they (Saul and his servant) went up the hill to the city, they found young maidens going out to draw water; and they said unto them, *Is the seer here?*" Saul then went according to the direction of these maidens, and met Samuel without knowing him, and said unto him, ver. 18, "Tell me, I pray thee, where the *seer's house is?* and Samuel answered Saul, and said, *I am the seer."*

As the writer of the book of Samuel relates these questions and answers, in the language or manner of speaking used in the time they are said to have been spoken, and as that manner of speaking was out of use when this author wrote, he found it necessary, in order to make the story understood, to explain the terms in which these questions and answers are spoken; and he does this in the 9th verse, when he says *"Before-time,* in Israel, when a man went to inquire of God, thus he spake, Come, and let us go to the seer; for he that is now called a prophet, was *before-time* called a seer."

This proves, as I have before said, that this story of Saul, Samuel and the asses, was an ancient story at the time the book of Samuel was written, and consequently that Samuel did not write it, and that that book is without authenticity.

But if we go further into those books the evidence is still more positive that Samuel is not the writer of them; for they relate things that did not happen till several years after the death of Samuel. Samuel died before Saul; for the 1st Samuel, chap. xxviii., tells that Saul and the witch of Endor conjured Samuel up after he was dead; yet the history of the matters contained in those books is extended through the remaining part of Saul's life, and to the latter end of the life of David, who succeeded Saul.

The account of the death and burial of Samuel (a thing which he could not write himself) is related in the 25th chapter of the first book of Samuel, and the chronology affixed to this chapter makes this to be 1060 years before Christ; yet the history of this *first* book is brought down to 1056 years before Christ; that is, to the death of Saul, which was not till four years after the death of Samuel.

The second book of Samuel begins with an account of things that did not happen till four years after Samuel was dead; for it begins with the reign of David, who succeeded Saul, and it goes on to the end of David's reign, which was forty-three years after the death of Samuel; and, therefore, the books are in themselves positive evidence that they were not written by Samuel.

I have now gone through all the books in the first part of the Bible to which the names of persons are affixed, as being the authors of those books, and which the Church, styling itself the Christian Church, has imposed upon the world as the writings of Moses, Joshua and Samuel, and I have detected and proved the falsehood of this imposition.

And now, ye priests of every description, who have preached and written against the former part of "The Age of Reason," what have ye to say? Will ye, with all this mass of evidence against you, and staring you in the face, still have the assurance to march into your pulpits and continue to impose these books on your congregations as the works of *inspired penmen,* and the Word of God, when it is as evident as demonstration can make truth appear that the persons who ye say are the authors are *not* the authors, and that ye know not who the authors are?

What shadow of pretense have ye now to produce for continuing the blasphemous fraud? What have ye still to offer against the pure and moral religion of Deism, in support of your system of falsehood, idolatry and pretended revelation? Had the cruel and murderous orders with which the Bible is filled, and the numberless torturing executions of men, women and children, in consequence of those orders, been ascribed to some friend whose memory you revered, you would have glowed with satisfaction at detecting the falsehood of the charge, and gloried in defending his injured fame.

Is it because ye are sunk in the cruelty of superstition, or feel no interest in the honor of your Creator, that ye listen to the horrid tales of the Bible, or hear them with callous indifference? The evidence I have produced, and shall produce in the course of this work, to prove that the Bible is without authority, will, while it wounds the stubbornness of a priest, relieve and tranquillize the minds of millions; it will free them from all those hard thoughts of the Almighty which priestcraft and the Bible had infused into their minds, and which stood in everlasting opposition to all their ideas of His moral justice and benevolence.

_I come now to the two books of Kings, and the two books of Chronicles. Those books are altogether historical, and are chiefly confined to the lives and actions of the Jewish kings, who in general were a parcel of rascals; but these are matters with which we have no more concern than we have with the Roman emperors or Homer's account of the Trojan War.

Besides which, as those works are anonymous, and as we know nothing of the writer, or of his character, it is impossible for us to know what degree of credit to give to the matters related therein. Like all other ancient histories, they appear to be a jumble of fable and of fact, and of probable and of improbable things; but which distance of time and place, and change of circumstances in the world, have rendered obsolete and uninteresting.

The chief use I shall make of those books will be that of comparing them with each other, and with other parts of the Bible, to show the confusion, contradiction and cruelty in this pretended Word of God.

The first book of Kings begins with the reign of Solomon, which, according to the Bible chronology, was 1015 years before Christ; and the second book ends 588 years before Christ, being a little after the reign of Zedekiah, whom Nebuchadnezzar, after taking Jerusalem and conquering the Jews, carried captive to Babylon. The two books include a space of 427 years.

The two books of Chronicles are a history of the same times, and in general of the same persons, by another author; for it would be absurd to suppose that the same author wrote the history twice over. The first book of Chronicles (after giving the genealogy from Adam to Saul, which takes up the first nine chapters), begins with the reign of David; and the last book ends as in the last book of Kings, soon after the reign of Zedekiah, about 588 years before Christ. The two last verses of the last chapter bring the history more forward 52 years, that is, to 536. But these verses do not belong to the book, as I shall show when I come to speak of the book of Ezra.

The two books of Kings, besides the history of Saul, David and Solomon, who reigned over *all* Israel, contain an abstract of the lives of 17 kings and one queen, who are styled kings of Judah, and of 19, who are styled kings of Israel; for the Jewish nation, immediately on the death of Solomon, split into two parties, who chose separate kings, and who carried on most rancorous wars against each other.

These two books are little more than a history of assassinations, treachery and wars. The cruelties that the Jews had accustomed themselves to practise on the Canaanites, whose country they had savagely invaded under a pretended gift from God, they afterward practised as furiously on each other. Scarcely half their kings died a natural death, and in some instances whole families were destroyed to secure possession to the successor, who, after a few years, and sometimes only a few months or less, shared the same fate. In the tenth chapter of the second book of Kings, an account is given of two baskets full of children's heads, seventy in number, being exposed at the entrance of the city; they were the children of Ahab, and were murdered by the order of Jehu, whom Elisha, the pretended man of God, had anointed to be king over Israel, on purpose to commit this bloody deed, and assassinate his predecessor.

And in the account of the reign of Menahem, one of the kings of Israel who had murdered Shallum, who had reigned but one month, it is said, II. Kings, chap. xv., ver. 16, that Menahem smote the city of Tiphsah, because they opened not the city to him, *and all the women therein that were with child he ripped up.*

Could we permit ourselves to suppose that the Almighty would distinguish any nation of people by the name of *His chosen people,* we must suppose that people to have been an example to all the rest of the world of the purest piety and humanity, and not such a nation of ruffians and cut-throats as the ancient Jews were; a people who, corrupted by and copying after such monsters and imposters as Moses and Aaron, Joshua, Samuel and David, had distinguished themselves above all others on the face of the known earth for barbarity and wickedness.

If we will not stubbornly shut our eyes and steel our hearts, it is impossible not to see, in spite of all that long-established superstition imposes upon the mind, that the flattering appellation of *His chosen people* is no other than a *lie* which the priests and leaders of the Jews had invented to cover the baseness of their own characters, and which Christian priests, sometimes as corrupt and often as cruel, have professed to believe.

The two books of Chronicles are a repetition of the same crimes, but the history is broken in several places by the author leaving out the reign of some of their kings; and in this, as well as in that of Kings, there is such a frequent transition from kings of Judah to kings of Israel, and from kings of Israel to kings of Judah, that the narrative is obscure in the reading.

In the same book the history sometimes contradicts itself; for example, in the second book of Kings, chap. i., ver. 17, we are told, but in rather ambiguous terms, that after the death of Ahaziah, king of Israel, Jehoram, or Joram (who was of the house of Ahab), reigned in his stead, in the *second year* of Jehoram, or Joram, son of Jehoshaphat, king of Judah; and in chap. viii., ver. 16, of the same book, it is said, and in the *fifth year* of Joram, the son of Ahab, king of Israel, Jehoshaphat being then king of Judah, began to reign; that is, one chapter says Joram of Judah began to reign in the *second year* of Joram of Israel; and the other chapter says that Joram of Israel began to reign in the *fifth year* of Joram of Judah.

Several of the most extraordinary matters related in one history, as having happened during the reign of such and such of their kings, are not to be found in the other, in relating the reign of the same king; for example, the two first rival kings, after the death of Solomon, were Rehoboam and Jeroboam; and in I. Kings, chaps. xii. and xiii., an account is given of Jeroboam making an offering of burnt incense, and that a man, who was there called a man of God, cried out against the altar, chap. xiii., ver. 2: "O altar, altar! thus saith the Lord; Behold, a child shall be born unto the house of David, Josiah by name; and upon thee shall he offer the priests of the high places that burn incense upon thee, and men's bones shall be burnt upon thee." Verse 3: "And it came to pass, when King Jeroboam heard the saying of the man of God, which had cried against the altar in Bethel, that he put forth his hand from the altar, saying, *Lay hold on him*. And his hand which he put out against him *dried up, so that he could not pull it in again to him.*"

One would think that such an extraordinary case as this (which is spoken of as a judgment), happening to the chief of one of the parties, and that at the first moment of the separation of the Israelites into two nations, would, if it had been true, have been recorded in both histories. But though men in latter times have believed *all that the prophets have said unto them,* it does not appear that these prophets or historians believed each other; they knew each other too well.

A long account also is given in Kings about Elijah. It runs through several chapters, and concludes with telling, II. Kings, chap. ii., ver. 11,

"And it came to pass, as they (Elijah and Elisha) still went on, and talked, that, behold, there appeared *a chariot of fire and horses of fire,* and parted them both asunder, and Elijah *went up by a whirlwind into heaven."* Hum! this the author of Chronicles, miraculous as the story is, makes no mention of, though he mentions Elijah by name; neither does he say anything of the story related in the second chapter of the same book of Kings, of a parcel of children calling Elisha *bald head, bald head;* and that this *man of God,* verse 24, "Turned back, and looked on them, *and cursed them in the name of the Lord;* and there came forth two she-bears out of the wood, and tore forty-and-two children of them."

He also passed over in silence the story told, II. Kings, chap. xiii., that when they were burying a man in the sepulchre where Elisha had been buried, it happened that the dead man, as they were letting him down (ver. 21), touched the bones of Elisha, and he (the dead man) *"revived and stood upon his feet."*

The story does not tell us whether they buried the man, notwithstanding he revived and stood upon his feet, or drew him up again. Upon all these stories the writer of Chronicles is as silent as any writer of the present day who did not choose to be accused of *lying,* or at least of romancing, would be about stories of the same kind.

But, however these two historians may differ from each other with respect to the tales related by either, they are silent alike with respect to those men styled prophets, whose writings fill up the latter part of the Bible.

Isaiah, who lived in the time of Hezekiah, is mentioned in Kings, and again in Chronicles, when these historians are speaking of that reign; but, except in one or two instances at most, and those very slightly, none of the rest are so much as spoken of, or even their existence hinted at; although, according to the Bible chronology, they lived within the time those histories were written; some of them long before.

If those prophets, as they are called, were men of such importance in their day as the compilers of the Bible and priests and commentators have since represented them to be, how can it be accounted for that not one of these histories should say anything about them?

The history in the books of Kings and of Chronicles is brought forward, as I have already said, to the year 588 before Christ; it will therefore be proper to examine which of these prophets lived before that period.

Here follows a table of all the prophets, with the times in which they lived before Christ, according to the chronology affixed to the first chapter of each of the books of the prophets; and also of the number of years they lived before the books of Kings and Chronicles were written.

TABLE OF THE PROPHETS

Names.	Years before Christ.	Years before Kings and Chronicles.	Observations.
Isaiah	760	172	mentioned.
Jeremiah	629	41	{ mentioned only in the last chap. of Chron.
Ezekiel	595	7	not mentioned.
Daniel	607	19	not mentioned.
Hosea	785	97	not mentioned.
Joel	800	212	not mentioned.
Amos	789	199	not mentioned.
Obadiah	789	199	not mentioned.
Jonah	862	274	see the note.[6]
Micah	750	162	not mentioned.
Nahum	713	125	not mentioned.
Habakkuk	620	38	not mentioned.
Zephaniah	630	42	not mentioned.
Haggai { after Zachariah { the year Malachi { 588			

This table is either not very honorable for the Bible historians, or not very honorable for the Bible prophets; and I leave to priests and commentators, who are very learned in little things, to settle the point of *etiquette* between the two, and to assign a reason why the authors of Kings and Chronicles have treated those prophets whom, in the former part of "The Age of Reason," I have considered as poets, with as much

---

[6] In II. Kings, chap. xiv., ver. 25, the name of Jonah is mentioned on account of the restoration of a tract of land by Jeroboam; but nothing further is said of him, nor is any allusion made to the book of Jonah, nor to his expedition to Nineveh, nor to his encounter with the whale.—*Author*.

degrading silence as any historian of the present day would treat Peter Pindar.

I have one observation more to make on the book of Chronicles, after which I shall pass on to review the remaining books of the Bible.

In my observations on the book of Genesis, I have quoted a passage from the 36th chapter, verse 31, which evidently refers to a time *after* that kings began to reign over the children of Israel; and I have shown that as this verse is verbatim the same as in Chronicles, chap. i, ver. 43, where it stands consistently with the order of history, which in Genesis it does not, that the verse in Genesis, and a great part of the 36th chapter, have been taken from Chronicles; and that the book of Genesis, though it is placed first in the Bible, and ascribed to Moses, has been manufactured by some unknown person after the book of Chronicles was written, which was not until at least eight hundred and sixty years after the time of Moses.

The evidence I proceed by to substantiate this is regular and has in it but two stages. First, as I have already stated that the passage in Genesis refers itself for *time* to Chronicles; secondly, that the book of Chronicles, to which this passage refers itself, was not *begun* to be written until at least eight hundred and sixty years after the time of Moses. To prove this, we have only to look into the thirteenth verse of the third chapter of the first book of Chronicles, where the writer, in giving the genealogy of the descendants of David, mentions Zedekiah; and it was in the time of Zedekiah that Nebuchadnezzar conquered Jerusalem, 588 years before Christ, and consequently more than 860 years after Moses.

Those who have superstitiously boasted of the antiquity of the Bible, and particularly of the books ascribed to Moses, have done it without examination, and without any other authority than that of one credulous man telling it to another; for, so far as historical and chronological evidence applies, the very first book in the Bible is not so ancient as the book of Homer by more than three hundred years, and is about the same age with Æsop's "Fables."

I am not contending for the morality of Homer; on the contrary, I think it a book of false glory, tending to inspire immoral and mischievous notions of honor; and with respect to Æsop, though the moral is in general just, the fable is often cruel; and the cruelty of the fable does more injury to the heart, especially in a child, than the moral does good to the judgment.

Having now dismissed Kings and Chronicles, I come to the next in course, the book of Ezra.

As one proof, among others I shall produce, to show the disorder in which this pretended word of God, the Bible, has been put together, and the uncertainty of who the authors were, we have only to look at the three first verses in Ezra, and the last two in Chronicles; for by what kind of cutting and shuffling has it been that the three first verses in Ezra should be the two last verses in Chronicles, or that the two last in Chronicles should be the three first in Ezra? Either the authors did not know their own works, or the compilers did not know the authors.

Two last verses of Chronicles.

Ver. 22. Now in the first year of Cyrus, king of Persia, that the word of the Lord, spoken by the mouth of Jeremiah, might be accomplished, the Lord stirred up the spirit of Cyrus, king of Persia, that he made a proclamation throughout all his kingdom, and put it also in writing, saying,

23. Thus saith Cyrus, king of Persia, All the kingdoms of the earth hath the Lord God of heaven given me: and he hath charged me to build him an house in Jerusalem, which is in Judah. Who is there among you of all his people? the Lord his God be with him, and let him go up.

Three first verses of Ezra.

Ver. 1. Now in the first year of Cyrus, king of Persia, that the word of the Lord, by the mouth of Jeremiah, might be fulfilled, the Lord stirred up the spirit of Cyrus, king of Persia, that he made a proclamation throughout all his kingdom, and put it also in writing, saying,

2. Thus saith Cyrus, king of Persia, the Lord God of heaven hath given me all the kingdoms of the earth; and he hath charged me to build him an house at Jerusalem, which is in Judah.

3. Who is there among you of all his people? his God be with him, and let him go up *to Jerusalem, which is in Judah, and build the house of the Lord God of Israel, (he is the God,) which is in Jerusalem.*

The last verse in Chronicles is broken abruptly, and ends in the middle of the phrase, with the word *up,* without signifying to what place. This abrupt break, and the appearance of the same verses, in different books, show, as I have already said, the disorder and ignorance in which the Bible has been put together, and that the compilers of it had no authority for what they were doing, nor we any authority for believing what they have done.[7]

The only thing that has any appearance of certainty in the book of Ezra, is the time in which it was written, which was immediately after the return of the Jews from the Babylonian captivity, about 536 years before Christ. Ezra (who, according to the Jewish commentators, is the same person as is called Esdras in the Apocrypha) was one of the persons who returned, and who, it is probable, wrote the account of that affair.

Nehemiah, whose book follows next to Ezra, was another of the returned persons; and who, it is also probable, wrote the account of the same affair in the book that bears his name. But these accounts are nothing to us, nor to any other persons, unless it be to the Jews, as a part of the history of their nation; and there is just as much of the word of God in these books as there is in any of the histories of France, or

[7] I observed, as I passed along, several broken and senseless passages in the Bible, without thinking them of consequence enough to be introduced in the body of the work; such as that, I. Samuel, chap. xiii. ver. 1, where it is said, "Saul reigned one year; and when he had reigned two years over Israel, Saul chose him three thousand men," etc. The first part of the verse, that Saul reigned one year, has no sense, since it does not tell us what Saul did, nor say anything of what happened at the end of that one year; and it is, besides, mere absurdity to say he reigned one year, when the very next phrase says he had reigned two; for if he had reigned two, it was impossible not to have reigned one.

Another instance occurs in Joshua, chap. v, where the writer tells us a story of an angel (for such the table of contents at the head of the chapter calls him) appearing unto Joshua; and the story ends abruptly, and without any conclusion. The story is as follows: Verse 13, "And it came to pass, when Joshua was by Jericho, that he lifted up his eyes and looked, and behold there stood a man over against him with his sword drawn in his hand; and Joshua went unto him and said unto him, Art thou for us or for our adversaries?" Verse 14, "And he said, Nay; but as captain of the hosts of the Lord am I now come. And Joshua fell on his face to the earth, and did worship, and said unto him, What saith my Lord unto his servant?" Verse 15, "And the captain of the Lord's host said unto Joshua, Loose thy shoe from off thy foot; for the place whereon thou standeth is holy. And Joshua did so." And what then? nothing, for here the story ends, and the chapter too.

Either the story is broken off in the middle, or it is a story told by some Jewish humorist, in ridicule of Joshua's pretended mission from God; and the compilers of the Bible, not perceiving the design of the story, have told it as a serious matter. As a story of humor and ridicule it has a great deal of point, for it pompously introduces an angel in the figure of a man, with a drawn sword in his hand, before whom Joshua falls on his face to the earth and worships (which is contrary to their second commandment); and then this most important embassy from heaven ends in telling Joshua to pull off his shoe. It might as well have told him to pull up his breeches.

It is certain, however, that the Jews did not credit everything their leaders told them, as appears from the cavalier manner in which they speak of Moses, when he was gone into the mount. "As for this Moses," say they, "we wot not what is become of him." Exod. chap. xxxii, ver. 1.—*Author.*

Rapin's "History of England," or the history of any other country. But even in matters of historical record, neither of those writers are to be depended upon. In the second chapter of Ezra, the writer gives a list of the tribes and families, and of the precise number of souls of each, that returned from Babylon to Jerusalem: and this enrollment of the persons so returned appears to have been one of the principal objects for writing the book; but in this there is an error that destroys the intention of the undertaking.

The writer begins his enrollment in the following manner, chap. ii., ver. 3: "The children of Parosh, two thousand one hundred seventy and four." Ver. 4, "The children of Shephatiah, three hundred seventy and two." And in this manner he proceeds through all the families; and in the 64th verse, he makes a total, and says, "The whole congregation together was *forty and two thousand three hundred and threescore.*"

But whoever will take the trouble of casting up the several particulars will find that the total is but 29,818; so that the error is 12,542.[8] What certainty, then, can there be in the Bible for anything?

Nehemiah, in like manner, gives a list of the returned families, and of the number of each family. He begins, as in Ezra, by saying, chap. vii., ver. 8, "The children of Parosh, two thousand three hundred seventy and two;" and so on through all the families. The list differs in several of the particulars from that of Ezra. In the 66th verse, Nehemiah makes a total, and says, as Ezra had said, "The whole congregation together was forty and two thousand three hundred and threescore." But the particulars of this list make a total of but 31,089, so that the error here is

---

[8] *Particulars of the Families from the second Chapter of Ezra.*

Chap. ii.		Bro't for. 12,243		Bro't for. 15,953		Bro't for. 24,144	
Verse 3	2172	Verse 14	2056	Verse 25	743	Verse 36	973
4	372	15	454	26	621	37	1052
5	775	16	98	27	122	38	1247
6	2812	17	323	28	223	39	1017
7	1254	18	112	29	52	40	74
8	945	19	223	30	156	41	128
9	760	20	95	31	1254	42	139
10	642	21	123	32	320	53	392
11	623	22	56	33	725	60	652
12	1222	23	128	34	345		
13	666	24	42	35	3630		
	12,243		15,953		24,144	Total,	29,818

—*Author*

11,271. These writers may do well enough for Bible-makers, but not for anything where truth and exactness is necessary.

The next book in course is the book of Esther. If Madame Esther thought it any honor to offer herself as a kept mistress to Ahasuerus, or as a rival to Queen Vashti who had refused to come to a drunken king in the midst of a drunken company, to be made a show of (for the account says they had been drinking seven days and were merry), let Esther and Mordecai look to that; it is no business of ours; at least it is none of mine; besides which the story has a great deal the appearance of being fabulous, and is also anonymous. I pass on to the book of Job.

The book of Job differs in character from all the books we have hitherto passed over. Treachery and murder make no part of this book; it is the meditations of a mind strongly impressed with the vicissitudes of human life, and by turns sinking under, and struggling against the pressure.

It is a highly wrought composition, between willing submission and involuntary discontent, and shows man, as he sometimes is, more disposed to be resigned than he is capable of being. Patience has but a small share in the character of the person of whom the book treats; on the contrary, his grief is often impetuous, but he still endeavors to keep a guard upon it, and seems determined in the midst of accumulating ills, to impose upon himself the hard duty of contentment.

I have spoken in a respectful manner of the book of Job in the former part of the "Age of Reason," but without knowing at that time what I have learned since, which is, that from all the evidence that can be collected the book of Job does not belong to the Bible.

I have seen the opinion of two Hebrew commentators, Abenezra and Spinoza, upon this subject. They both say that the book of Job carries no internal evidence of being a Hebrew book; that the genius of the composition and the drama of the piece are not Hebrew; that it has been translated from another language into Hebrew, and that the author of the book was a Gentile; that the character represented under the name of Satan (which is the first and only time this name is mentioned in the Bible) does not correspond to any Hebrew idea, and that the two convocations which the Deity is supposed to have made of those whom the poem calls Sons of God, and the familiarity which this supposed Satan is stated to have with the Deity, are in the same case.

It may also be observed, that the book shows itself to be the production of a mind cultivated in science, which the Jews, so far from being famous for, were very ignorant of. The allusions to objects of natural philosophy are frequent and strong, and are of a different cast to anything in the books known to be Hebrew.

The astronomical names, Pleiades, Orion and Arcturus, are Greek and not Hebrew names, and it does not appear from anything that is to be found in the Bible that the Jews knew anything of astronomy, or that they studied it; they had no translation of those names into their own language, but adopted the names as they found them in the poem.

That the Jews did translate the literary productions of the Gentile nations into the Hebrew language, and mix them with their own, is not a matter of doubt; the thirty-first chapter of Proverbs is an evidence of this; it is there said, v. 1: *"The words of King Lemuel, the prophecy that his mother taught him."* This verse stands as a preface to the Proverbs that follow, and which are not the proverbs of Solomon, but of Lemuel; and this Lemuel was not one of the kings of Israel, nor of Judah, but of some other country, and consequently a Gentile.

The Jews, however, have adopted his proverbs, and as they cannot give any account who the author of the book of Job was, nor how they came by the book, and as it differs in character from the Hebrew writings, and stands totally unconnected with every other book and chapter in the Bible, before it and after it, it has all the circumstantial evidence of being originally a book of the Gentiles.[9]

The Bible-makers and those regulators of time, the chronologists, appear to have been at a loss where to place and how to dispose of the book of Job; for it contains no one historical circumstance, nor allusion to any, that might serve to determine its place in the Bible.

But it would not have answered the purpose of these men to have informed the world of their ignorance, and, therefore, they have affixed

---

[9] The prayer known by the name of *Agur's prayer,* in the 30th chapter of Proverbs, immediately preceding the proverbs of Lemuel, and which is the only sensible, well-conceived and well-expressed prayer in the Bible, has much the appearance of being a prayer taken from the Gentiles. The name of Agur occurs on no other occasion than this; and he is introduced, together with the prayer ascribed to him, in the same manner, and nearly in the same words, that Lemuel and his proverbs are introduced in the chapter that follows. The first verse of the 30th chapter says, "The words of Agur, the son of Jakeh, even the prophecy." Here the word prophecy is used in the same application it has in the following chapter of Lemuel, unconnected with any thing of prediction. The prayer of Agur is in the 8th and 9th verses, "Remove far from me vanity and lies; give me neither riches nor poverty; feed me with food convenient for me; lest I be full and deny thee, and say, Who is the Lord? or lest I be poor and steal, and take the name of my God in vain." This has not any of the marks of being a Jewish prayer, for the Jews never prayed but when they were in trouble. and never for anything but victory, vengeance or riches.—*Author.*

it to the era of 1520 years before Christ, which is during the time the Israelites were in Egypt, and for which they have just as much authority and no more than I should have for saying it was a thousand years before that period. The probability, however, is that it is older than any book in the Bible; and it is the only one that can be read without indignation or disgust.

We know nothing of what the ancient Gentile world (as it is called) was before the time of the Jews, whose practise has been to calumniate and blacken the character of all other nations; and it is from the Jewish accounts that we have learned to call them heathens..

But, as far as we know to the contrary, they were a just and moral people, and not addicted, like the Jews, to cruelty and revenge, but of whose profession of faith we are unacquainted. It appears to have been their custom to personify both virtue and vice by statues and images, as is done nowadays both by statuary and by paintings; but it does not follow from this that they worshipped them, any more than we do.

I pass on to the book of Psalms, of which it is not necessary to make much observation. Some of them are moral, and others are very revengeful; and the greater part relates to certain local circumstances of the Jewish nation at the time they were written, with which we have nothing to do.

It is, however, an error or an imposition to call them the Psalms of David. They are a collection, as song-books are nowadays, from different song-writers, who lived at different times. The 137th Psalm could not have been written till more than 400 years after the time of David, because it was written in commemoration of an event, the captivity of the Jews in Babylon, which did not happen till that distance of time. *"By the rivers of Babylon we sat down; yea, we wept, when we remembered Zion. We hanged our harps upon the willows, in the midst thereof; for there they that carried us away captive required of us a song, saying, Sing us one of the songs of Zion."* As a man would say to an American, or to a Frenchman, or to an Englishman, "Sing us one of your American songs, or of your French songs, or of your English songs."

This remark, with respect to the time this Psalm was written, is of no other use than to show (among others already mentioned) the general imposition the world has been under in respect to the authors of the Bible.

No regard has been paid to time, place and circumstance, and the names of persons have been affixed to the several books, which it was as impossible they should write as that a man should walk in procession at his own funeral.

The Book of Proverbs. These, like the Psalms, are a collection, and that from authors belonging to other nations than those of the Jewish nation, as I have shown in the observations upon the book of Job; besides which some of the proverbs ascribed to Solomon did not appear till two hundred and fifty years after the death of Solomon; for it is said in the 1st verse of the 25th chapter, *"These are also proverbs of Solomon, which the men of Hezekiah, king of Judah, copied out."*

It was two hundred and fifty years from the time of Solomon to the time of Hezekiah. When a man is famous and his name is abroad, he is made the putative father of things he never said or did, and this, most probably, has been the case with Solomon. It appears to have been the fashion of that day to make proverbs, as it is now to make jest-books and father them upon those who never saw them.

The book of Ecclesiastes, or the Preacher, is also ascribed to Solomon, and that with much reason, if not with truth. It is written as the solitary reflections of a worn-out debauchee, such as Solomon was, who, looking back on scenes he can no longer enjoy, cries out, *"All is vanity!"*

A great deal of the metaphor and of the sentiment is obscure, most probably by translation; but enough is left to show they were strongly pointed in the original.[10] From what is transmitted to us of the character of Solomon, he was witty, ostentatious, dissolute and at last melancholy. He lived fast, and died, tired of the world, at the age of fifty-eight years.

Seven hundred wives and three hundred concubines are worse than none, and, however it may carry with it the appearance of heightened enjoyment, it defeats all the felicity of affection by leaving it no point to fix upon. Divided love is never happy. This was the case with Solomon, and if he could not, with all his pretensions to wisdom, discover it beforehand, he merited, unpitied, the mortification he afterward endured.

In this point of view, his preaching is unnecessary, because, to know the consequences, it is only necessary to know the case. Seven hundred wives, and three hundred concubines would have stood in place of the whole book. It was needless, after this, to say that all was vanity and

---

[10] *Those that look out of the window shall be darkened,* is an obscure figure in translation for loss of sight.—*Author.*

vexation of spirit; for it is impossible to derive happiness from the company of those whom we deprive of happiness.

To be happy in old age, it is necessary that we accustom ourselves to objects that can accompany the mind all the way through life, and that we take the rest as good in their day. The mere man of pleasure is miserable in old age, and the mere drudge in business is but little better; whereas, natural philosophy, mathematical and mechanical science are a continual source of tranquil pleasure, and in spite of the gloomy dogmas of priests and of superstition, the study of those things is the study of the true theology; it teaches man to know and to admire the Creator, for the principles of science are in the creation, and are unchangeable and of divine origin.

Those who knew Benjamin Franklin will recollect that his mind was ever young, his temper ever serene; science, that never grows gray, was always his mistress. He was never without an object, for when we cease to have an object, we become like an invalid in a hospital waiting for death.

Solomon's Songs are amorous and foolish enough, but which wrinkled fanaticism has called divine. The compilers of the Bible have placed these songs after the book of Ecclesiastes, and the chronologists have affixed to them the era of 1014 years before Christ, at which time Solomon, according to the same chronology, was nineteen years of age, and was then forming his seraglio of wives and concubines.

The Bible-makers and the chronologists should have managed this matter a little better, and either have said nothing about the time, or chosen a time less inconsistent with the supposed divinity of those songs; for Solomon was then in the honeymoon of one thousand debaucheries.

It should also have occurred to them that, as he wrote, if he did write, the book of Ecclesiastes long after these songs, and in which he exclaims, that all is vanity and vexation of spirit, that he included those songs in that description. This is the more probable, because he says, or somebody for him, Ecclesiastes, chap. ii. ver. 8, *"I gat me men singers and women singers* (most probably to sing those songs), *as musical instruments and that of all sorts;* and behold (ver. 11), all was vanity and vexation of spirit." The compilers, however, have done their work but by halves, for as they have given us the songs, they should have given us the tunes, that we might sing them.

The books called the books of the Prophets fill up all the remaining parts of the Bible; they are sixteen in number, beginning with Isaiah, and ending with Malachi, of which I have given a list in the observations upon Chronicles. Of these sixteen prophets, all of whom, except the three last, lived within the time the books of Kings and Chronicles were written, two only, Isaiah and Jeremiah, are mentioned in the history of those books. I shall begin with those two, reserving what I have to say on the general character of the men called prophets to another part of the work.

Whoever will take the trouble of reading the book ascribed to Isaiah will find it one of the most wild and disorderly compositions ever put together; it has neither beginning, middle nor end; and, except a short historical part and a few sketches of history in two or three of the first chapters, is one continued, incoherent, bombastical rant, full of extravagant metaphor, without application, and destitute of meaning; a school-boy would scarcely have been excusable for writing such stuff; it is (at least in the translation) that kind of composition and false taste that is properly called prose run mad.

The historical part begins at the 36th chapter, and is continued to the end of the 39th chapter. It relates to some matters that are said to have passed during the reign of Hezekiah, king of Judah; at which time Isaiah lived. This fragment of history begins and ends abruptly; it has not the least connection with the chapter that precedes it, nor with that which follows it, nor with any other in the book.

It is probable that Isaiah wrote this fragment himself, because he was an actor in the circumstances it treats of; but, except this part, there are scarcely two chapters that have any connection with each other; one is entitled, at the beginning of the first verse, "The burden of Babylon;" another, "The burden of Moab;" another, "The burden of Damascus;" another, "The burden of Egypt;" another, "The burden of the desert of the sea;" another, "The burden of the valley of vision" [11]—as you would say, "The story of the Knight of the Burning Mountain," "The story of Cinderella or The Glass Slipper"; the story of "The Sleeping Beauty in the Woods," etc., etc.

I have already shown, in the instance of the two last verses of Chronicles, and the three first in Ezra, that the compilers of the Bible mixed and confounded the writings of different authors with each other, which alone, were there no other cause, is sufficient to destroy the authenticity of any compilation, because it is more than presumptive evidence that

---

[11] See beginning of chapters xiii, xv, xvii, xix, xxi and xxii.—*Author.*

the compilers were ignorant who the authors were. A very glaring instance of this occurs in the book ascribed to Isaiah; the latter part of the 44th chapter and the beginning of the 45th, so far from having been written by Isaiah, could only have been written by some person who lived at least a hundred and fifty years after Isaiah was dead.

These chapters are a compliment to Cyrus, who permitted the Jews to return to Jerusalem from the Babylonian captivity, to rebuild Jerusalem and the temple, as is stated in Ezra. The last verse of the 44th chapter and the beginning of the 45th, are in the following words: *"That saith of Cyrus; He is my shepherd, and shall perform all my pleasure; even saying to Jerusalem, Thou shalt be built, and to the temple, Thy foundation shall be laid. Thus saith the Lord to His anointed, to Cyrus, whose right hand I have holden, to subdue nations before him; and I will loose the loins of kings, to open before him the two-leaved gates, and the gates shall not be shut; I will go before thee,"* etc.

What audacity of church and priestly ignorance it is to impose this book upon the world as the writing of Isaiah, when Isaiah, according to their own chronology, died soon after the death of Hezekiah, which was 693 years before Christ, and the decree of Cyrus, in favor of the Jews returning to Jerusalem, was, according to the same chronology, 536 years before Christ, which is a distance of time between the two of 162 years.

I do not suppose that the compilers of the Bible made these books, but rather that they picked up some loose anonymous essays, and put them together under the names of such authors as best suited their purpose. They have encouraged the imposition, which is next to inventing it, for it was impossible but they must have observed it.

When we see the studied craft of the Scripture-makers, in making every part of this romantic book of school-boy's eloquence bend to the monstrous idea of a Son of God begotten by a ghost on the body of a virgin, there is no imposition we are not justified in suspecting them of. Every phrase and circumstance is marked with the barbarous hand of superstitious torture, and forced into meanings it was impossible they could have. The head of every chapter and the top of every page are blazoned with the names of Christ and the Church, that the unwary reader might suck in the error before he began to read.

"Behold a virgin shall conceive, and bear a son," Isaiah, chap. vii. ver. 14, has been interpreted to mean the person called Jesus Christ, and his mother Mary, and has been echoed through Christendom for more

than a thousand years; and such has been the rage of this opinion that scarcely a spot in it but has been stained with blood, and marked with desolation in consequence of it. Though it is not my intention to enter into controversy on subjects of this kind, but to confine myself to show that the Bible is spurious, and thus, by taking away the foundation, to overthrow at once the whole structure of superstition raised thereon, I will, however, stop a moment to expose the fallacious application of this passage.

Whether Isaiah was playing a trick with Ahaz, king of Judah, to whom this passage is spoken, is no business of mine; I mean only to show the misapplication of the passage, and that it has no more reference to Christ and his mother than it has to me and my mother.

The story is simply this: The king of Syria and the king of Israel (I have already mentioned that the Jews were split into two nations, one of which was called Judah, the capital of which was Jerusalem, and the other Israel), made war jointly against Ahaz, king of Judah, and marched their armies toward Jerusalem. Ahaz and his people became alarmed, and the account says, ver. 2, "*And his heart was moved, and the heart of his people, as the trees of the wood are moved with the wind.*"

In this situation of things, Isaiah addresses himself to Ahaz, and assures him in the *name of the Lord* (the cant phrase of all the prophets) that these two kings should not succeed against him; and to satisfy Ahaz that this should be the case, tells him to ask a sign. This, the account says, Ahaz declined doing, giving as a reason that he would not tempt the Lord; upon which Isaiah, who is the speaker, says, ver. 14, "Therefore the Lord himself shall give you a sign, *Behold, a virgin shall conceive, and bear a son*"; and the 16th verse says, "*For before this child shall know to refuse the evil, and choose the good, the land that thou abhorrest* [or dreadest, meaning Syria and the kingdom of Israel], *shall be forsaken of both her kings.*" Here then was the sign, and the time limited for the completion of the assurance or promise, namely, before this child should know to refuse the evil and choose the good.

Isaiah having committed himself thus far, it became necessary to him, in order to avoid the imputation of being a false prophet and the consequence thereof, to take measures to make this sign appear. It certainly was not a difficult thing, in any time of the world, to find a girl with child, or to make her so, and perhaps Isaiah knew of one beforehand; for I do not suppose that the prophets of that day were any more to be trusted than the priests of this. Be that, however, as it may, he says in the next chapter, ver. 2, "And I took unto me faithful witnesses to record, Uriah the priest, and Zechariah the son of Jeberechiah, and *I went unto the prophetess, and she conceived and bare a son.*"

Here, then, is the whole story, foolish as it is, of this child and this virgin; and it is upon the barefaced perversion of this story, that the book of Matthew, and the impudence and sordid interests of priests in later times, have founded a theory which they call the Gospel; and have applied this story to signify the person they call Jesus Christ, begotten, they say, by a ghost, whom they call holy, on the body of a woman, engaged in marriage, and afterward married, whom they call a virgin, 700 years after this foolish story was told; a theory which, speaking for myself, I hesitate not to disbelieve, and to say, is as fabulous and as false as God is true.[12]

But to show the imposition and falsehood of Isaiah, we have only to attend to the sequel of this story, which, though it is passed over in silence in the book of Isaiah, is related in the 28th chapter of the second Chronicles, and which is, that instead of these two kings failing in their attempt against Ahaz, king of Judah, as Isaiah had pretended to foretell in the name of the Lord, they succeeded; Ahaz was defeated and destroyed, a hundred and twenty thousand of his people were slaughtered, Jerusalem was plundered, and two hundred thousand women, and sons and daughters, carried into captivity. Thus much for this lying prophet and impostor, Isaiah, and the book of falsehoods that bears his name.

I pass on to the book of Jeremiah. This prophet, as he is called, lived in the time that Nebuchadnezzar besieged Jerusalem, in the reign of Zedekiah, the last king of Judah; and the suspicion was strong against him that he was a traitor in the interests of Nebuchadnezzar. Everything relating to Jeremiah shows him to have been a man of an equivocal character; in his metaphor of the potter and the clay, chap. xviii., he guards his prognostications in such a crafty manner as always to leave himself a door to escape by, in case the event should be contrary to what he had predicted.

In the 7th and 8th verses of that chapter he makes the Almighty to say, "At what instant I shall speak concerning a nation, and concerning

---

[12] In the 14th verse of the 7th chapter, it is said that the child should be called Immanuel; but this name was not given to either of the children otherwise than as a character which the word signifies. That of the prophetess was called Maher-shalal-hash-baz, and that of Mary was called Jesus.—*Author.*

a kingdom, to pluck up, and to pull down, and destroy it. If that nation, against whom I have prcnounced, turn from their evil, I will repent of the evil that I thought to do unto them." Here was a proviso against one side of the case; now for the other side.

Verses 9 and 10, "And at what instant I shall speak concerning a nation, and concerning a kingdom, to build and to plant it, if it do evil in my sight, that it obey not my voice; then I shall repent of the good wherewith I said I would benefit them." Here is a proviso against the other side; and, according to this plan of prophesying, a prophet could never be wrong, however mistaken the Almighty might be. This sort of absurd subterfuge, and this manner of speaking of the Almighty, as one would speak of a man, is consistent with nothing but the stupidity of the Bible.

As to the authenticity of the book, it is only necessary to read it in order to decide positively that, though some passages recorded therein may have been spoken by Jeremiah, he is not the author of the book. The historical parts, if they can be called by that name, are in the most confused condition; the same events are several times repeated, and that in a manner different, and sometimes in contradiction to each other; and this disorder runs even to the last chapter, where the history upon which the greater part of the book has been employed begins anew, and ends abruptly.

The book has all the appearance of being a medley of unconnected anecdotes respecting persons and things of that time, collected together in the same rude manner as if the various and contradictory accounts that are to be found in a bundle of newspapers respecting persons and things of the present day were put together without date, order or explanation. I will give two or three examples of this kind.

It appears, from the account of the 37th chapter, that the army of Nebuchadnezzar, which is called the army of the Chaldeans, had besieged Jerusalem some time, and on their hearing that the army of Pharaoh, of Egypt, was marching against them they raised the siege and retreated for a time.

It may here be proper to mention, in order to understand this confused history, that Nebuchadnezzar had besieged and taken Jerusalem during the reign of Jehoiakim, the predecessor of Zedekiah; and that it was Nebuchadnezzar who had made Zedekiah king, or rather viceroy; and that this second siege, of which the book of Jeremiah treats, was in consequence of the revolt of Zedekiah against Nebuchadnezzar. This will in some measure account for the suspicion that affixes to Jeremiah of being a traitor in the interest of Nebuchadnezzar, whom Jeremiah calls, in the 43d chapter, ver. 10, the servant of God. The 11th verse of this chapter (the 37th), says, "And it came to pass, that, when the army of the Chaldeans was broken up from Jerusalem, for fear of Pharaoh's army, that Jeremiah went forth out of Jerusalem, to go (as this account states) into the land of Benjamin, to separate himself thence in the midst of the people, and when he was in the gate of Benjamin, a captain of the ward was there, whose name was Irijah, the son of Shelemiah, the son of Hananiah, and he took Jeremiah the prophet, saying, Thou fallest away to the Chaldeans. Then said Jeremiah, It is false; I fall not away to the Chaldeans." Jeremiah being thus stopped and accused, was, after being examined, committed to prison on suspicion of being a traitor, where he remained, as is stated in the last verse of this chapter.

But the next chapter gives an account of the imprisonment of Jeremiah which has no connection with this account, but ascribes his imprisonment to another circumstance, and for which we must go back to the 21st chapter. It is there stated, ver. 1, that Zedekiah sent Pashur, the son of Malchiah, and Zephaniah, the son of Maaseiah the priest, to Jeremiah to inquire of him concerning Nebuchadnezzar, whose army was then before Jerusalem; and Jeremiah said unto them, ver. 8 and 9, "Thus saith the Lord, Behold I set before you the way of life, and the way of death; he that abideth in this city shall die by the sword, and by the famine, and by the pestilence; but he that goeth out and falleth to the Chaldeans that besiege you, he shall live, and his life shall be unto him for a prey."

This interview and conference breaks off abruptly at the end of the 10th verse of the 21st chapter; and such is the disorder of this book that we have to pass over sixteen chapters, upon various subjects, in order to come at the continuation and event of this conference, and this brings us to the first verse of the 38th chapter, as I have just mentioned.

The 38th chapter opens with saying, "Then Shephatiah, the son of Mattan; Gedaliah, the son of Pashur; and Jucal, the son of Shelemiah; and Pashur, the son of Malchiah (here are more persons mentioned than in the 21st chapter), heard the words that Jeremiah had spoken unto all the people, saying, *Thus saith the Lord, He that remaineth in this city, shall die by the sword, by the famine, and by the pestilence; but he that goeth forth to the Chaldeans shall live, for he shall have his*

life for a prey, and shall live" (which are the words of the conference);
therefore (they say to Zedekiah), "We beseech thee, let us put this man
to death, *for thus he weakeneth the hands of the men of war that remain
in this city, and the hands of all the people in speaking such words unto
them; for this man seeketh not the welfare of the people, but the hurt."*
And at the 6th verse it is said, "Then took they Jeremiah, and cast him·
into the dungeon of Malchiah."

These two accounts are different and contradictory. The one ascribes
his imprisonment to his attempt to escape out of the city; the other to
his preaching and prophesying in the city; the one to his being seized by
the guard at the gate; the other to his being accused before Zedekiah,
by the conferees.[13]

In the next chapter (the 39th) we have another instance of the disordered state of this book; for notwithstanding the siege of the city by
Nebuchadnezzar has been the subject of several of the preceding chapters, particularly the 37th and 38th, the 39th chapter begins as if not a
word had been said upon the subject; and as if the reader was to be
informed of every particular respecting it, for it begins with saying,

[13] I observed two chapters, 16th and 17th, in the first book of Samuel, that contradict
each other with respect to David, and the manner he became acquainted with Saul; as
the 37th and 38th chapters of the book of Jeremiah contradict each other with respect to
the cause of Jeremiah's imprisonment.

In the 16th chapter of Samuel, it is said, that an evil spirit of God troubled Saul, and
that his servants advised him (as a remedy) "to seek out a man who was a cunning player
upon the harp." And Saul said [ver. 17], "Provide me now a man that can play well, and
bring *him* to me. Then answered one of the servants, and said, Behold I have seen a son
of Jesse the Bethlehemite, *that is* cunning in playing, and a mighty valiant man, and
a man of war, and prudent in matters, and a comely person, and the Lᴏʀᴅ is with him.
Wherefore Saul sent messengers unto Jesse, and said, "Send me David thy son." "And
[ver. 21] David came to Saul, and stood before him, and he loved him greatly, and he
became his armor-bearer. And when the evil spirit from God was upon Saul [ver. 23]
David took an harp, and played with his hand: so Saul was refreshed, and was well."

But the next chapter [17] gives an account, all different to this, of the manner that Saul
and David became acquainted. Here it is ascribed to David's encounter with Golia[t]h,
when David was sent by his father to carry provision to his brethren in the camp. In the 55th
verse of this chapter it is said, "And when Saul saw David go forth against the Philistine
[Golia[t]h], he said unto Abner, the captain of the host, Abner, whose son is this youth?
And Abner said, *As* thy soul liveth, O king, I cannot tell. And the king said, Enquire thou
whose son the stripling *is*. And as David returned from the slaughter of the Philistine,
Abner took him, and brought him before Saul with the head of the Philistine in his hand.
And Saul said to him, Whose son *art* thou, *thou* young man? And David answered, *I am*
the son of thy servant Jesse the Bethlehemite." These two accounts belie each other, because each of them supposes Saul and David not to have known each other before. This
book, the Bible, is too ridiculous even for criticism.—*Author.*

ver. 1, "In the ninth year of Zedekiah, king of Judah, in the tenth month, came Nebuchadnezzar, king of Babylon, and all his army, against Jerusalem, and they besieged it," etc.

But the instance in the last chapter (the 52d) is still more glaring, for though the story has been told over and over again, this chapter still supposes the reader not to know anything of it, for it begins by saying, ver. 1, *"Zedekiah was one and twenty years old when he began to reign, and he reigned eleven years in Jerusalem, and his mother's name was Hamutal, the daughter of Jeremiah of Libnah. (Ver. 4.) And it came to pass in the ninth year of his reign, in the tenth month, in the tenth day of the month, that Nebuchadnezzar, king of Babylon, came, he and all his army, against Jerusalem, and pitched against it, and built forts against it,"* etc.

It is not possible that any one man, and more particularly Jeremiah, could have been the writer of this book. The errors are such as could not have been committed by any person sitting down to compose a work. Were I, or any other man, to write in such a disordered manner, nobody would read what was written; and everybody would suppose that the writer was in a state of insanity. The only way, therefore, to account for this disorder is that the book is a medley of detached, unauthenticated anecdotes put together by some stupid book-maker under the name of Jeremiah, because many of them refer to him and to the circumstances of the times he lived in.

Of the duplicity, and of the false prediction of Jeremiah, I shall mention two instances, and then proceed to review the remainder of the Bible.

It appears from the 38th chapter, that when Jeremiah was in prison, Zedekiah sent for him, and at this interview, which was private, Jeremiah pressed it strongly on Zedekiah to surrender himself to the enemy. *"If,"* says he (ver. 17), *"thou wilt assuredly go forth unto the king of Babylon's princes, then thy soul shall live,"* etc. Zedekiah was apprehensive that what passed at this conference should be known, and he said to Jeremiah (ver. 25), "If the princes [meaning those of Judah] hear that I have talked with thee, and they come unto thee, and say unto thee, Declare unto us now what thou hast said unto the king; hide it not from us, and we will not put thee to death; and also what the king said unto thee; then thou shalt say unto them, I presented my supplication before the king, that he would not cause me to return to Jonathan's house to die there. Then came all the princes unto Jeremiah, and asked him: and *he told them according to all the words the king had commanded."*

Thus, this man of God, as he is called, could tell a lie or very strongly prevaricate, when he supposed it would answer his purpose; for certainly he did not go to Zedekiah to make his supplication, neither did he make it; he went because he was sent for, and he employed that opportunity to advise Zedekiah to surrender himself to Nebuchadnezzar.

In the 34th chapter is a prophecy of Jeremiah to Zedekiah, in these words (ver. 2), "Thus saith the Lord, Behold I will give this city into the hands of the king of Babylon, and he shall burn it with fire; and thou shalt not escape out of his hand, but shalt surely be taken, and delivered into his hand; and thine eyes shall behold the eyes of the king of Babylon, and he shall speak with thee mouth to mouth, and thou shalt go to Babylon. *Yet hear the word of the Lord, O Zedekiah, king of Judah, Thus saith the Lord, of thee, Thou shalt not die by the sword, but thou shalt die in peace; and with the burnings of thy fathers, the former kings which were before thee, so shall they burn odors for thee, and they will lament thee, saying, Ah, lord; for I have pronounced the word, saith the Lord."*

Now, instead of Zedekiah beholding the eyes of the king of Babylon, and speaking with him mouth to mouth, and dying in peace, and with the burning of odors, as at the funeral of his fathers (as Jeremiah had declared the Lord himself had pronounced), the reverse, according to the 52nd chapter, was the case; it is there said (ver. 10), "And the king of Babylon slew the son of Zedekiah before his eyes; then he put out the eyes of Zedekiah, and the king of Babylon bound him in chains, and carried him to Babylon, and put him in prison till the day of his death." What, then, can we say of these prophets, but that they were impostors and liars?

As for Jeremiah, he experienced none of those evils. He was taken into favor by Nebuchadnezzar, who gave him in charge to the captain of the guard (chap. xxxix. ver. 12), "Take him (said he) and look well to him, and do him no harm; but do unto him even as he shall say unto thee." Jeremiah joined himself afterward to Nebuchadnezzar, and went about prophesying for him against the Egyptians, who had marched to the relief of Jerusalem while it was besieged. Thus much for another of the lying prophets, and the book that bears his name.

I have been the more particular in treating of the books ascribed to

Isaiah and Jeremiah, because those two are spoken of in the books of Kings and Chronicles, which the others are not. The remainder of the books ascribed to the men called prophets I shall not trouble myself much about, but take them collectively into the observations I shall offer on the character of the men styled prophets.

In the former part of "The Age of Reason," I have said that the word prophet was the Bible word for poet, and that the flights and metaphors of Jewish poets have been foolishly erected into what are now called prophecies. I am sufficiently justified in this opinion, not only because the books called the prophecies are written in poetical language, but because there is no word in the Bible, except it be the word prophet, that describes what we mean by a poet.

I have also said that the word signifies a performer upon musical instruments, of which I have given some instances, such as that of a company of prophets prophesying with psalteries, with tabrets, with pipes, with harps, etc., and that Saul prophesied with them, I. Sam., chap. x., ver. 5.

It appears from this passage, and from other parts in the book of Samuel, that the word prophet was confined to signify poetry and music; for the person who was supposed to have a visionary insight into concealed things, was not a prophet but a *seer* [14] (I. Sam., chap. ix., ver. 9); and it was not till after the word *seer* went out of use (which most probably was when Saul banished those he called wizards) that the profession of the seer, or the art of seeing, became incorporated into the word prophet.

According to the *modern* meaning of the words prophet and prophesying, it signifies foretelling events to a great distance of time, and it became necessary to the inventors of the Gospel to give it this latitude of meaning, in order to apply or to stretch what they call the prophecies of the Old Testament to the times of the New; but according to the Old Testament, the prophesying of the seer, and afterward of the prophet, so far as the meaning of the word seer, incorporated into that of prophet, had reference only to things of the time then passing, or very closely connected with it, such as the event of a battle they were going to engage in, or of a journey, or of any enterprise they were going

---

[14] I know not what is the Hebrew word that corresponds to the word seer in English; but I observe it is translated into French by *la voyant*, from the verb *voir*, to *see;* and which means the person who *sees*, or the seer.—*Author.*

The Hebrew word for *Seer*, in I Samuel ix., is *chozéh*, the gazer.—*Editor.*

to undertake, or of any circumstance then pending, or of any difficulty they were then in; all of which had immediate reference to themselves (as in the case already mentioned of Ahaz and Isaiah with respect to the expression, *"Behold a virgin shall conceive and bear a son"*), and not to any distant future time.

It was that kind of prophesying that corresponds to what we call fortune-telling, such as casting nativities, predicting riches, fortunate or unfortunate marriages, conjuring for lost goods, etc.; and it is the fraud of the Christian Church, not that of the Jews, and the ignorance and the superstition of modern, not that of ancient, times, that elevated those poetical, musical, conjuring, dreaming, strolling gentry into the rank they have since had.

But, besides this general character of all the prophets, they had also a particular character. They were in parties, and they prophesied for or against, according to the party they were with, as the poetical and political writers of the present day write in defense of the party they associate with against the other.

After the Jews were divided into two nations, that of Judah and that of Israel, each party had its prophets, who abused and accused each other of being false prophets, lying prophets, impostors, etc.

The prophets of the party of Judah prophesied against the prophets of the party of Israel; and those of the party of Israel against those of Judah. This party prophesying showed itself immediately on the separation under the first two rival kings, Rehoboam and Jeroboam.

The prophet that cursed or prophesied against the altar that Jeroboam had built in Bethel was of the party of Judah, where Rehoboam was king; and he was waylaid on his return home, by a prophet of the party of Israel, who said unto him (I. Kings, chap. x.), *"Art thou the man of God that came from Judah? and he said, I am."* Then the prophet of the party of Israel said to him, *"I am a prophet also, as thou art* [signifying of Judah], *and an angel spake unto me by the word of the Lord, saying, Bring him back with thee into thine house, that he may eat bread and drink water: but* (says the 18th verse) *he lied unto him."*

This event, however, according to the story, is that the prophet of Judah never got back to Judah, for he was found dead on the road, by the contrivance of the prophet of Israel, who, no doubt, was called a true prophet by his own party, and the prophet of Judah a lying prophet.

In the third chapter of the second of Kings, a story is related of prophesying or conjuring that shows, in several particulars, the character of a prophet. Jehoshaphat, king of Judah, and Jehoram, king of Israel, had for a while ceased their party animosity, and entered into an alliance; and these two, together with the king of Edom, engaged in a war against the king of Moab.

After uniting and marching their armies, the story says, they were in great distress for water; upon which Jehoshaphat said, *"Is there not here a prophet of the Lord, that we may inquire of the Lord by him? and one of the servants of the king of Israel said, Here is Elisha."* [Elisha was one of the party of Judah.] *"And Jehoshaphat, the king of Judah, said, The word of the Lord is with him."*

The story then says, that these three kings went down to Elisha; and when Elisha (who, as I have said, was a Judahmite prophet) saw the king of Israel, he said unto him, *"What have I to do with·thee? get thee to the prophets of thy father, and to the prophets of thy mother. And the king of Israel said unto him, Nay, for the Lord hath called these three kings together, to deliver them into the hand of Moab."* [Meaning because of the distress they were in for water.] Upon which Elisha said, *"As the Lord of hosts liveth, before whom I stand, surely,.were it not that I regard the presence of Jehoshaphat, the king of Judah, I would not look towards thee, nor see thee."* Here is all the venom and vulgarity of a party prophet. We have now to see the performance, or manner of prophesying.

Verse 15. *"Bring me* (said Elisha), *a minstrel: And it came to pass, when the minstrel played, that the hand of the Lord came upon him."* Here is the farce of the conjurer. Now for the prophecy: *"And Elisha said,* [singing most probably to the tune he was playing,] *Thus saith the Lord, make this valley full of ditches";* which was just telling them what every countryman could have told them, without either fiddle or farce, that the way to get water was to dig for it.

But as every conjurer is not famous alike for the same thing, so neither were those prophets; for though all of them, at least those I have spoken of, were famous for lying, some of them excelled in cursing. Elisha, whom I have just mentioned, was a chief in this branch of prophesying; it was he that cursed the forty-two children in the name of the Lord, whom the two she-bears came and devoured. We are to suppose that those children were of the party of Israel; but as those who will curse will lie, there is just as much credit to be given to this story of Elisha's two she-bears as there is to that of the Dragon of Wantley, of whom it is said:

"Poor children three devoured he,
That could not with him grapple;
And at one sup he ate them up,
As a man would eat an apple."

There was another description of men called prophets that amused themselves with dreams and visions; but whether by night or by day we know not. These, if they were not quite harmless, were but little mischievous. Of this class are:

Ezekiel and Daniel; and the first question upon those books, as upon all the others, is, are they genuine? that is, were they written by Ezekiel and Daniel?

Of this there is no proof, but so far as my own opinion goes, I am more inclined to believe they were than that they were not. My reasons for this opinion are as follows: First, Because those books do not contain internal evidence to prove they were not written by Ezekiel and Daniel, as the books ascribed to Moses, Joshua, Samuel, etc. prove they were not written by Moses, Joshua, Samuel, etc.

Secondly, Because they were not written till after the Babylonian captivity began, and there is good reason to believe that not any book in the Bible was written before that period; at least it is proveable from the books themselves, as I have already shown, that they were not written till after the commencement of the Jewish monarchy.

Thirdly, Because the manner in which the books ascribed to Ezekiel and Daniel are written agrees with the condition these men were in at the time of writing them.

Had the numerous commentators and priests, who have foolishly employed or wasted their time in pretending to expound and unriddle those books, been carried into captivity, as Ezekiel and Daniel were, it would have greatly improved their intellects in comprehending the reason for this mode of writing, and have saved them the trouble of racking their invention, as they have done, to no purpose; for they would have found that themselves would be obliged to write whatever they had to write respecting their own affairs or those of their friends or of their country, in a concealed manner, as those men have done.

These two books differ from all the rest, for it is only these that are filled with accounts of dreams and visions; and this difference arose from the situation the writers were in as prisoners of war, or prisoners of state, in a foreign country, which obliged them to convey even the most trifling information to each other, and all their political projects or opinions, in obscure and metaphorical terms. They pretended to have dreamed dreams and seen visions, because it was unsafe for them to speak facts or plain language.

We ought, however, to suppose that the persons to whom they wrote understood what they meant, and that it was not intended anybody else should. But these busy commentators and priests have been puzzling their wits to find out what it was not intended they should know, and with which they have nothing to do.

Ezekiel and Daniel were carried prisoners to Babylon under the first captivity, in the time of Jehoiakim, nine years before the second captivity in the time of Zedekiah.

The Jews were still numerous, and had considerable force at Jerusalem; and as it is natural to suppose that men in the situation of Ezekiel and Daniel would be meditating the recovery of their country and their own deliverance, it is reasonable to suppose that the accounts of dreams and visions with which those books are filled are no other than a disguised mode of correspondence, to facilitate those objects —it served them as a cipher or secret alphabet. If they are not this, they are tales, reveries and nonsense; or, at least, a fanciful way of wearing off the wearisomeness of captivity; but the presumption is they are the former.

Ezekiel begins his book by speaking of a vision of *cherubims* and of a *wheel within a wheel,* which he says he saw by the river Chebar, in the land of his captivity. Is it not reasonable to suppose, that by the cherubims he meant the temple at Jerusalem, where they had figures of cherubims? And by a wheel within a wheel (which, as a figure, has always been understood to signify political contrivance) the project or means of recovering Jerusalem?

In the latter part of this book he supposes himself transported to Jerusalem and into the temple; and he refers back to the vision on the river Chebar, and says (chap. xliii, ver. 3), that this last vision was like the vision on the river Chebar; which indicates that those pretended dreams and visions had for their object the recovery of Jerusalem, and nothing further.

As to the romantic interpretations and applications, wild as the dreams and visions they undertake to explain, which commentators and priests have made of those books, that of converting them into things which they call prophecies, and making them bend to times and circumstances as far remote even as the present day, it shows the fraud or the extreme folly to which credulity or priestcraft can go.

Scarcely anything can be more absurd than to suppose that men situated as Ezekiel and Daniel were, whose country was overrun and in the possession of the enemy, all their friends and relations in captivity abroad, or in slavery at home, or massacred, or in continual danger of it; scarcely anything, I say, can be more absurd than to suppose that such men should find nothing to do but that of employing their time and their thoughts about what was to happen to other nations a thousand or two thousand years after they were dead; at the same time, nothing is more natural than that they should meditate the recovery of Jerusalem and their own deliverance; and that this was the sole object of all the obscure and apparently frantic writings contained in those books.

In this sense, the mode of writing used in those two books, being forced by necessity, and not adopted by choice, is not irrational; but, if we are to view the books as prophecies, they are false. In the 29th chapter of Ezekiel, speaking of Egypt, it is said (ver. 11), *"No foot of man shall pass through it, nor foot of beast shall pass through it; neither shall it be inhabited for forty years."* This is what never came to pass, and consequently it is false, as all the books I have already reviewed are: I here close this part of the subject.

In the former part of "The Age of Reason" I have spoken of Jonah, and of the story of him and the whale. A fit story for ridicule, if it was written to be believed; or of laughter, if it was intended to try what credulity could swallow; for if it could swallow Jonah and the whale, it could swallow anything.

But, as is already shown in the observations on the book of Job and of Proverbs, it is not always certain which of the books in the Bible are originally Hebrew, or only translations from the books of the Gentiles into Hebrew; and as the book of Jonah, so far from treating of the affairs of the Jews, says nothing upon that subject, but treats altogether of the Gentiles, it is more probable that it is a book of the Gentiles than of the Jews, and that it has been written as a fable, to expose the nonsense and satirize the vicious and malignant character of a Bible prophet, or a predicting priest.

Jonah is represented, first, as a disobedient prophet, running away from his mission, and taking shelter aboard a vessel of the Gentiles, bound from Joppa to Tarshish; as if he ignorantly supposed, by such a paltry contrivance, he could hide himself where God could not find him. The vessel is overtaken by a storm at sea, and the mariners, all of whom are Gentiles, believing it to be a judgment, on account of some one on board who had committed a crime, agreed to cast lots to discover the offender, and the lot fell upon Jonah. But, before this, they had cast all their wares and merchandise overboard to lighten the vessel, while Jonah, like a stupid fellow, was fast asleep in the hold.

After the lot had designated Jonah to be the offender, they questioned him to know who and what he was? and he told them *he was a Hebrew;* and the story implies that he confessed himself to be guilty.

But these Gentiles, instead of sacrificing him at once, without pity or mercy, as a company of Bible prophets or priests would have done by a Gentile in the same case, and as it is related Samuel had done by Agag, and Moses by the women and children, they endeavored to save him, though at the risk of their own lives, for the account says, *"Nevertheless* [that is, though Jonah was a Jew and a foreigner, and the cause of all their misfortunes and the loss of their cargo], *the men rowed hard to bring it* [*the boat*] *to land, but they could not, for the sea wrought and was tempestuous against them."*

Still they were unwilling to put the fate of the lot into execution, and they cried (says the account) unto the Lord, saying (ver. 14), *"We beseech Thee, O Lord, we beseech Thee, let us not perish for this man's life, and lay not upon us innocent blood; for Thou, O Lord, hast done as it pleased Thee."* Meaning, thereby, that they did not presume to judge Jonah guilty, since that he might be innocent; but that they considered the lot that had fallen upon him as a decree of God, or as it *pleased God.*

The address of this prayer shows that the Gentiles worshipped one *Supreme Being,* and that they were not idolaters, as the Jews represented them to be. But the storm still continuing and the danger increasing, they put the fate of the lot into execution, and cast Jonah into the sea, where, according to the story, a great fish swallowed him up whole and alive.

We have now to consider Jonah securely housed from the storm in the fish's belly. Here we are told that he prayed; but the prayer is a made-up prayer, taken from various parts of the Psalms, without any connection or consistency, and adapted to the distress, but not at all to the condition Jonah was in. It is such a prayer as a Gentile, who might know something of the Psalms, could copy out for him.

This circumstance alone, were there no other, is sufficient to indicate that the whole is a made-up story. The prayer, however, is supposed to have answered the purpose, and the story goes on (taking up at the same time the cant language of a Bible prophet), saying: (chap. ii, ver. 10), *"And the Lord spake unto the fish, and it vomited out Jonah upon the dry land."*

Jonah then received a second mission to Nineveh, with which he sets out; and we have now to consider him as a preacher. The distress he is represented to have suffered, the remembrance of his own disobedience as the cause of it, and the miraculous escape he is supposed to have had, were sufficient, one would conceive, to have impressed him with sympathy and benevolence in the execution of his mission; but, instead of this, he enters the city with denunciation and malediction in his mouth, crying (chap. iii, ver. 4): *"Yet forty days, and Nineveh shall be overthrown."*

We have now to consider this supposed missionary in the last act of his mission; and here it is that the malevolent spirit of a Bible-prophet, or of a predicting priest, appears in all that blackness of character that men ascribe to the being they call the devil.

Having published his predictions, he withdrew, says the story, to the East side of the city. But for what? Not to contemplate, in retirement, the mercy of his Creator to himself or to others, but to wait, with malignant impatience, the destruction of Nineveh.

It came to pass, however, as the story relates, that the Ninevites reformed, and that God, according to the Bible phrase, repented Him of the evil He had said He would do unto them, and did it not. This, saith the first verse of the last chapter, *"displeased Jonah exceedingly, and he was very angry."* His obdurate heart would rather that all Nineveh should be destroyed, and every soul, young and old, perish in its ruins, than that his prediction should not be fulfilled.

To expose the character of a prophet still more, a gourd is made to grow up in the night, that promised him an agreeable shelter from the heat of the sun, in the place to which he had retired, and the next morning it dies.

Here the rage of the prophet becomes excessive, and he is ready to destroy himself. *"It is better, said he, for me to die than to live."* This brings on a supposed expostulation between the Almighty and the prophet, in which the former says, *"Doest thou well to be angry for the gourd? And Jonah said, I do well to be angry even unto death; Then, said the Lord, Thou hast had pity on the gourd, for which thou hast*

not labored, neither madest it grow; which came up in a night, and
perished in a night; and should not I spare Nineveh that great city,
in which are more than threescore thousand persons that cannot dis-
cern between their right hand and their left hand?"

Here is both the winding up of the satire and the moral of the fable.
As a satire, it strikes against the character of all the Bible prophets,
and against all the indiscriminate judgments upon men, women and
children, with which this lying book, the Bible, is crowded; such as
Noah's flood, the destruction of the cities of Sodom and Gomorrah, the
extirpation of the Canaanites, even to the sucking infants and women
with child, because the same reflection, *that there are more than three-*
score thousand persons that cannot discern between their right hand and
their left hand, meaning young children, apply to all the cases. It
satirizes also the supposed partiality of the Creator for one nation more
than for another.

As a moral, it preaches against the malevolent spirit of prediction;
for as certainly as a man predicts ill, he becomes inclined to wish it.
The pride of having his judgment right hardens his heart, till at last
he beholds with satisfaction, or sees with disappointment, the accomplishment or the failure of his predictions.

The book ends with the same kind of strong and well-directed point
against prophets, prophecies and indiscriminate judgment, as the chapter
that Benjamin Franklin made for the Bible, about Abraham and the
stranger, ends against the intolerant spirit of religious persecution. Thus
much for the book of Jonah.

Of the poetical parts of the Bible, that are called prophecies, I have
spoken in the former part of "The Age of Reason," and already in this,
where I have said that the word *prophet* is the Bible word for *poet,* and
that the flights and metaphors of those poets, many of which have
become obscure by the lapse of time and the change of circumstances,
have been ridiculously erected into things called prophecies, and applied
to purposes the writers never thought of.

When a priest quotes any of those passages, he unriddles it agreeably
to his own views, and imposes that explanation upon his congregation
as the meaning of the writer. The *whore of Babylon* has been the common whore of all the priests, and each has accused the other of keeping
the strumpet; so well do they agree in their explanations.

There now remain only a few books, which they call books of the
lesser prophets, and as I have already shown that the greater are im-

postors, it would be cowardice to disturb the repose of the little ones. Let them sleep, then, in the arms of their nurses, the priests, and both be forgotten together.

I have now gone through the Bible, as a man would go through a wood with an axe on his shoulder and fell trees. Here they lie; and the priests, if they can, may replant them. They may, perhaps, stick them in the ground, but they will never make them grow. I pass on to the books of the New Testament.

CHAPTER II

Turning to the New Testament

THE New Testament, they tell us, is founded upon the prophecies of the Old; if so, it must follow the fate of its foundation.

As it is nothing extraordinary that a woman should be with child before she was married, and that the son she might bring forth should be executed, even unjustly, I see no reason for not believing that such a woman as Mary, and such a man as Joseph, and Jesus existed; their mere existence is a matter of indifference about which there is no ground either to believe or to disbelieve, and which comes under the common head of, *It may be so; and what then?*

The probability, however, is that there were such persons, or at least such as resembled them in part of the circumstances, because almost all romantic stories have been suggested by some actual circumstance; as the adventures of Robinson Crusoe, not a word of which is true, were suggested by the case of Alexander Selkirk.

It is not the existence, or non-existence, of the persons that I trouble myself about; it is the fable of Jesus Christ, as told in the New Testament, and the wild and visionary doctrine raised thereon, against which I contend. The story, taking it as it is told, is blasphemously obscene.

It gives an account of a young woman engaged to be married, and while under this engagement she is, to speak plain language, debauched by a ghost, under the impious pretense (Luke, chap. i., ver. 35), that *"the Holy Ghost shall come upon thee, and the power of the Highest shall overshadow thee."* Notwithstanding which, Joseph afterward marries her, cohabits with her as his wife, and in his turn rivals the ghost. This is putting the story into intelligible language, and when told in this manner, there is not a priest but must be ashamed to own it.[15]

Obscenity in matters of faith, however wrapped up, is always a token of fable and imposture; for it is necessary to our serious belief of God that we do not connect it with stories that run, as this does, into ludicrous interpretations. This story is upon the face of it, the same kind of story as that of Jupiter and Leda, or Jupiter and Europa, or any of the amorous adventures of Jupiter; and shows, as is already stated in the former part of "The Age of Reason," that the Christian faith is built upon the heathen mythology.

As the historical parts of the New Testament, so far as concerns Jesus Christ, are confined to a very short space of time, less than two years, and all within the same country, and nearly to the same spot, the discordance of time, place and circumstance, which detects the fallacy of the books of the Old Testament, and proves them to be impositions, cannot be expected to be found here in the same abundance. The New Testament compared with the Old, is like a farce of one act, in which there is not room for very numerous violations of the unities. There are, however, some glaring contradictions, which, exclusive of the fallacy of the pretended prophecies, are sufficient to show the story of Jesus Christ to be false.

I lay it down as a position which cannot be controverted, first, that the *agreement* of all the parts of a story does not prove that story to be true, because the parts may agree and the whole may be false; secondly, that the *disagreement* of the parts of a story proves *the whole cannot be true*. The agreement does not prove true, but the disagreement proves falsehood positively.

The history of Jesus Christ is contained in the four books ascribed to Matthew, Mark, Luke and John. The first chapter of Matthew begins with giving a genealogy of Jesus Christ; and in the third chapter of Luke there is also given a genealogy of Jesus Christ. Did those two agree, it would not prove the genealogy to be true, because it might, nevertheless, be a fabrication; but as they contradict each other in every particular, it proves falsehood absolutely.

If Matthew speaks truth, Luke speaks falsehood, and if Luke speaks truth, Matthew speaks falsehood; and as there is no authority for be-

[15] Mary, the supposed virgin-mother of Jesus, had several other children, sons and daughters. See Matthew, chap. xiii, verses 55, 56.—*Author.*

lieving one more than the other, there is no authority for believing
either; and if they cannot be believed even in the very first thing they
say and set out to prove, they are not entitled to be believed in anything
they say afterward.

Truth is a uniform thing; and as to inspiration and revelation, were
we to admit it, it is impossible to suppose it can be contradictory. Either,
then, the men called apostles are impostors, or the books ascribed to
them have been written by other persons and fathered upon them, as is
the case in the Old Testament.

The book of Matthew gives (chap. i., ver. 6) a genealogy by name
from David up through Joseph, the husband of Mary, to Christ; and
makes there to be *twenty-eight* generations. The book of Luke gives also
a genealogy by name from Christ, through Joseph, the husband of Mary,
down to David, and makes there to be *forty-three* generations; besides
which, there are only the two names of David and Joseph that are alike
in the two lists.

I here insert both genealogical lists, and for the sake of perspicuity
and comparison, have placed them both in the same direction, that is
from Joseph down to David.

Now, if these men, Matthew and Luke, set out with a falsehood
between them (as these two accounts show they do) in the very commencement of their history of Jesus Christ, and of whom and what he
was, what authority (as I have before asked) is there left for believing
the strange things they tell us afterward? If they cannot be believed
in their account of his natural genealogy, how are we to believe them
when they tell us he was the Son of God begotten by a ghost, and that
an angel announced this in secret to his mother? If they lied in one
genealogy, why are we to believe them in the other?

If his natural genealogy be manufactured, which it certainly is, why
are we not to suppose that his celestial genealogy is manufactured also,
and that the whole is fabulous? Can any man of serious reflection
hazard his future happiness upon the belief of a story naturally impossible, repugnant to every idea of decency, and related by persons already
detected of falsehood? Is it not more safe that we stop ourselves at the
plain, pure and unmixed belief of one God, which is Deism, than that
we commit ourselves on an ocean of improbable, irrational, indecent
and contradictory tales?

The first question, however, upon the books of the New Testament,
as upon those of the Old, is: Are they genuine? Were they written by

Genealogy according to Matthew		Genealogy according to Luke	
Christ	23 Josaphat	Christ	23 Neri
2 Joseph	24 Asa	2 Joseph	24 Melchi
3 Jacob	25 Abia	3 Heli	25 Addi
4 Matthan	26 Roboam	4 Matthat	26 Cosam
5 Eleazar	27 Solomon	5 Levi	27 Elmodam
6 Eliud	28 David [16]	6 Melchi	28 Er
7 Achim		7 Janna	29 Jose
8 Sadoc		8 Joseph	30 Eliezer
9 Azor		9 Mattathias	31 Jorim
10 Eliakim		10 Amos	32 Matthat
11 Abiud		11 Naum	33 Levi
12 Zorobabel		12 Esli	34 Simeon
13 Salathiel		13 Nagge	35 Juda
14 Jechonias		14 Maath	36 Joseph
15 Josias		15 Mattathias	37 Jonan
16 Amon		16 Semei	38 Eliakim
17 Manasses		17 Joseph	39 Melea
18 Ezekias		18 Juda	40 Menan
19 Achaz		19 Joanna	41 Mattatha
20 Joatham		20 Rhesa	42 Nathan
21 Ozias		21 Zorobabel	43 David
22 Joram		22 Salathiel	

the persons to whom they are ascribed? for it is upon this ground only that the strange things related therein have been credited. Upon this point there is no *direct proof for or against,* and all that this state of a case proves is *doubtfulness,* and doubtfulness is the opposite of belief. The state, therefore, that the books are in, proves against themselves as far as this kind of proof can go.

[16] From the birth of David to the birth of Christ is upwards of 1080 years; and as the lifetime of Christ is not included, there are but 27 full generations. To find, therefore, the average age of each person mentioned in the list, at the time his first son was born, it is only necessary to divide 1080 years by 27, which gives 40 years for each person. As the lifetime of man was then but of the same extent it is now, it is an absurdity to suppose that 27 following generations should all be old bachelors, before they married; and the more so, when we are told, that Solomon, the next in succession to David, had a house full of wives and mistresses before he was twenty-one years of age. So far from this genealogy being a solemn truth, it is not even a reasonable lie. This list of Luke gives about twenty-six years for the average age, and this is too much.—*Author.*

But exclusive of this, the presumption is that the books called the Evangelists, and ascribed to Matthew, Mark, Luke and John, were not written by Matthew, Mark, Luke and John, and that they are impositions. The disordered state of the history in those four books, the silence of one book upon matters related in the other, and the disagreement that is to be found among them, implies that they are the production of some unconnected individuals, many years after the things they pretend to relate, each of whom made his own legend; and not the writings of men living intimately together, as the men called the apostles are supposed to have done—in fine, that they have been manufactured, as the books of the Old Testament have been, by other persons than those whose names they bear.

The story of the angel announcing what the Church calls the *immaculate conception* is not so much as mentioned in the books ascribed to Mark and John; and is differently related in Matthew and Luke. The former says the angel appeared to Joseph; the latter says it was to Mary; but either Joseph or Mary was the worst evidence that could have been thought of, for it was others that should have testified *for them,* and not they for themselves.

Were any girl that is now with child to say, and even to swear it, that she was gotten with child by a ghost, and that an angel told her so, would she be believed? Certainly she would not. Why, then, are we to believe the same thing of another girl, whom we never saw, told by nobody knows who, nor when, nor where? How strange and inconsistent it is, that the same circumstance that would weaken the belief even of a probable story should be given as a motive for believing this one, that has upon the face of it every token of absolute impossibility and imposture!

The story of Herod destroying all the children under two years old belongs altogether to the book of Matthew; not one of the rest mentions anything about it. Had such a circumstance been true, the universality of it must have made it known to all the writers, and the thing would have been too striking to have been omitted by any.

This writer tells us that Jesus escaped this slaughter because Joseph and Mary were warned by an angel to flee with him unto Egypt; but he forgot to make any provision for John, who was then under two years of age. John, however, who stayed behind, fared as well as Jesus, who fled; and, therefore, the story circumstantially belies itself.

Not any two of these writers agree in reciting, *exactly in the same words,* the written inscription, short as it is, which they tell us was put over Christ when he was crucified; and besides this, Mark says: He was crucified at the third hour (nine in the morning), and John says it was the sixth hour (twelve at noon).[17]

The inscription is thus stated in these books:

MATTHEW .... *This is Jesus, the King of the Jews.*
MARK .... *The King of the Jews.*
LUKE .... *This is the King of the Jews.*
JOHN .... *Jesus of Nazareth, King of the Jews.*

We may infer from these circumstances, trivial as they are, that those writers, whoever they were, and in whatever time they lived, were not present at the scene. The only one of the men called apostles who appears to have been near the spot was Peter, and when he was accused of being one of Jesus' followers, it is said (Matthew, chap. xxvi., ver. 74), *"Then he [Peter] began to curse and to swear, saying, I know not the man!"* yet we are now called upon to believe the same Peter, convicted, by their own account, of perjury. For what reason, or on what authority, shall we do this?

The accounts that are given of the circumstances that they tell us attended the crucifixion are differently related in these four books.

The book ascribed to Matthew says (chap. xxvii, v. 45), *"Now from the sixth hour there was darkness over all the land unto the ninth hour."* (Ver. 51, 52, 53), *"And, behold, the veil of the temple was rent in twain from the top to the bottom; and the earth did quake, and the rocks rent; and the graves were opened; and many bodies of the saints which slept arose, and came out of the graves after his resurrection, and went into the holy city and appeared unto many."* Such is the account which this dashing writer of the book of Matthew gives, but in which he is not supported by the writers of the other books.

The writer of the book ascribed to Mark, in detailing the circumstances of the crucifixion, makes no mention of any earthquake, nor of the rocks rending, nor of the graves opening, nor of the dead men walking out. The writer of the book of Luke is silent also upon the same

---

[17] According to John, the sentence was not passed till about the sixth hour (noon), and, consequently, the execution could not be till the afternoon; but Mark says expressly, that he was crucified at the third hour (nine in the morning), chap. xv, verse 25. John, chap. xix, verse 14.—*Author.*

points. And as to the writer of the book of John, though he details all the circumstances of the crucifixion down to the burial of Christ, he says nothing about either the darkness—the veil of the temple—the earthquake—the rocks—the graves—nor the dead men.

Now, if it had been true that those things had happened, and if the writers of these books had lived at the time they did happen, and had been the persons they are said to be, namely, the four men called apostles, Matthew, Mark, Luke and John, it was not possible for them, as true historians, even without the aid of inspiration, not to have recorded them.

The things, supposing them to have been facts, were of too much notoriety not to have been known, and of too much importance not to have been told. All these supposed apostles must have been witnesses of the earthquake, if there had been any; for it was not possible for them to have been absent from it; the opening of the graves and the resurrection of the dead men, and their walking about the city, is of still greater importance than the earthquake.

An earthquake is always possible and natural, and proves nothing; but this opening of the graves is supernatural, and directly in point to their doctrine, their cause and their apostleship. Had it been true, it would have filled up whole chapters of those books, and been the chosen theme and general chorus of all the writers; but instead of this, little and trivial things, and mere prattling conversations of, *he said this,* and *he said that,* are often tediously detailed, while this, most important of all, had it been true, is passed off in a slovenly manner by a single dash of the pen, and that by one writer only and not so much as hinted at by the rest.

It is an easy thing to tell a lie, but it is difficult to support the lie after it is told. The writer of the book of Matthew should have told us who the saints were that came to life again and went into the city, and what became of them afterward, and who it was that saw them—for he is not hardy enough to say he saw them himself; whether they came out naked, and all in natural buff, he-saints and she-saints; or whether they came full dressed, and where they got their dresses; whether they went to their former habitations, and reclaimed their wives, their husbands and their property, and how they were received; whether they entered ejectments for the recovery of their possessions, or brought actions of *crim. con.* against the rival interlopers; whether they remained on earth, and followed their former occupation of preaching or working; or whether they died again, or went back to their graves alive and buried themselves.

Strange, indeed, that an army of saints should return to life and nobody know who they were, nor who it was that saw them, and that not a word more should be said upon the subject, nor these saints have anything to tell us!

Had it been the prophets who (as we are told) had formerly prophesied of these things, *they* must have had a *great deal* to say. They could have told us everything and we should have had posthumous prophecies, with notes and commentaries upon the first, a little better at least than we have now. Had it been Moses and Aaron and Joshua and Samuel and David, not an unconverted Jew had remained in all Jerusalem. Had it been John the Baptist, and the saints of the time then present, everybody would have known them, and they would have out-preached and out-famed all the other apostles. But, instead of this, these saints were made to pop up, like Jonah's gourd in the night, for no purpose at all but to wither in the morning. Thus much for this part of the story.

The tale of the resurrection follows that of the crucifixion, and in this as well as in that, the writers, whoever they were, disagree so much as to make it evident that none of them were there.

The book of Matthew states that when Christ was put in the sepulchre, the Jews applied to Pilate for a watch or a guard to be placed over the sepulchre, to prevent the body being stolen by the disciples; and that, in consequence of this request, the sepulchre *was made sure, sealing the stone* that covered the mouth, and setting a watch.

But the other books say nothing about this application, nor about the sealing, nor the guard, nor the watch; and, according to their accounts, there were none. Matthew, however, follows up this part of the story of the guard or the watch with a second part that I shall notice in the conclusion, as it serves to detect the fallacy of those books.

The book of Matthew continues its account, and says (chap. xxviii., ver. 1) that at the end of the Sabbath, as it began to dawn toward the first day of the week, came Mary Magdalene and the other Mary, to see the sepulchre. Mark says it was sun-rising, and John says it was dark. Luke says it was Mary Magdalene and Joanna, and Mary, the mother of James, and other women, that came to the sepulchre; and John states that Mary Magdalene came alone. So well do they agree about their first evidence! they all, however, appear to have known most about Mary Magdalene; she was a woman of a large acquaintance, and it was not an ill conjecture that she might be upon the stroll.

The book of Matthew goes on to say (ver. 2), "And behold there was a great earthquake, for the angel of the Lord descended from heaven, and came and rolled back the stone from the door, and sat upon it." But the other books say nothing about any earthquake, nor about the angel rolling back the stone and sitting upon it, and according to their account, there was no angel sitting there. Mark says the angel was within the sepulchre, sitting on the right side. Luke says there were two, and they were both standing up; and John says they were both sitting down, one at the head and the other at the feet.

Matthew says that the angel that was sitting upon the stone on the outside of the sepulchre told the two Marys that Christ was risen, and that the women went away quickly. Mark says that the women, upon seeing the stone rolled away and wondering at it, went into the sepulchre, and that it was the angel that was sitting within on the right side that told them so. Luke says it was the two angels that were standing up; and John says it was Jesus Christ himself that told it to Mary Magdalene, and that she did not go into the sepulchre, but only stooped down and looked in.

Now, if the writers of those four books had gone into a court of justice to prove an *alibi* (for it is of the nature of an alibi that is here attempted to be proved, namely, the absence of a dead body by supernatural means), and had they given their evidence in the same contradictory manner as it is here given, they would have been in danger of having their ears cropped for perjury, and would have justly deserved it. Yet this is the evidence, and these are the books that have been imposed upon the world as being given by divine inspiration and as the unchangeable Word of God.

The writer of the book of Matthew, after giving this account, relates a story that is not to be found in any of the other books, and which is the same I have just before alluded to.

"Now," says he [that is, after the conversation the women had with the angel sitting upon the stone], "behold some of the watch [meaning the watch that he had said had been placed over the sepulchre] came into the city, showed unto the chief priests all the things that were done; and when they were assembled with the elders and had taken counsel they gave large money unto the soldiers, saying, Say ye, His disciples came by night, and stole him away while we *slept;* and if this come to the governor's ears, we will persuade him, and secure you. So they took the money, and did as they were taught; and this saying [that his disciples stole him away] is commonly reported among the Jews until this day."

The expression, *until this day,* is an evidence that the book ascribed to Matthew was not written by Matthew, and that it had been manufactured long after the time and things of which it pretends to treat; for the expression implies a great length of intervening time. It would be inconsistent in us to speak in this manner of anything happening in our own time. To give, therefore, intelligible meaning to the expression, we must suppose a lapse of some generations at least, for this manner of speaking carries the mind back to ancient time.

The absurdity also of the story is worth noticing; for it shows the writer of the book of Matthew to have been an exceedingly weak and foolish man. He tells a story that contradicts itself in point of possibility; for though the guard, if there were any, might be made to say that the body was taken away while they were *asleep,* and to give that as a reason for their not having prevented it, that same sleep must also have prevented their knowing how and by whom it was done, and yet they were made to say that it was the disciples who did it.

Were a man to tender his evidence of something that he should say was done, and of the manner of doing it, and of the persons who did it, while he was asleep, and could know nothing of the matter, such evidence could not be received; it will do well enough for Testament evidence, but not for anything where truth is concerned.

I come now to that part of the evidence in those books that respects the pretended appearance of Christ after this pretended resurrection.

The writer of the book of Matthew relates that the angel that was sitting on the stone at the mouth of the sepulchre said to the two Marys (chap. xxviii, ver. 7), *"Behold Christ has gone before you into Galilee, there shall ye see him; lo, I have told you."* And the same writer at the next two verses (8, 9), makes Christ himself to speak to the same purpose to these women immediately after the angel had told it to them, and that they ran quickly to tell it to the disciples; and at the 16th verse it is said, *"Then the eleven disciples went away into Galilee, into a mountain where Jesus had appointed them; and when they saw him, they worshiped him."*

But the writer of the book of John tells us a story very different to this; for he says (chap. xx., ver. 19), *"Then the same day at evening, being the first day of the week* [that is, the same day that Christ is said to have risen], *when the doors were shut, where the disciples were assembled, for fear of the Jews, came Jesus and stood in the midst of them."*

According to Matthew the eleven were marching to Galilee to meet Jesus in a mountain, by his own appointment, at the very time when, according to John, they were assembled in another place, and that not by appointment, but in secret, for fear of the Jews.

The writer of the book of Luke contradicts that of Matthew more pointedly than John does; for he says expressly that the meeting was in *Jerusalem* the evening of the same day that he [Christ] rose, and that the *eleven* were *there*. See Luke, chap. xxiv, ver. 13, 33.

Now, it is not possible, unless we admit these supposed disciples the right of willful lying, that the writer of those books could be any of the eleven persons called disciples; for if, according to Matthew, the eleven went into Galilee to meet Jesus in a mountain by his own appointment, on the same day that he is said to have risen, Luke and John must have been two of that eleven; yet the writer of Luke says expressly, and John implies as much, that the meeting was that same day in a house in Jerusalem; and, on the other hand, if, according to Luke and John, the *eleven* were assembled in a house in Jerusalem, Matthew must have been one of that eleven; yet Matthew says the meeting was in a mountain in Galilee, and consequently the evidence given in those books destroys each other.

The writer of the book of Mark says nothing about any meeting in Galilee; but he says (chap. xvi, ver. 12), that Christ, after his resurrection, appeared in another form to two of them as they walked into the country, and that these two told it to the residue, who would not believe them.

Luke also tells a story in which he keeps Christ employed the whole day of this pretended resurrection until the evening, and which totally invalidates the account of going to the mountain in Galilee. He says that two of them, without saying which two, went that same day to a village called Emmaus, three score furlongs (seven miles and a half) from Jerusalem, and that Christ, in disguise, went with them, and stayed with them unto the evening, and supped with them, and then vanished out of their sight, and re-appeared that same evening at the meeting of the eleven in Jerusalem.

This is the contradictory manner in which the evidence of this pretended re-appearance of Christ is stated; the only point in which the writers agree is the skulking privacy of that re-appearance; for whether it was in the recess of a mountain in Galilee, or a shut-up house in Jerusalem, it was still skulking. To what cause, then, are we to assign this skulking? On the one hand it is directly repugnant to the supposed or pretended end—that of convincing the world that Christ was risen; and, on the other hand, to have asserted the publicity of it would have exposed the writers of those books to public detection, and, therefore, they have been under the necessity of making it a private affair.

As to the account of Christ being seen by more than five hundred at once, it is Paul only who says it, and not the five hundred who say it for themselves. It is, therefore, the testimony of but one man, and that, too, of a man who did not, according to the same account, believe a word of the matter himself at the time it is said to have happened.

His evidence, supposing him to have been the writer of the 15th chapter of Corinthians, where this account is given, is like that of a man who comes into a court of justice to swear that what he had sworn before is false. A man may often see reason, and he has, too, always the right of changing his opinion; but this liberty does not extend to matters of fact.

I now come to the last scene, that of the ascension into heaven. Here all fear of the Jews, and of everything else, must necessarily have been out of the question: it was that which, if true, was to seal the whole, and upon which the reality of the future mission of the disciples was to rest for proof.

Words, whether declarations or promises, that passed in private, either in the recess of a mountain in Galilee, or in a shut-up house in Jerusalem, even supposing them to have been spoken, could not be evidence in public; it was therefore necessary that this last scene should preclude the possibility of denial and dispute, and that it should be, as I have stated in the former part of "The Age of Reason," as public and as visible as the sun at noonday; at least it ought to have been as public as the crucifixion is reported to have been. But to come to the point.

In the first place, the writer of the book of Matthew does not say a syllable about it; neither does the writer of the book of John. This being the case, is it possible to suppose that those writers, who affect to be even minute in other matters, would have been silent upon this, had it been true?

The writer of the book of Mark passes it off in a careless, slovenly manner, with a single dash of the pen, as if he was tired of romancing or ashamed of the story. So also does the writer of Luke. And even between these two there is not an apparent agreement as to the place where his final parting is said to have been.

The book of Mark says that Christ appeared to the eleven as they sat at meat, alluding to the meeting of the eleven at Jerusalem; he then states the conversation that he says passed at that meeting; and immediately after says (as a schoolboy would finish a dull story) *"So then, after the Lord had spoken unto them, he was received up into heaven and sat on the right hand of God."*

But the writer of Luke says, that the ascension was from Bethany; that *he* [Christ] *led them out as far as Bethany, and was parted from them, and was carried up into heaven.* So also was Mahomet; and as to Moses, the apostle Jude says (ver. 9) *"that Michael and the devil disputed about his body."* While we believe such fables as these, or either of them, we believe unworthily of the Almighty.

I have now gone through the examination of the four books ascribed to Matthew, Mark, Luke and John; and when it is considered that the whole space of time from the crucifixion to what is called the ascension is but a few days, apparently not more than three or four, and that all the circumstances are reported to have happened nearly about the same spot, Jerusalem, it is, I believe, impossible to find in any story upon record so many and such glaring absurdities, contradictions and falsehoods as are in those books. They are more numerous and striking than I had any expectation of finding when I began this examination, and far more so than I had any idea of when I wrote the former part of "The Age of Reason."

I had neither Bible nor Testament to refer to, nor could I procure any. My own situation, even as to existence, was becoming every day more precarious, and as I was willing to leave something behind me on the subject, I was obliged to be quick and concise.

The quotations I then made were from memory only, but they are correct; and the opinions I have advanced in that work are the effect of the most clear and long-established conviction that the Bible and the Testament are impositions upon the world, that the fall of man, the account of Jesus Christ being the Son of God, and of his dying to appease the wrath of God, and of salvation by that strange means are all fabulous inventions, dishonorable to the wisdom and power of the

Almighty; that the only true religion is Deism, by which I then meant, and mean now, the belief of one God, and an imitation of His moral character, or the practise of what are called moral virtues—and that it was upon this only (so far as religion is concerned) that I rested all my hopes of happiness hereafter. So I say now—and so help me God.

But to return to the subject. Though it is impossible, at this distance of time, to ascertain as a fact who were the writers of those four books (and this alone is sufficient to hold them in doubt, and where we doubt we do not believe), it is not difficult to ascertain negatively that they were not written by the persons to whom they are ascribed. The contradictions in those books demonstrate two things:

First, that the writers could not have been eye-witnesses and ear-witnesses of the matters they relate, or they would have related them without those contradictions; and consequently that the books have not been written by the persons called apostles, who are supposed to have been witnesses of this kind.

Secondly, that the writers, whoever they were, have not acted in concerted imposition; but each writer separately and individually for himself, and without the knowledge of the other.

The same evidence that applies to prove the one, applies equally to prove both those cases; that is, that the books were not written by the men called apostles, and also that they are not a concerted imposition. As to inspiration, it is altogether out of the question; we may as well attempt to unite truth and falsehood as inspiration and contradiction.

If four men are eye-witnesses and ear-witnesses to a scene, they will, without any concert between them, agree as to time and place when and where that scene happened. Their individual knowledge of the *thing,* each one knowing it for himself, renders concert totally unnecessary; the one will not say it was in a mountain in the country, and the other at a house in town: the one will not say it was at sunrise, and the other that it was dark. For in whatever place it was, at whatever time it was, they know it equally alike.

And, on the other hand, if four men concert a story, they will make their separate relations of that story agree and corroborate with each other to support the whole. *That* concert supplies the want of fact in the one case, as the knowledge of the fact supersedes, in the other case, the necessity of a concert.

The same contradictions, therefore, that prove that there has been no concert, prove also that the reporters had no knowledge of the fact (or rather of that which they relate as a fact), and detect also the falsehood of their reports. These books, therefore, have neither been written by the men called apostles, nor by impostors in concert. How then have they been written?

I am not one of those who are fond of believing there is much of that which is called willful lying, or lying originally, except in the case of men setting up to be prophets, as in the Old Testament; for prophesying is lying professionally. In almost all other cases, it is not difficult to discover the progress by which even simple supposition, with the aid of credulity, will, in time, grow into a lie, and at last be told as a fact; and whenever we can find a charitable reason for a thing of this kind, we ought not to indulge a severe one.

The story of Jesus Christ appearing after he was dead is the story of an apparition, such as timid imaginations can always create in vision, and credulity believe. Stories of this kind had been told of the assassination of Julius Caesar, not many years before; and they generally have their origin in violent deaths, or in the execution of innocent persons.

In cases of this kind, compassion lends its aid and benevolently stretches the story. It goes on a little and a little further till it becomes *a most certain truth*. Once start a ghost and credulity fills up the history of its life and assigns the cause of its appearance! One tells it one way, another another way, till there are as many stories about the ghost and about the proprietor of the ghost, as there are about Jesus Christ in these four books.

The story of the appearance of Jesus Christ is told with that strange mixture of the natural and impossible that distinguishes legendary tale from fact. He is represented as suddenly coming in and going out when the doors were shut, and of vanishing out of sight and appearing again, as one would conceive of an unsubstantial vision; then again he is hungry, sits down to meat and eats his supper. But as those who tell stories of this kind never provide for all the cases, so it is here; they have told us that when he arose he left his grave clothes behind him; but they have forgotten to provide other clothes for him to appear in afterward, or to tell us what he did with them when he ascended—whether he stripped them off, or went up clothes and all.

In the case of Elijah, they have been careful enough to make him throw down his mantle; how it happened not to be burned in the chariot of fire they also have not told us. But as imagination supplies all deficiencies of this kind, we may suppose, if we please, that it was made of salamander's wool.

Those who are not much acquainted with ecclesiastical history may suppose that the book called the New Testament has existed ever since the time of Jesus Christ, as they suppose that the books ascribed to Moses have existed ever since the time of Moses. But the fact is historically otherwise. There was no such book as the New Testament till more than three hundred years after the time that Christ is said to have lived.

At what time the books ascribed to Matthew, Mark, Luke and John began to appear is altogether a matter of uncertainty. There is not the least shadow of evidence of who the persons were that wrote them, nor at what time they were written; and they might as well have been called by the names of any of the other supposed apostles, as by the names they are now called. The originals are not in the possession of any Christian Church existing, any more than the two tables of stone written on, they pretend, by the finger of God, upon Mount Sinai, and given to Moses, are in the possession of the Jews. And even if they were, there is no possibility of proving the handwriting in either case.

At the time those books were written there was no printing, and consequently there could be no publication, otherwise than by written copies, which any man might make or alter at pleasure, and call them originals.[18] Can we suppose it is consistent with the wisdom of the Almighty, to commit Himself and His will to man upon such precarious means as these, or that it is consistent we should pin our faith upon such uncertainties? We cannot make, nor alter, nor even imitate so much as one blade of grass that He has made, and yet we can make or alter *words of God* as easily as words of man.

About three hundred and fifty years after the time that Christ is

[18] The former part of "The Age of Reason" has not been published two years, and there is already an expression in it that is not mine. The expression is, *The book of Luke was carried by a majority of one voice only*. It may be true, but it is not I that have said it. Some person, who might know of the circumstance, has added it in a note at the bottom of the page of some of the editions, printed either in England or in America; and the printers, after that, have placed it into the body of the work, and made me the author of it. If this has happened within such a short space of time, notwithstanding the aid of printing, which prevents the alteration of copies individually, what may not have happened in a much greater length of time, when there was no printing, and when any man who could write could make a written copy, and call it an original by Matthew, Mark, Luke or John?—*Author*.

said to have lived, several writings of the kind I am speaking of were scattered in the hands of divers individuals; and as the Church had begun to form itself into a hierarchy, or church government, with temporal powers, it set itself about collecting them into a code, as we now see them, called *The New Testament*. They decided by vote, as I have before said in the former part of "The Age of Reason," which of those writings, out of the collection they had made, should be the *Word of God,* and which should not. The rabbins of the Jews had decided, by vote, upon the books of the Bible before.

As the object of the Church, as is the case in all national establishments of churches, was power and revenue, and terror the means it used, it is consistent to suppose that the most miraculous and wonderful of the writings they had collected stood the best chance of being voted. And as to the authenticity of the books, the *vote stands in the place of it,* for it can be traced no higher.

Disputes, however, ran high among the people then calling themselves Christians; not only as to points of doctrine, but as to the authenticity of the books. In the contest between the persons called St. Augustine and Fauste, about the year 400, the latter says: "The books called the Evangelists have been composed long after the times of the apostles by some obscure men, who, fearing that the world would not give credit to their relation of matters of which they could not be informed, have published them under the names of the apostles, and which are so full of sottishness and discordant relations, that there is neither agreement nor connection between them."

And in another place, addressing himself to the advocate of those books, as being the Word of God, he says, "It is thus that your predecessors have inserted in the Scriptures of our Lord many things, which, though they carry his name agree not with his doctrine. This is not surprising, *since that we have often proved* that these things have not been written by himself, nor by his apostles, but that for the greater part they are founded upon *tales,* upon *vague reports,* and put together by I know not what, half-Jews, but with little agreement between them, and which they have nevertheless published under the names of the apostles of our Lord, and have thus attributed to them their own *errors and their lies."* [19]

---

[19] I have these two extracts from Boulanger's "Life of Paul," written in French. Boulanger has quoted them from the writings of Augustine against Fauste, to which he refers.— *Author.*

The reader will see by these extracts, that the authenticity of the books of the New Testament was denied, and the books treated as tales, forgeries, and lies, at the time they were voted to be the Word of God.[20] But the interest of the Church, with the assistance of the fagot, bore down the opposition and at last suppressed all investigation.

Miracles followed upon miracles, if we will believe them, and men were taught to say they believed whether they believed or not. But (by way of throwing in a thought) the French Revolution has excommunicated the Church from the power of working miracles; she has not been able, with the assistance of all her saints, to work *one* miracle since the Revolution began; and as she never stood in greater need than now, we may, without the aid of divination, conclude that all her former miracles were tricks and lies.

When we consider the lapse of more than three hundred years intervening between the time that Christ is said to have lived and the time the New Testament was formed into a book, we must see, even without the assistance of historical evidence, the exceeding uncertainty there is of its authenticity. The authenticity of the book of Homer, so far as regards the authorship, is much better established than that of the New Testament, though Homer is a thousand years the most ancient.

It is only an exceedingly good poet that could have written the book of Homer, and therefore few men only could have attempted it; and a man capable of doing it would not have thrown away his own fame by

[20] Boulanger, in his "Life of Paul" has collected from the ecclesiastical histories, and from the writings of the fathers, as they are called, several matters which show the opinions that prevailed among the different sects of Christians at the time the *Testament,* as we now see it, was voted to be the Word of God. The following extracts are from the second chapter of that work.

The Marcionists (a Christian sect) assumed that the evangelists were filled with falsities. The Manicheans, who formed a very numerous sect at the commencement of Christianity, *rejected as false all the New Testament,* and showed other writings quite different that they gave for authentic. The Cerinthians, like the Marcionists, admitted not the Acts of the Apostles. The Encratites, and the Sévénians, adopted neither the Acts nor the Epistles of Paul. Chrysostom, in a homily which he made upon the Acts of the Apostles, says that in his time, about the year 400, many people knew nothing either of the author or of the book. St. Irene, who lived before that time, reports that the Valentinians, like several other sects of Christians, accused the Scriptures of being filled with imperfections, errors and contradictions. The Ebionites, or Nazarines, who were the first Christians, rejected all the Epistles of Paul and regarded him as an impostor. They report, among other things, that he was originally a pagan, that he came to Jerusalem, where he lived some time; and that having a mind to marry the daughter of the high priest, he caused himself to be circumcised; but that not being able to obtain her, he quarreled with the Jews and wrote against circumcision, and against the observance of the Sabbath, and against all the legal ordinances.—*Author.*

giving it to another. In like manner, there were but few that could have composed Euclid's "Elements," because none but an exceedingly good geometrician could have been the author of that work.

But with respect to the books of the New Testament, particularly such parts as tell us of the resurrection and ascension of Christ, any person who could tell a story of an apparition, or of a *man's walking,* could have made such books; for the story is most wretchedly told. The chance, therefore, of forgery in the Testament, is millions to one greater than in the case of Homer or Euclid.

Of the numerous priests or parsons of the present day, bishops and all, every one of them can make a sermon, or translate a scrap of Latin, especially if it has been translated a thousand times before; but is there any among them. that can write poetry like Homer, or science like Euclid? The sum total of a person's learning, with very few exceptions, is *a b ab,* and *hic, hæc, hoc;* and their knowledge of science is three times one is *one;* and this is more than sufficient to have enabled them, had they lived at the time, to have written all the books of the New Testament.

As the opportunities of forgeries were greater, so also was the inducement. A man could gain no advantage by writing under the name of Homer or Euclid; if he could write equal to them, it would be better that he wrote under his own name; if inferior, he could not succeed. Pride would prevent the former, and impossibility the latter. But with respect to such books as compose the New Testament, all the inducements were on the side of the forgery. The best imagined history that could have been made, at the distance of two or three hundred years after the time, could not have passed for an original under the name of the real writer; the only chance of success lay in forgery, for the church wanted pretense for its new doctrine, and truth and talents were out of the question.

But as is not uncommon (as before observed) to relate stories of persons *walking* after they are dead, and of ghosts and apparitions of such as have fallen by some violent or extraordinary means; and as the people of that day were in the habit of believing such things, and of the appearance of angels and also of devils, and of their getting into people's insides and shaking them like a fit of an ague, and of their being cast out again as if by an emetic—(Mary Magdalene, the book of Mark tells us, had brought up, or been brought to bed of seven devils)— it was nothing extraordinary that some story of this kind should get abroad of the person called Jesus Christ, and become afterward the foundation of the four books ascribed to Matthew, Mark, Luke and John.

Each writer told the tale as he heard it, or thereabouts, and gave to his book the name of the saint or the apostle whom tradition had given as the eye-witness. It is only upon this ground that the contradiction in those books can be accounted for; and if this be not the case, they are downright impositions, lies and forgeries, without even the apology of credulity.

That they have been written by a sort of half Jews, as the foregoing quotations mention, is discernible enough. The frequent references made to that chief assassin and impostor, Moses, and to the men called prophets, establish this point; and, on the other hand, the church has complemented the fraud of admitting the Bible and the Testament to reply to each other.

Between the Christian Jew and the Christian Gentile, the thing called a prophecy and the thing prophesied, the type and the thing typified, the sign and the thing signified have been industriously rummaged up and fitted together like old locks and pick-lock keys.

The story foolishly enough told of Eve and the serpent, and naturally enough as to the enmity between men and serpents (for the serpent always bites about the *heel,* because it cannot reach higher; and the man always knocks the serpent about the *head,* as the most effectual way to prevent its biting),[21] this foolish story, I say, has been made into a prophecy, a type, and a promise to begin with; and the lying imposition of Isaiah to Ahaz, *That a virgin shall conceive and bear a son,* as a sign that Ahaz should conquer, when the event was that he was defeated (as already noticed in the observations on the book of Isaiah), has been perverted and made to serve as a winder-up.

Jonah and the whale are also made into a sign or a type. Jonah is Jesus, and the whale is the grave; for it is said (and they have made Christ to say it of himself), Matt. chap. xii, ver. 40, "For as Jonah was *three days* and *three nights* in the whale's belly, so shall the Son of Man be *three days* and *three nights* in the heart of the earth."

But it happens, awkwardly enough, that Christ, according to their account, was but one day and two nights in the grave; about 36 hours, instead of 72; that is, the Friday night, the Saturday, and the Saturday

---

[21] It shall bruise thy *head* and thou shalt bruise his *heel.* Genesis, chap. iii, verse 15.— *Author.*

night; for they say he was up on the Sunday morning by sunrise, or before. But as this fits quite as well as the *bite* and the *kick* in Genesis, or the *virgin* and her *son* in Isaiah, it will pass in the lump of *orthodox* things. Thus much for the historical part of the Testament and its evidences.

Epistles of Paul.—The epistles ascribed to Paul, being fourteen in number, almost fill up the remaining part of the Testament. Whether those epistles were written by the person to whom they are ascribed is a matter of no great importance, since the writer, whoever he was, attempts to prove his doctrine by argument. He does not pretend to have been witness to any of the scenes told of the resurrection and the ascension, and he declares that he had not believed them.

The story of his being struck to the ground as he was journeying to Damascus has nothing in it miraculous or extraordinary; he escaped with life, and that is more than many others have done who have been struck with lightning; and that he should lose his sight for three days, and be unable to eat or drink during that time, is nothing more than is common in such conditions. His companions that were with him appear not to have suffered in the same manner, for they were well enough to lead him the remainder of the journey; neither did they pretend to have seen any vision.

The character of the person called Paul, according to the accounts given of him, has in it a great deal of violence and fanaticism; he had persecuted with as much heat as he preached afterward; the stroke he had received had changed his thinking, without altering his constitution; and either as a Jew or a Christian, he was the same zealot. Such men are never good moral evidences of any doctrine they preach. They are always in extremes, as well of actions as of belief.

The doctrine he sets out to prove by argument is the resurrection of the same body, and he advances this as an evidence of immortality. But so much will men differ in their manner of thinking, and in the conclusions they draw from the same premises, that this doctrine of the resurrection of the same body, so far from being an evidence of immortality, appears to me to furnish an evidence against it; for if I have already died in this body, and am raised again in the same body in which I have lived, it is a presumptive evidence that I shall die again.

That resurrection no more secures me against the repetition of dying, than an ague-fit, when passed, secures me against another. To believe, therefore, in immortality, I must have a more elevated idea than is contained in the gloomy doctrine of the resurrection.

Besides, as a matter of choice, as well as of hope, I had rather have a better body and a more convenient form than the present. Every animal in the creation excels us in something. The winged insects, without mentioning doves or eagles, can pass over more space and with greater ease in a few minutes than man can in an hour. The glide of the smallest fish, in proportion to its bulk, exceeds us in motion almost beyond comparison, and without weariness.

Even the sluggish snail can ascend from the bottom of a dungeon, where a man, by the want of that ability, would perish; and a spider can launch itself from the top, as a playful amusement. The personal powers of man are so limited, and his heavy frame so little constructed to extensive enjoyment, that there is nothing to induce us to wish the opinion of Paul to be true. It is too little for the magnitude of the scene—too mean for the sublimity of the subject.

But all other arguments apart, the *consciousness of existence* is the only conceivable idea we have of another life, and the continuance of that consciousness is immortality. The consciousness of existence, or the knowing that we exist, is not necessarily confined to the same form, nor to the same matter, even in this life.

We have not in all cases the same form, nor in any case the same matter that composed our bodies twenty or thirty years ago; and yet we are conscious of being the same persons. Even legs and arms, which make up almost half the human frame, are not necessary to the consciousness of existence. These may be lost or taken away, and the full consciousness of existence remain; and were their place supplied by wings, or other appendages, we cannot conceive that it would alter our consciousness of existence.

In short, we know not how much, or rather how little, of our composition it is, and how exquisitely fine that little is, that creates in us this consciousness of existence; and all beyond that is like the pulp of a peach, distinct and separate from the vegetative speck in the kernel.

Who can say by what exceedingly fine action of fine matter it is that a thought is produced in what we call the mind? And yet that thought when produced, as I now produce the thought I am writing, is capable of becoming immortal, and is the only production of man that has that capacity.

Statues of marble or brass will perish; and statues made in imitation of them are not the same statues, nor the same workmanship, any more than the copy of a picture is the same picture. But print and reprint a thought a thousand times over, and that with materials of any kind —carve it into wood or engrave it in stone, the thought is eternally and identically the same thought in every case. It has a capacity of unimpaired existence, unaffected by change of matter, and is essentially distinct and of a nature different from everything else that we know or can conceive.

If, then, the thing produced has in itself a capacity of being immortal, it is more than a token that the power that produced it, which is the selfsame thing as consciousness of existence, can be immortal also; and that as independently of the matter it was first connected with, as the thought is of the printing or writing it first appeared in. The one idea is not more difficult to believe than the other, and we can see that one is true.

That the consciousness of existence is not dependent on the same form or the same matter is demonstrated to our senses in the works of the creation, as far as our senses are capable of receiving that demonstration. A very numerous part of the animal creation preaches to us, far better than Paul, the belief of a life hereafter. Their little life resembles an earth and a heaven—a present and a future state, and comprises, if it may be so expressed, immortality in miniature.

The most beautiful parts of the creation to our eye are the winged insects, and they are not so originally. They acquire that form and that inimitable brilliancy by progressive changes. The slow and creeping caterpillar-worm of to-day passes in a few days to a torpid figure and a state resembling death; and in the next change comes forth in all the miniature magnificence of life, a splendid butterfly.

No resemblance of the former creature remains; everything is changed; all his powers are new, and life is to him another thing. We cannot conceive that the consciousness of existence is not the same in this state of the animal as before; why then must I believe that the resurrection of the same body is necessary to continue to me the consciousness of existence hereafter?

In the former part of "The Age of Reason" I have called the Creation the only true and real Word of God; and this instance, or this text, in the Book of Creation, not only shows to us that this thing may be so, but that it is so; and that the belief of a future state is a rational belief, corroborated by facts visible in the Creation; for it is not more difficult to believe that we shall exist hereafter in a better state and form than at present, than that a worm should become a butterfly, and quit the dunghill for the atmosphere, if we did not know it as a fact.

As to the doubtful jargon ascribed to Paul in the 15th chapter of I. Corinthians, which makes part of the burial service of some Christian sectaries, it is as destitute of meaning as the tolling of the bell at the funeral; it explains nothing to the understanding—it illustrates nothing to the imagination, but leaves the reader to find any meaning if he can. "All flesh [says he] is not the same flesh. There is one flesh of men; another of beasts; another of fishes; and another of birds." And what then?—nothing. A cook could have said as much.

"There are also [says he] bodies celestial, and bodies terrestrial; the glory of the celestial is one, and the glory of the terrestrial is another." And what then?—nothing. And what is the difference? nothing that he has told. "There is [says he] one glory of the sun, and another glory of the moon, and another glory of the stars." And what then?—nothing; except that he says that *one star differeth from another star in glory,* instead of distance; and he might as well have told us that the moon did not shine so bright as the sun.

All this is nothing better than the jargon of a conjuror, who picks up phrases he does not understand, to confound the credulous people who have come to have their fortune told. Priests and conjurors are of the same trade.

Sometimes Paul affects to be a naturalist and to prove his system of resurrection from the principles of vegetation. "Thou fool [says he], that which thou sowest is not quickened, except it die." To which one might reply in his own language and say, "Thou fool, Paul, that which thou sowest is not quickened, except it die not; for the grain that dies in the ground never does, and cannot vegetate. It is only the living grains that produce the next crop." But the metaphor, in any point of view, is no simile. It is succession, and not resurrection.

The progress of an animal from one state of being to another, as from a worm to a butterfly, applies to the case; but this of the grain does not, and shows Paul to have been what he says of others, *a fool.*

Whether the fourteen epistles ascribed to Paul were written by him or not is a matter of indifference; they are either argumentative or dogmatical; and as the argument is defective and the dogmatical part is merely presumptive, it signifies not who wrote them.

And the same may be said for the remaining parts of the Testament. It is not upon the epistles, but upon what is called the Gospel, contained in the four books ascribed to Matthew, Mark, Luke and John, and upon the pretended prophecies, that the theory of the Church calling itself the Christian Church is founded. The epistles are dependent upon those, and must follow their fate; for if the story of Jesus Christ be fabulous, all reasoning founded upon it as a supposed truth must fall with it.

We know from history that one of the principal leaders of this Church, Athanasius, lived at the time the New Testament was formed; [22] and we know also, from the absurd jargon he left us under the name of a creed, the character of the men who formed the New Testament; and we know also from the same history that the authenticity of the books of which it is composed was denied at the time. It was upon the vote of such men as Athanasius, that the Testament was decreed to be the Word of God; and nothing can present to us a more strange idea than that of decreeing the word of God by vote.

Those who rest their faith upon such authority put man in the place of God, and have no true foundation for future happiness; credulity, however, is not a crime, but it becomes criminal by resisting conviction. It is strangling in the womb of the conscience the efforts it makes to ascertain truth. We should never force belief upon ourselves in anything.

I here close the subject of the Old Testament and the New. The evidence I have produced to prove them forgeries is extracted from the books themselves, and acts, like a two-edged sword, either way. If the evidence be denied, the authenticity of the scriptures is denied with it, for it is scripture evidence; and if the evidence be admitted, the authenticity of the books is disproved. The contradictory impossibilities contained in the Old Testament and the New put them in the case of a man who swears for and against. Either evidence convicts him of perjury, and equally destroys reputation.

Should the Bible and the New Testament hereafter fall, it is not I that have done it. I have done no more than extracted the evidence from the confused mass of matter with which it is mixed, and arranged that evidence in a point of light to be clearly seen and easily comprehended; and, having done this, I leave the reader to judge for himself, as I have judged for myself.

---

[22] Athanasius died, according to the Church chronology, in the year 371.—*Author.*

CHAPTER III

CONCLUSION

IN THE former part of "The Age of Reason" I have spoken of the three frauds, *mystery, miracle* and *prophecy;* and as I have seen nothing in any of the answers to that work that in the least affects what I have there said upon those subjects, I shall not encumber this Second Part with additions that are not necessary.

I have spoken also in the same work upon what is called *revelation,* and have shown the absurd misapplication of that term to the books of the Old Testament and the New; for certainly revelation is out of the question in reciting anything of which man has been the actor or the witness.

That which a man has done or seen needs no revelation to tell him he has done it or seen it, for he knows it already; nor to enable him to tell it or to write it. It is ignorance or imposition to apply the term revelation in such cases; yet the Bible and Testament are classed under this fraudulent description of being all *revelation.*

Revelation then, so far as the term has relation between God and man, can only be applied to something which God reveals of His *will* to man; but though the power of the Almighty to make such a communication is necessarily admitted, because to that power all things are possible, yet the thing so revealed (if anything ever was revealed, and which, by the bye, it is impossible to prove) is revelation to the person *only to whom it is made.*

His account of it to another person is not revelation; and whoever puts faith in that account, puts it in the man from whom the account comes; and that man may have been deceived, or may have dreamed it, or he may be an impostor and may lie.

There is no possible criterion whereby to judge of the truth of what he tells, for even the morality of it would be no proof of revelation. In all such cases the proper answer would be, *"When it is revealed to me, I will believe it to be a revelation; but it is not, and cannot be incumbent upon me to believe it to be revelation before; neither is it proper that I should take the word of man as the Word of God, and put man in the place of God."*

This is the manner in which I have spoken of revelation in the former part of "The Age of Reason"; and which, while it reverentially admits revelation as a possible thing, because, as before said, to the Almighty all things are possible, it prevents the imposition of one man upon another, and precludes the wicked use of pretended revelation.

But though, speaking for myself, I thus admit the possibility of revelation, I totally disbelieve that the Almighty ever did communicate anything to man, by any mode of speech, in any language, or by any kind of vision, or appearance, or by any means which our senses are capable of receiving, otherwise than by the universal display of Himself in the works of the creation, and by that repugnance we feel in ourselves to bad actions, and the disposition to do good ones.

The most detestable wickedness, the most horrid cruelties, and the greatest miseries that have afflicted the human race have had their origin in this thing called revelation, or revealed religion. It has been the most dishonorable belief against the character of the Divinity, the most destructive to morality and the peace and happiness of man that ever was propagated since man began to exist.

It is better, far better, that we admitted, if it were possible, a thousand devils to roam at large, and to preach publicly the doctrine of devils, if there were any such, than that we permitted one such impostor and monster as Moses, Joshua, Samuel and the Bible prophets, to come with the pretended world of God in his mouth and have credit among us.

Whence arose all the horrid assassinations of whole nations of men, women and infants, with which the Bible is filled, and the bloody persecutions and tortures unto death, and religious wars, that since that time have laid Europe in blood and ashes—whence rose they but from this impious thing called revealed religion, and this monstrous belief that God has spoken to man? The lies of the Bible have been the cause of the one, and the lies of the Testament of the other.

Some Christians pretend that Christianity was not established by the sword; but of what period of time do they speak? It was impossible that twelve men could begin with the sword; they had not the power; but no sooner were the professors of Christianity sufficiently powerful to employ the sword than they did so, and the stake and fagot, too; and Mahomet could not do it sooner. By the same spirit that Peter cut off the ear of the high priest's servant (if the story be true), he would have cut off his head, and the head of his master, had he been able.

Besides this, Christianity founds itself originally upon the Bible, and the Bible was established altogether by the sword, and that in the worst use of it—not to terrify, but to extirpate. The Jews made no converts; they butchered all. The Bible is the sire of the Testament, and both are called the *Word of God*. The Christians read both books; the ministers preach from both books; and this thing called Christianity is made up of both. It is then false to say that Christianity was not established by the sword.

The only sect that has not persecuted are the Quakers, and the only reason that can be given for it is that they are rather Deists than Christians. They do not believe much about Jesus Christ, and they call the Scriptures a dead letter.[23] Had they called them by a worse name, they had been nearer the truth.

It is incumbent on every man who reverences the character of the Creator, and who wishes to lessen the catalogue of artificial miseries, and remove the cause that has sown persecutions thick among mankind, to expel all ideas of revealed religion, as a dangerous heresy and an impious fraud.

What is that we have learned from this pretended thing called revealed religion? Nothing that is useful to man, and everything that is dishonorable to his Maker. What is it the Bible teaches us?—rapine, cruelty, and murder. What is it the Testament teaches us?—to believe that the Almighty committed debauchery with a woman engaged to be married, and the belief of this debauchery is called faith.

As to the fragments of morality that are irregularly and thinly scattered in these books, they make no part of this pretended thing, revealed religion. They are the natural dictates of conscience, and the bonds by which society is held together, and without which it cannot exist, and are nearly the same in all religions and in all societies.

The Testament teaches nothing new upon this subject, and where it attempts to exceed, it becomes mean and ridiculous. The doctrine of not retaliating injuries is much better expressed in Proverbs, which is a collection as well from the Gentiles as the Jews, than it is in the Testament. It is there said (Proverbs xxv, ver. 21), *"If thine enemy be hungry, give him bread to eat; and if he be thirsty, give him water to drink"*; [24] but

---

[23] Paine's acquaintance with the Quakers, it must be remembered, was with the sect to which his father belonged, and whose doctrines he correctly refers to.—*Editor.*

[24] According to what is called Christ's sermon on the mount, in the book of Matthew, where, among some other good things, a great deal of this feigned morality is introduced, it is there expressly said, that the doctrine of forbearance, or of not retaliating injuries, was not any part of the doctrine of the Jews; but as this doctrine is found in Proverbs it must, according to that statement, have been copied from the Gentiles, from

when it said, as in the Testament, *"If a man smite thee on the right cheek, turn to him the other also";* it is assassinating the dignity of forbearance, and sinking man into a spaniel.

Loving of enemies is another dogma of feigned morality, and has besides no meaning. It is incumbent on man, as a moralist, that he does not revenge an injury; and it is equally as good in a political sense, for there is no end to retaliation, each retaliates on the other, and calls it justice; but to love in proportion to the injury, if it could be done, would be to offer a premium for crime. Besides, the word *enemies* is too vague and general to be used in a moral maxim, which ought always to be clear and defined, like a proverb.

If a man be the enemy of another from mistake and prejudice, as in the case of religious opinions, and sometimes in politics, that man is different to an enemy at heart with a criminal intention; and it is incumbent upon us, and it contributes also to our own tranquillity, that we put the best construction upon a thing that it will bear. But even this erroneous motive in him makes no motive for love on the other part; and to say that we can love voluntarily, and without a motive, is morally and physically impossible.

Morality is injured by prescribing to it duties that, in the first place, are impossible to be performed; and, if they could be, would be productive of evil; or, as before said, be premiums for crime. The maxim *of doing as we would be done unto* does not include this strange doctrine of loving enemies; for no man expects to be loved himself for his crime or for his enmity.

Those who preach this doctrine of loving their enemies are in general the greatest persecutors, and they act consistently by so doing; for the doctrine is hypocritical, and it is natural that hypocrisy should act the reverse of what it preaches.

For my own part I disown the doctrine, and consider it as a feigned or fabulous morality; yet the man does not exist that can say I have persecuted him, or any man, or any set of men, either in the American Revolution or in the French Revolution; or that I have, in any case,

---

whom Christ had learned it. Those men, whom Jewish and Christian idolators have abusively called heathens, had much better and clearer ideas of justice and morality than are to be found in the Old Testament, so far as it is Jewish; or in the New. The answer of Solon on the question, Which is the most perfect popular government? has never been exceeded by any man since his time, as containing a maxim of political morality. "That," says he, *"where the least injury done to the meanest individual, is considered as an insult on the whole constitution."* Solon lived about 500 years before Christ.—*Author.*

returned evil for evil. But it is not incumbent on man to reward a bad action with a good one, or to return good for evil; and wherever it is done, it is a voluntary act and not a duty.

It is also absurd to suppose that such doctrine can make any part of a revealed religion. We imitate the moral character of the Creator by forbearing with each other, for He forbears with all; but this doctrine would imply that He loved man, not in proportion as he was good, but as he was bad.

If we consider the nature of our condition here, we must see there is no occasion for such a thing as *revealed religion*. What is it we want to know? Does not the creation, the universe we behold, preach to us the existence of an Almighty Power that governs and regulates the whole? And is not the evidence that this creation holds out to our senses infinitely stronger than anything we can read in a book that any impostor might make and call the Word of God? As for morality, the knowledge of it exists in every man's conscience.

Here we are. The existence of an Almighty Power is sufficiently demonstrated to us, though we cannot conceive, as it is impossible we should, the nature and manner of its existence. We cannot conceive how we came here ourselves, and yet we know for a fact that we are here.

We must know also that the Power that called us into being, can, if He pleases, and when He pleases, call us to account for the manner in which we have lived here; and, therefore, without seeking any other motive for the belief, it is rational to believe that He will, for we know beforehand that He can. The probability or even possibility of the thing is all that we ought to know; for if we knew it as a fact, we should be the mere slaves of terror; our belief would have no merit, and our best actions no virtue.

Deism, then, teaches us, without the possibility of being deceived, all that is necessary or proper to be known. The creation is the Bible of the Deist. He there reads, in the handwriting of the Creator himself, the certainty of His existence and the immutability of His power, and all other Bibles and Testaments are to him forgeries.

The probability that we may be called to account hereafter will, to a reflecting mind, have the influence of belief; for it is not our belief or our disbelief that can make or unmake the fact. As this is the state we are in, and which it is proper we should be in, as free agents, it is the fool only, and not the philosopher, or even the prudent man, that would live as if there were no God.

But the belief of a God is so weakened by being mixed with the strange fable of the Christian creed, and with the wild adventures related in the Bible, and of the obscurity and obscene nonsense of the Testament, that the mind of man is bewildered as in a fog. Viewing all these things in a confused mass, he confounds fact with fable; and as he cannot believe all, he feels a disposition to reject all.

But the belief of a God is a belief distinct from all other things, and ought not to be confounded with any. The notion of a Trinity of Gods has enfeebled the belief of one God. A multiplication of beliefs acts as a division of belief; and in proportion as anything is divided it is weakened.

Religion, by such means, becomes a thing of form, instead of fact—of notion, instead of principles; morality is banished to make room for an imaginary thing called faith, and this faith has its origin in a supposed debauchery; a man is preached instead of a God; an execution is an object for gratitude; the preachers daub themselves with blood, like a troop of assassins, and pretend to admire the brilliancy it gives them; they preach a humdrum sermon on the merits of the execution; then praise Jesus Christ for being executed, and condemn the Jews for doing it. A man, by hearing all this nonsense lumped and preached together, confounds the God of the Creation with the imagined God of the Christians, and lives as if there were none.

Of all the systems of religion that ever were invented, there is none more derogatory to the Almighty, more unedifying to man, more repugnant to reason, and more contradictory in itself, than this thing called Christianity. Too absurd for belief, too impossible to convince, and too inconsistent for practise, it renders the heart torpid, or produces only atheists and fanatics. As an engine of power, it serves the purpose of despotism; and as a means of wealth, the avarice of priests; but so far as respects the good of man in general, it leads to nothing here or hereafter.

The only religion that has not been invented, and that has in it every evidence of divine originality, is pure and simple Deism. It must have been the first, and will probably be the last, that man believes. But pure and simple Deism does not answer the purpose of despotic governments. They cannot lay hold of religion as an engine, but by mixing it with human inventions, and making their own authority a part; neither does it answer the avarice of priests, but by incorporating themselves and their functions with it, and becoming, like the government, a party in the system. It is this that forms the otherwise mysterious connection of Church and State; the Church humane, and the State tyrannic.

Were man impressed as fully and as strongly as he ought to be with the belief of a God, his moral life would be regulated by the force of that belief; he would stand in awe of God and of himself, and would not do the thing that could not be concealed from either. To give this belief the full opportunity of force, it is necessary that it acts alone. This is Deism. But when, according to the Christian Trinitarian scheme, one part of God is represented by a dying man, and another part, called the Holy Ghost, by a flying pigeon, it is impossible that belief can attach itself to such wild conceits.[25]

It has been the scheme of the Christian Church, and of all the other invented systems of religion, to hold man in ignorance of the Creator, as it is of Governments to hold man in ignorance of his rights. The systems of the one are as false as those of the other, and are calculated for mutual support.

The study of theology, as it stands in Christian churches, is the study of nothing; it is founded on nothing; it rests on no principles; it proceeds by no authorities; it has no data; it can demonstrate nothing; and it admits of no conclusion. Not any thing can be studied as a science, without our being in possession of the principles upon which it is founded; and as this is not the case with Christian theology, it is therefore the study of nothing.

Instead then of studying theology, as is now done out of the Bible and Testament, the meanings of which books are always controverted and the authenticity of which is disproved, it is necessary that we refer to the Bible of the Creation. The principles we discover there are eternal and of divine origin; they are the foundation of all the science that exists in the world, and must be the foundation of theology.

We can know God only through His works. We cannot have a conception of any one attribute but by following some principle that leads to it. We have only a confused idea of His power, if we have not the means of comprehending something of its immensity. We can have no idea of His wisdom, but by knowing the order and manner in which it

[25] The book called the book of Matthew says (chap. iii, verse 16), that *the Holy Ghost descended in the shape of a dove*. It might as well have said a goose; the creatures are equally harmless, and the one is as much of a nonsensical lie as the other. The second of Acts, ver. 2, 3, says that it descended in a mighty *rushing wind*, in the shape of *cloven tongues*, perhaps it was cloven feet. Such absurd stuff is only fit for tales of witches and wizards.—*Author*

acts. The principles of science lead to this knowledge; for the Creator of man is the Creator of science, and it is through that medium that man can see God, as it were, face to face.

Could a man be placed in a situation, and endowed with the power of vision, to behold at one view, and to contemplate deliberately, the structure of the universe; to mark the movements of the several planets, the cause of their varying appearances, the unerring order in which they revolve, even to the remotest comet; their connection and dependence on each other, and to know the system of laws established by the Creator, that governs and regulates the whole, he would then conceive, far beyond what any church theology can teach him, the power, the wisdom, the vastness, the munificence of the Creator; he would then see, that all the knowledge man has of science, and that all mechanical arts by which he renders his situation comfortable here, are derived from that source; his mind, exalted by the scene, and convinced by the fact, would increase in gratitude as it increased in knowledge; his religion or his worship would become united with his improvement as a man; any employment he followed, that had any connection with the principles of the creation, as everything of agriculture, of science and of the mechanical arts has, would teach him more of God, and of the gratitude he owes to Him, than any theological Christian sermon he now hears.

Great objects inspire great thoughts; great munificence excites great gratitude; but the groveling tales and doctrines of the Bible and the Testament are fit only to excite contempt.

Though man cannot arrive, at least in this life, at the actual scene I have described, he can demonstrate it, because he has a knowledge of the principles upon which the creation is constructed.[26] We know that the

---

[26] The Bible-makers have undertaken to give us, in the first chapter of Genesis, an account of the Creation; and in doing this, they have demonstrated nothing but their ignorance. They make there to have been three days and three nights, evenings and mornings, before there was a sun; when it is the presence or absence of the sun that is the cause of day and night, and what is called his rising and setting that of morning and evening. Besides, it is a puerile and pitiful idea, to suppose the Almighty to say, Let there be light. It is the imperative manner of speaking that a conjuror uses when he says to his cups and balls, Presto, begone, and most probably has been taken from it; as Moses and his rod are a conjuror and his wand. Longinus calls this expression the sublime; and, by the same rule, the conjuror is sublime too, for the manner of speaking is expressively and grammatically the same. When authors and critics talk of the sublime, they see not how nearly it borders on the ridiculous. The sublime of the critics, like some parts of Edmund Burke's "Sublime and Beautiful," is like a wind-mill just visible in a fog, which imagination might distort into a flying mountain, or an archangel, or a flock of wild geese.—*Author.*

greatest works can be represented in model, and that the universe can be represented by the same means.

The same principles by which we measure an inch, or an acre of ground, will measure to millions in extent. A circle of an inch diameter has the same geometrical properties as a circle that would circumscribe the universe.

The same properties of a triangle that will demonstrate upon paper the course of a ship, will do it on the ocean; and when applied to what are called the heavenly bodies, will ascertain to a minute the time of an eclipse, though these bodies are millions of miles from us. This knowledge is of divine origin, and it is from the Bible of the Creation that man has learned it, and not from the stupid Bible of the Church, that teacheth man nothing.

All the knowledge man has of science and of machinery, by the aid of which his existence is rendered comfortable upon earth, and without which he would be scarcely distinguishable in appearance and condition from a common animal, comes from the great machine and structure of the universe.

The constant and unwearied observations of our ancestors upon the movements and revolutions of the heavenly bodies, in what are supposed to have been the early ages of the world, have brought this knowledge upon earth. It is not Moses and the prophets, nor Jesus Christ, nor his apostles, that have done it. The Almighty is the great mechanic of the creation; the first philosopher and original teacher of all science. Let us, then, learn to reverence our master, and let us not forget the labors of our ancestors.

Had we, at this day, no knowledge of machinery, and were it possible that man could have a view, as I have before described, of the structure and machinery of the universe, he would soon conceive the idea of constructing some at least of the mechanical works we now have; and the idea so conceived would progressively advance in practice. Or could a model of the universe, such as is called an orrery, be presented before him and put in motion, his mind would arrive at the same idea.

Such an object and such a subject would, while it improved him in knowledge useful to himself as a man and a member of society, as well as entertaining, afford far better matter for impressing him with a knowledge of, and a belief in, the Creator, and of the reverence and gratitude that man owes to Him, than the stupid texts of the Bible and of the Testament, from which, be the talents of the preacher what they may, only stupid sermons can be preached.

If man must preach, let him preach something that is edifying, and from texts that are known to be true.

The Bible of the Creation is inexhaustible in texts. Every part of science, whether connected with the geometry of the universe, with the systems of animal and vegetable life, or with the properties of inanimate matter, is a text as well for devotion as for philosophy—for gratitude as for human improvement. It will perhaps be said, that if such a revolution in the system of religion takes place, every preacher ought to be a philosopher. *Most certainly;* and every house of devotion a school of science.

It has been by wandering from the immutable laws of science, and the light of reason, and setting up an invented thing called revealed religion, that so many wild and blasphemous conceits have been formed of the Almighty.

The Jews have made Him the assassin of the human species to make room for the religion of the Jews. The Christians have made Him the murderer of Himself and the founder of a new religion, to supersede and expel the Jewish religion. And to find pretense and admission for these things, they must have supposed His power or His wisdom imperfect, or His will changeable; and the changeableness of the will is imperfection of the judgment.

The philosopher knows that the laws of the Creator have never changed with respect either to the principles of science or the properties of matter. Why, then, is it supposed they have changed with respect to man?

I here close the subject. I have shown in all the foregoing parts of this work that the Bible and the Testament are impositions and forgeries; and I leave the evidence I have produced in proof of it to be refuted, if any one can do it; and I leave the ideas that are suggested in the conclusion of the work to rest on the mind of the reader; certain, as I am, that when opinions are free, either in matters of government or religion, truth will finally and powerfully prevail.